Christoph Keller

PARANOMIA

CONTENTS

Paranomia

Grey Magic

Æther

Anarcheology

Small Survey on Nothingness

Paranomia

Spector Books

P—for Paranomia

Disambiguation:
Paranomia may refer to:

- The medical condition *verbal paraphasia*, an aspect of aphasia, characterized by the incorrect naming of objects
- A misspelling of the 1986 Art of Noise single *Paranoimia*
- A translation of "para nomos" (alongside the normative), a term in Greek philosophy, meaning *transgression, wickedness, lawlessness*

(Wikipedia entry for Paranomia)

A—for Aphasia

According to the *American Heritage Medical Dictionary*, Paranomia *is a form of Aphasia in which objects are called by the wrong names.*

At the same time that I was taking university classes in philosophy and comparative literature, I began working with disabled people in the course of my civil service. One of my patients, a craftsman in his fifties, had suffered from a stroke and temporarily exhibited severe disturbances in his motor speech center. It was called the tip-of-the-tongue phenomenon: when for example cards with little drawings, or objects like a spoon, were presented to him, he would actually retrieve the correct word from his memory, but involuntarily—at the very last moment—vocalize instead either "Dortmund" (the name of a town in Germany) or "Donnerstag" (which means Thursday in German). This semantic slip was so disarming and comical that at times both the patient and I had to laugh during the therapeutic sessions.

An object wrongly addressed triggers a multitude of associations in the imagination of a listener. This is the anarchic momentum of paranomia in its linguistic form: that it radically questions the relation between signifier and signified.

R—for Riddle

When experimenting with forms I often use writing because it is a quick way to sketch ideas. This sometimes takes the form of riddles. One, for example, is a four-line poem describing human thought as an immense tree, "the tree of thought," which grows on and on from the trunk to the branches that follow in sequence. Us humans climb hand over hand from one branch to another, from one theory to the next, so to speak—only we shall never be able to leave the tree of thought! This is not meant as a metaphor. What is interesting for me, instead, is that by describing the fatality of not being able to leave the tree of thought, one has paradoxically already created an image for the possibility of doing so.

A—for Alcibiades

In his death, as in his life, Alcibiades combines every sort of paranomia. He is imagined to transgress all the limits—of sex and gender, national, social, and political—that define Athenian citizenship. His behavior breaks all the "rules" of sexuality: the distinction between erastes and eromenos, the stigma against male passivity, the essential divide between masculine and feminine. Likewise, his political behavior blurs the line between democratic ambition and tyrannical aspirations. (...) This bifurcation of Alcibiades's character in the speeches for and against him reflects the ambivalence of his contemporaries: when Timon the Misanthrope said to Alcibiades, "You do well to grow, child, for you will grow to be a great pain to all the Athenians," some who heard laughed, others cursed, and some took it very much to heart.

(From Victoria Wohl, *Love among the Ruins: The Erotics of Democracy in Classical Athens*, 2003)

N—for Narration

A film, first of all, tells the story of its conditions of production.

(Opening title of the video *Small Survey on Nothingness*, 2014)

O—for Outer Space

Verifiably outer space is not a thing-in-itself, but our own organ of perception—with which the organs of our body are connected in a way that is only seemingly interrupted by our skin.

(From the preface of Salomo Friedlaender/Mynona, *Katechismus der Magie*, 1925)

Our body extends ethereally into the cosmos, the skin is not its true boundary.

(From Salomo Friedlaender/Mynona, *Graue Magie*, 1922)

M—for Myth

Although I am going to talk about what I have written, my books and papers and so on, unfortunately I forget what I have written practically as soon as it is finished. There is probably going to be some trouble about that. But nevertheless I think there is also something significant about it, in that I don't have the feeling that I write my books. I have the feeling that my books get written through me and that once they have got across me I feel empty and nothing is left.

(Claude Lévi-Strauss, from the introduction to *Myth and Meaning*, 1978)

I—for Immaterial

There is a work by the avant-garde musician and artist Tony Conrad, which I like a lot and once heard him talk about. It is called This Artwork is its Name. *The artwork is its own title, and its title is* This Artwork is its Name. *The work is not printed on paper, nor made into a neon sign. This artwork is just its name. Conrad said that for him, the work expands its own tautological space, in which it exists.*

(Transcript of the artist talk "The Bosphorus of My Mind," which took place at Platform Garanti, Istanbul, on January 2, 2009)

A—for Anarcheology

This is a theoretical and practical attitude concerning the non-necessity of all power, and to distinguish this position of the non-necessity of power as a principle of intelligibility of knowledge itself, it would be rather obvious to use the word "anarchy" or "anarchism," which is not suitable, so I'll make a wordplay and as wordplays are not very fashionable nowadays—let's go a little bit against the grain and make a play on words (which is also... well, mine are very bad, I recognize that). Then I will tell you that what I propose is rather a kind of Anarcheology.

(Michel Foucault, *Du gouvernement des vivants,* 1980)

Christoph Keller

On Stammering

From a conversation between
Christoph Keller and Joseph Vogl

Christoph Keller

So, where I would like to start from with regards to "stammering" is actually something that I have often experienced myself, but also that I witnessed once with Jacques Rancière at one of his talks. He spoke in English, and towards the end he was asked something by a member of the audience. As he received the question, there was a sudden twitch that coursed through his body—and from this corporeal event, an answer then emerged, halting at first, but which ended up being a complete philosophical thought. I found that extremely remarkable to see, this becoming-language or coming-to-language in the body. So we can start with that, perhaps, as an opening image. And then as a second image, juxtaposed with this, Ludwig Wittgenstein's *Tractatus Logico-Philosophicus*, which ends with the phrase "whereof one cannot speak, thereof one must be silent." And I think, one could counter this point allegorically; that, whereof one cannot speak, one must first, as it were, stammer. So finding something new, or something which one seeks to conceive and express in language, in fact proceeds automatically by way of stammering.

Joseph Vogl

Well, it is possible to approach stammering from various angles. Perhaps to begin with, there is a historical approach, and thereby also a historico-conceptual approach. In this regard, it would be important to keep in mind that in Greek, the translation of "to stammer" is actually *barbaros.* The differentiation between those who took part in the *polis*, in political life—that is, the *zoon politikon*—on the one hand, and all those who did not participate in it, on the other, was an utterly cardinal difference, a categorical differentiation in Greek antiquity. Those who did not belong to the polis were either something more than human, closer to the Gods, or otherwise something less than human—that is, closer to animals. And, in some way, the barbarian also belonged on this spectrum, as the person who is without place or order, as the one who possesses neither a space of order nor a space of emplacement, and who for the Greeks, in some sense, emitted animal noises. And that was stammering, "barbaros." Thus, with stammering we diverge in a certain sense from the anthropomorphic, departing from this, if you will, mythical plane. In stammering, language takes on a form that is something less than human. And we could also say that in the process, language is deterritorialized. That is, it loses its syntactic order, it becomes semantically blurred, and it also becomes phonetically blurred. So in various regards, stammering implies a loss of differentiation. That would be, I think, a first point, which would also, if you like, explain the shame that is associated with stammering, or even more strongly, with the almost pathological concept of stuttering. The shame that is associated with it is at root the shame of something which departs from the protective form of the human being, which exposes itself, in a way, as such corresponding to a physiological remnant, a noise that belongs less to the tools of speech than to the tools of eating, or a language which—and this may be a really important aspect here—essentially loses communicative substrata. Or rather, it is a communicative disturbance. If this is conceived of as an initial systematic aspect, one could say that stammering or stuttering—though I actually prefer stammering—is a disturbance in the communication with oneself and with others. And that which reveals itself in this disturbance is in fact something physiological, is an obstacle which articulates itself physiologically...

CK

I would like to try to turn this around, because for me, stammering—and perhaps you might even agree with me here—is not just a transitional state which leads from speech to stammering, but also from stammering to speech, as I earlier described in the case of Jacques Rancière. Stammering would then be the antecedent to fluent speech. And all speaking would also emerge, in a certain sense, from stammering. It may be that we only learn to suppress this stammering, but in principle then it would be a kind of "gathering of thoughts." Which is very similar to your book *On Tarrying*, in which tarrying is virtually the antecedent of an action. I would like to throw light on the concept of stammering from this angle.

JV

Another extremely important aspect here is that stammering represents an interesting marking on the various axes of language. One could say that the direction of spoken language is prescribed by a syntagma, which is to say, by a continuous chain of syntactical units, and that decisions must be made at every link of the chain, that a choice must be made from the paradigm. Continuous speech, then, means making choices vis-à-vis each part of the sentence, each syntagma, each paradigm, thereby endowing speech with direction—a direction which is prescribed, for instance, by the verb, by definition, etc., but also through semantic linkages. Here, stammering occupies an interesting position, because in a sense, it shifts the sentence—and hence also the trajectory of the utterance—into a state of suspension, into a peculiar hesitation or indecision. The trajectory is interrupted, and in fact, stammering is often associated with the start of a search process. A search process in which, for example, various alternative possibilities for continuing arise. In such cases, a sentence which might conclude either positively or negatively, that is to say, in a negation or in an affirmation, seems suddenly to allow both possibilities to appear simultaneously. It is conceivable that at a certain point, various images surface which exhibit various shadings, for example with regard to semantics.

And at each of these points, stammering introduces a kind of carousel of possibilities, and represents a gain in, as well as an impairment of, quality—namely an exit from communication, for example, an intensification of communication with the self in the form of a question, or the like. It is not therefore just a subtraction, but also a multiplication, specifically one of possibilities.

In stammering, then, the direction of continuation, the trajectory of the sentence, of the utterance, and not least of all of a movement of thought, in fact remains open. Which is why stammering has in this regard the character of a potentization of that which is spoken. Which is to say, precisely not only of a depotentization, in the sense that communication is interrupted, but of a potentization where a wealth of meaning is in a sense present and the specification of the process of selection has not yet come to a conclusion.

CK

Barnett Newman, for example, in his essay "The First Man Was an Artist," writes that the first utterance of humanity was actually not a factual statement, but rather a poetic exclamation—an attempt to linguistically address something unknown, something inconceivable, something new. As an artist I am interested in the poetic, this possibility of expressing something new with language via the detour of stammering—via the suspension, which you have mentioned as well. For me this suspension is the moment in which one does not yet wish to commit to one way of expressing something in language. It is effectively the holding open of all possibilities.

JV

A similar question was reflected upon in the eighteenth century in a variety of narratives concerning the origins of language—in the supposition that the first phoneme was an onomatopoetic utterance, which is to say the Rousseauian natural phoneme, an "ah" or an "oh," or simple onomatopoeia, which is in some sense preverbal and of course above all pre-conceptual. Something similar is found in Nietzsche, who said, for example, that first there was an image, then a phoneme related to that image—the concept emerged only after a long filtering process. And here too, stammering is, if you will, actually positioned prior to the ordering and directional force of the conceptual (that is to say, assuming that stammering is a mere phonetic phenomenon still devoid of syntactic continuity, as yet undetermined by syntactic determinations).

Here, too, we could say that it does not necessarily generate a zero point, but instead the most extreme intensity, in which concepts themselves are set into suspension.

Formulated somewhat differently, one could say that insistently present in stammering is meaning, but that this meaning does not yet exist. Conspicuous in stammering, hence, is an insistent potential for meaning.

CK

Great! Well that's already a first conceptual rapprochement. But now I would like to divert your attention to something else: a sentence written by Karl Jaspers, which says that the emergence of language is a leap, and that language is an absolute limit for us. So the emergence of language is of course a leap from a historical standpoint, but also ontogenetically: the child comes to language by way of stammering. Can we put it like that?

JV

I would say that stammering—which interests you, and which perhaps interests me as well—can emerge in the first place only under the condition that language exists, and secondly under the condition that speech is possible. Stammering, then, about which we have just spoken, is something which is engendered only under the preconditions of a language system, or of language as such. And I believe (even if one states it cautiously, or even incautiously) that this would also be the artistic side of things. Gilles Deleuze, for instance, has made this clear on the basis of a variety of examples, with reference to Proust, to Cummings, to Kafka, to Sacher-Masoch—that artistic language begins where the internal, the immanent capacity of a language to stammer in some sense becomes the artistic motor. Which also means that in friction, in phonemic friction, in asyntactical formulations (or even in grammatical sentences such as Bartleby's famous "I would prefer not to," which functions as an interruption), that at all such points, interruptions are incorporated whose linguistic potential, ultimately, engender that which Deleuze refers to as "the new."

An important aspect, I believe, is the fact that at least for a certain form of modern literature, for example (and we could probably say the same for modern art), certain central operations consist in reductions of the ordering gestalt of the world. And hence in the returning of the world (an existent and, so to speak, linguistically established world) to a condition which one might refer to as becoming: one in which the world develops embryonic aspects, is no longer present in the form of predetermined structures. And stammering (Deleuze says that stammering also consists precisely in the act of bringing an entire language itself to a state of stammering) would have precisely this form, would reduce stable relationships in the world, constructions.

And of course, stammering would then mark out something along the lines of a connection failure, as in film editing. In a certain sense, one could say that the films of the Nouvelle Vague stammer, for example when it is unclear how we are moving from one shot to the next. Or when it is clear that the transition from one shot to the next is being presented in multiple ways. There is a wonderful scene in Godard which enacts this. The question here is: how does one pass through a door? In *Le mépris* (1963), Michel Piccoli opens a door, steps through it, and closes it behind him. Then the next time: the same door. Michel Piccoli stops, opens the door, and you realize suddenly that in the middle, the glass window, which is to say the door panel, is missing. He passes through the space of the absent door panel, leaving the door closed. And the third time, he does both, he opens the door and passes through the space of the absent door panel. He has now enacted all three possibilities: first, to pass from one room into another; second, to deal with the door; and third, to surpass this threshold. And I think that a similar form is associated with the connection failure, where it becomes clear that progress or continuity through space, for example (through metric space as well) is interrupted and becomes entangled in errancy. And I believe that this erratic quality, this errancy into indecisiveness, this "ah" of stammering is quite important, and leads to a structure of indecision in which the stability of the world, the structuration of the world and the fact, for example, that the door exists, becomes bracketed, so to speak.

CK

It is possible that through stammering one actually hints at something normative, where non-stammering, the continuity of speech, would then be the normative. In your film example, this is represented by the doors, the existence of which is not challenged until precisely this "stammering" is produced in the film, through which the existence of these very doors, or of the object at all, is then pushed back and forth and is thereby analyzed. And this process takes the object itself out of the world, so to speak, and interrogates it in a poetic manner.

JV

As a system condition, basically, stammering is remote from a condition of equilibrium. It might be possible to compare this more clearly with a chaotic system, which is to say, with that which the mathematician Benoît Mandelbrot, for example, attempted to describe. An interesting contemporary physicist, a physical chemist, Ilya Prigogine, describes how turbulent systems—for instance liquids characterized by the presence of laminar currents, which is to say by currents within which sudden interruptions occur, resulting in turbulence—are not entirely unordered. In fact, it is a question of a relatively organized system, albeit one remote from a state of equilibrium, of a state in which (and precisely this formula is used by Ilya Prigogine) "the system tarries." It is impossible to determine how a given state is capable of leading to a given future state of the system. Instead, all possible states of the system are brought into play, which leads to the circumstance that there is no probable—that is to say, no "normally probable"—future progression.

Instead, we find a hyperbolic state of the system in which even processes of probability become fully irregular. And this "tarrying system," where the transition from one state to another is unclear, is remote from a condition of equilibrium. To this extent, it could be said that linguistic conditions of equilibrium, too—which is to say their balance—may be suspended.

CK

I find this formulation of the "tarrying system of fluids" fascinating, because in it, the scientist seems to "subjectivize," to a certain extent, the medium or nature in a way that we might expect from artists rather than from scientists. Nature, in the form of a fluid, is said to tarry, which is more or less a human characteristic.

On the possibility of two opposing facts in stammering, I also think of C. G. Jung, who, speaking about religions, said something along the lines of: they remain strong so long as they can absorb and bear contradictions. And as soon as they cease to be able to do that, they become dogmatic and thus lose the strength which actually constitutes them as religions.

JV

Every system, it seems to me, when it displays a certain tendency toward self-reproduction, when a system develops an immanent intelligence in order to, in a certain sense, propagate itself (and this pertains as much to economic as to social systems), must have margins through which contacts with the environment (in addition to all notions of closure, all ideas of delimitation, and so forth) are endowed with manifest openings—which is to say, flexible ends, frayed edges, and so on. Gilles Deleuze once asked: Why does capitalism function so well? Because everything leaks, because there are holes everywhere, and because despite this, although nothing functions, it always continues.

To turn disturbances toward functionality—this is an elementary definition of cybernetic systems, for example, which maintain themselves by incorporating disturbances. Basically, every disturbance is an opportunity for optimizing the system.

But there is, I think, another interesting aspect to stuttering or stammering. In a marginal remark, Lévi-Strauss indicates that in various indigenous

North American myths, stammering or stuttering is associated with stumbling. This means that since both speaking and walking are forms of forward motion, it becomes possible to establish a certain congruence or analogy between different disturbances of forward motion. And in many cases, the one who stammers is also the one who stumbles. Stumbling is often triggered by stammering, and vice versa.

CK

But in many cultures it is precisely the stumblers, or those who stammer, who are taken to be proximate to the Gods or to divinity. And that manifests itself then, for example, in glossolalia, about which Felicitas D. Goodman has written a great deal, so this connection between stammering and transcendence...

JV

This would provide us with another way of zeroing in on that which occurs during stammering: glossolalia or so-called speaking in tongues is not actually the speaking of a language, but instead the speaking of languages.

That which is articulated there, in a kind of Pentecost miracle, is the simultaneous speaking together of various languages, no one of which remains identifiable. Languages are positioned in relations of intensive friction with one another, and therefore stammering would be, as a matter of definition, not a case of "not speaking," of "not speaking a certain language or of not enunciating a specific sentence," but instead a kind of guide to a glossolalian "speaking languages in the plural." As though it were, so to speak, a pluralization of the speaking of a language in stammering.

If we spoke of the branching out or bifurcation which takes place in stammering, then this actually means not merely that the continuity of speech as such is called into question, the forward movement of the sentence, is not just a question of the interruption of semantic and syntactic structures, but instead that language itself is now pluralized in the process. Just as in glossolalia, where it is not a question of nothing being spoken, but instead of the fact that no one language is recognizable.

Perhaps we should say more about this, because I mentioned the analogy between stumbling and stammering: it is interesting that precisely in biomechanics, for example in attempts to describe human locomotion, that the human gait is not characterized normatively as the performance of upright walking, but instead as the continual avoidance of falling. To take a step, then, means to resist the gravitational force of the body in a falling state, so that walking is nothing else but a perpetual interruption of falling. And of course, the act of speech, of speaking continuously, could also be conceptualized as a continual interception of stammering or stuttering. The interesting twist here would be that the norms of correct speech, and hence syntax, grammar, semantics, etc., would no longer be taken as the guiding elements of continuous speech, but on the contrary, the interruptions, the disturbances, which is to say not the constants, but the variables, which surface there. And this could result in an interesting theory of language, if we say that language, the command of speech or of language in speech, is defined less in terms of unitary forms which are hence associated with corresponding constants, but conversely in terms of interruptions, failures of connection, etc., which is to say, of the stuttering which must be perpetually intercepted within language in order for speech to proceed.

CK

In relation to language, that would mean that there is initially an antecedent to that which is verbalized, which would more or less like to find its way to verbalization, and it is in this very process that stammering comes about. That really fascinates me. I'm trying to draw a connection to my exhibition "Verbal/ Nonverbal" (Esther Schipper, Berlin, 2010). It deals with states of trance, and these are—as, for example, some hypnotists maintain—rather the basic states of being, and conscious utterances are only very exceptional configurations.
I would like to pick up on your image of walking, which is almost just a permanent forestalling of falling. In this way, conscious speech, as it were, would be a permanent forestalling of falling back into a pre-verbal state, which, however, is actually the basic state. Because the conscious state always requires an effort, namely that of a permanent response.

JV

And hence, the knowledge of the Structuralists, of course—which is to say the Structuralists who emerged from the so-called "linguistic turn," but also those who grasped the unconscious of linguistic structures; Lacan, for example. Of course, they know very well that in order to speak at all, one must not wish to speak. Intentional speech, then, is a speech which interrupts itself. In fact,

I can speak continuously only under the condition that I do not reflect upon how one utterance is linked to the next. Otherwise, speech cannot function. Which means that speech actually functions under the condition of reduced consciousness, that it functions, so to speak, "unconsciously." Kleist is a terrific experimenter in this area, when he writes, for example, about how Mirabeau, standing before the French Revolutionary Assembly, all of a sudden, through a kind of explosion, no longer reflected, no longer framed his ideas, but instead—as though animated by an electrical spark—delivered the speech which captivated everyone. And I think this is absolutely decisive, that a heightened sense of consciousness hinders speech.

Just as one of the great schizophrenic thinkers, Daniel Paul Schreber, spoke about so-called *Denkungsgedanken* (not-thinking-of-anything-thoughts), which inhibited thought. Assuming we take this seriously, that means of course that what manifests itself in stammering is not a reduced consciousness, but instead, on the contrary, a heightened consciousness.

This means that if consciousness is associated with volition, and if volition is related to the affirmation of a decision, then we find that it is in fact the highest degree of consciousness, which is to say of a volitional force, and hence of decision-making potential, which hinders the continuous progress of speech.

Stammering, then, would represent not a reduction of consciousness, but on the contrary, an almost catastrophic eruption of the awareness of language.

CK

Just as it is said of schizophrenics that they possess a certain lucidity, dealing with language in such a way, that it... breaks... well now I am stammering myself, somewhat. And we can presume that this is no coincidence, that it is precisely those who operate around such a threshold that are able to perceive the normative element in language very clearly, and that the transgressions they make there are in no way arbitrary.

JV

I would be very cautious there... and I don't really know enough about this... so I would call for a certain amount of caution there...

CK

(laughs) Yes, well that's why I was stammering.

JV

Of course, there is also the other extreme, catatonia, in which nothing at all happens any longer. But if schizoid conditions (intended not in the pathological sense, but instead in an ethnological, in a behavioral-technical sense) play a role here, then you could say that stammering and the forms of expression associated with it have to do with problems of coherence, that it exposes these problems and possibly leads toward a solution.

And problems of coherence may be located at a variety of levels. A condition may emerge (for example through the use of a concept like that of "man" or something similar) in which the existence of a norm represents a definitive problem of coherence. Because this concept can no longer be accommodated within a certain world, where it lies like an unwieldy beam, a steel girder that can no longer be adapted to these structures. Which is to say, one is confronted by a problem of coherence which must be resolved, and this may involve insanely complicated constructions.

There is the celebrated case of a schizophrenic who was also analyzed by Deleuze, among others. Of someone who was incapable of speaking English, his mother tongue. He could speak, then, only by avoiding his native language.

Now this individual, who referred to himself as a student of languages, was extraordinarily educated—he knew Hebrew, could speak various Slavic languages, German, other Romance languages, and of course French—and he managed (and, again, this approaches the edge of glossolalia) to frame words and sentences which sounded English but which were composed of words and phonemes from all other possible languages. His performance, then, resembled a mimicry of English, in which however no word, no trace, no phoneme, and therefore no unit of meaning was still decipherable as English.

In a sense, this represents an approach to a problem of coherence, to solving an almost irresolvable problem of coherence, namely the normative ordering of the so-called mother tongue (which is to say English as the language of the mother), in a sense of banishing the mother from language.

And as a result, we find completely different combinations which in a sense traverse the entire map, linguistic combinations which achieve one thing: to generate a language that sounds like English, but from which the mother has been expelled—a language where she does not exist.

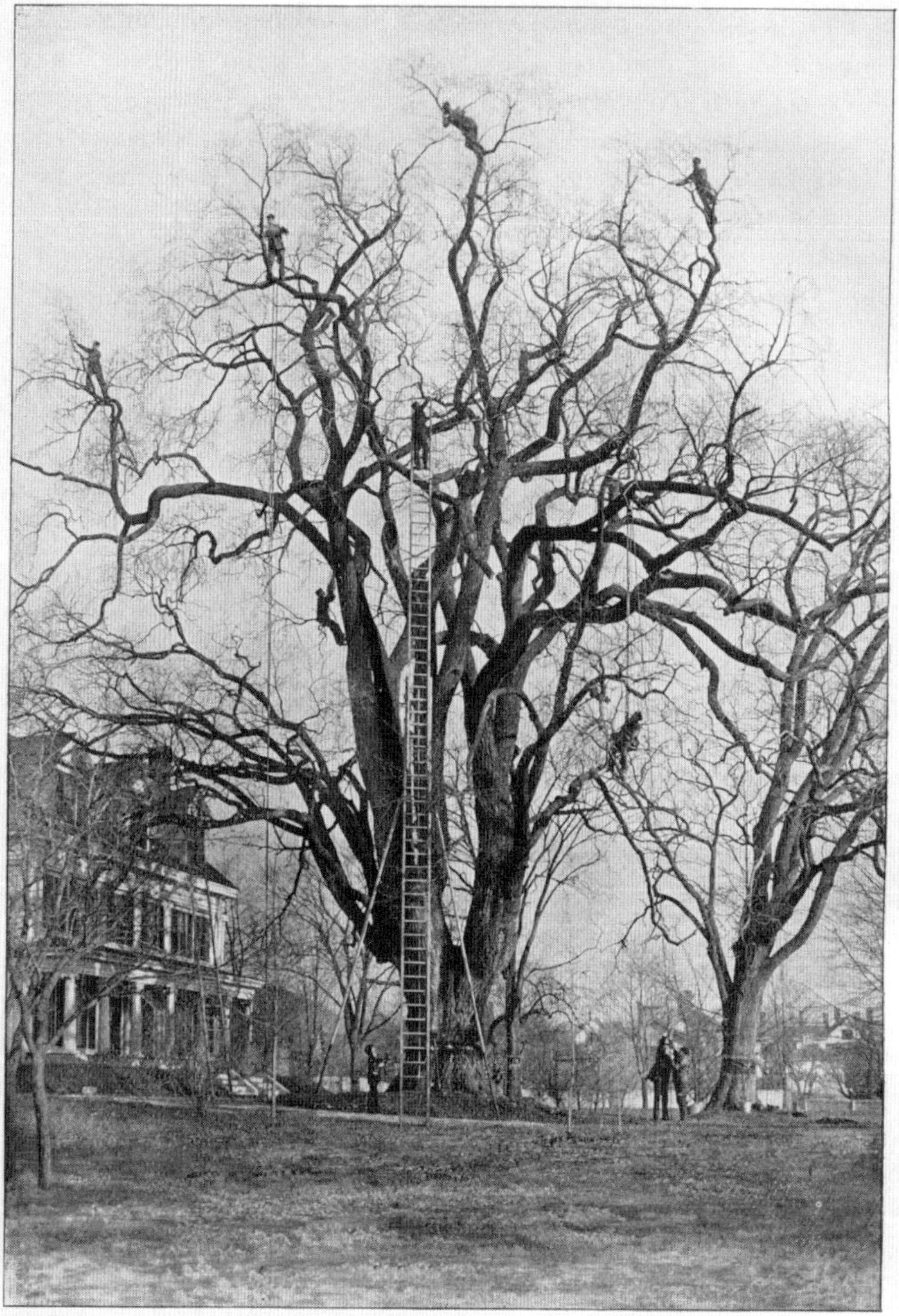

PLATE XXXVI. Men at work on the Dexter elm, Malden. From a photograph.

Christoph Keller

The Trouvelot Story

Étienne Léopold Trouvelot (December 26, 1827–April 22, 1895) was a French artist, astronomer, and amateur entomologist, who became famous for the unfortunate introduction of the Gypsy Moth into North America.

In the mid-1860s, Trouvelot imported Gypsy Moth egg masses from Europe to the United States, raising their larvae in the garden behind his house in Massachusetts. Trouvelot's interest in breeding the moths remains unknown. By mistake, some of the larvae eventually escaped into the nearby woods. Aware of the environmental problem he might have caused, Trouvelot alerted other entomologists right away. However, the situation was underestimated and at first no effective measures were taken to prevent the species's spread.

Not long after this incident, Trouvelot gave up entomology and turned to astronomy. His interest in the field apparently developed after witnessing several auroras around 1870. Being an excellent draughtsman, he was able to accurately illustrate the astronomical observations that he made with large refractor telescopes. Soon he gained recognition for his remarkable drawings and paintings of a wide range of subjects, such as solar prominences, stellar constellations, and galaxies. At the time, the choice between astronomic illustrations by artists versus the new medium of photography became the subject of scientific debate. Trouvelot's work served as an example for the proponents of drawing; the proponents of photography, however, eventually prevailed.

Trouvelot left the United States in 1882 and moved back to France, where he joined the Meudon astronomical observatory near Paris. The magnitude of the problem he had caused by releasing the Gypsy Moth became evident only a few years later, when the local authorities in Massachusetts named the Gypsy Moth as a serious threat to the region's forests. Attempts were made to eradicate it with traps, pest control, and even with flame-throwers. But in the end these efforts were all unsuccessful. To this day, the Gypsy Moth continues to spread its range on the North American continent.

Some of Trouvelot's late photographic works found their way into the art world long after his death, when they were printed in the fifth issue of the surrealist magazine *Minotaure* by its editor, André Breton, in 1934. Those images were photograms of electrical discharges on photographic paper, with titles such as *Étincelle électrique directe, obtenu avec une bobine de Ruhmkorff* (Direct electrical spark, obtained with a Ruhmkorff coil).

Oscillating between the spheres of art and science, Trouvelot can be seen as a symptomatic as well as tragic figure of the late nineteenth century—not only because he was a gifted artist in a declining craft, who became famous for causing the world's first well-documented ecological catastrophe unleashed by a single man—but ultimately because he was a visionary in a time when visions were rapidly changing.

Étienne Léopold Trouvelot's works and life story were one of the entry points to the exhibition "Æther — from Cosmology to Consciousness" by Christoph Keller in Espace 315 at the Centre Pompidou in Paris, 2011.

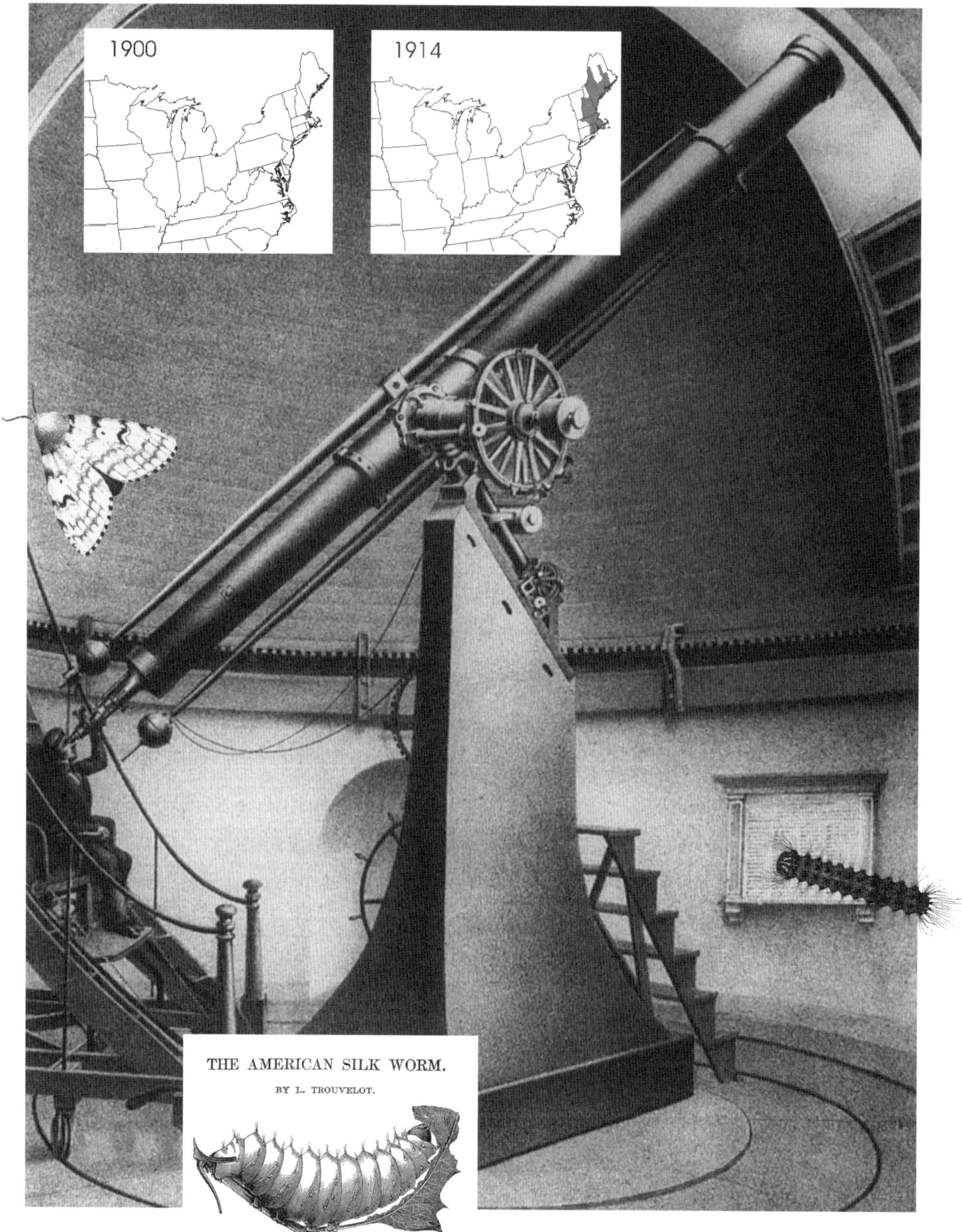
1900
1914
THE AMERICAN SILK WORM.
BY L. TROUVELOT.

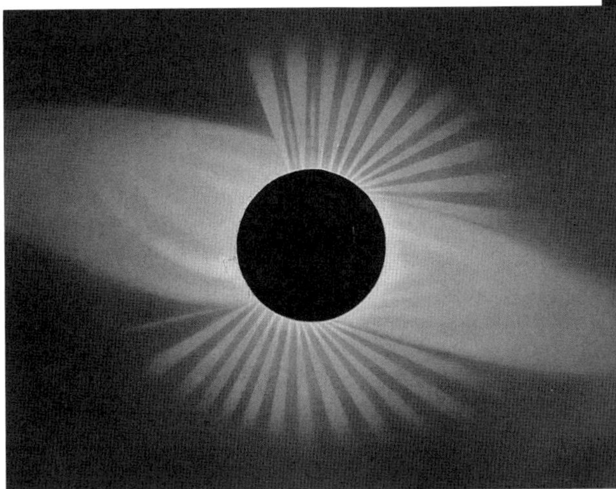

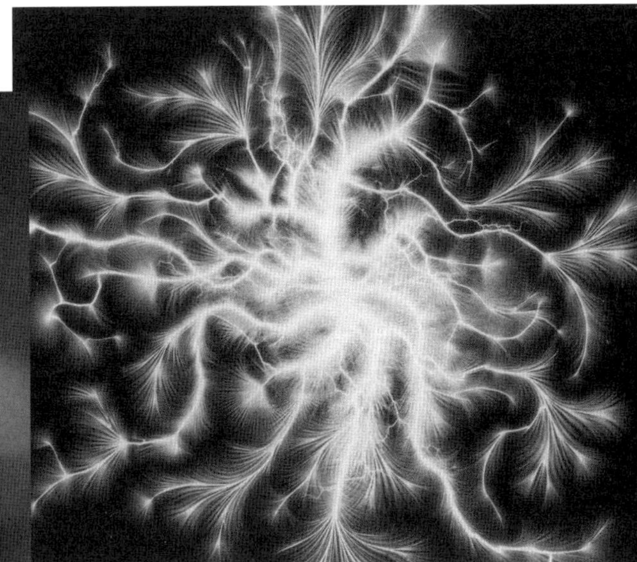

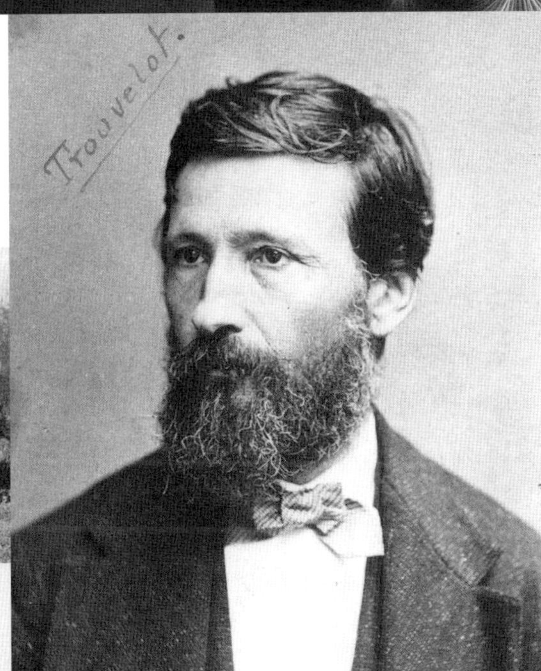
Trouvelot.

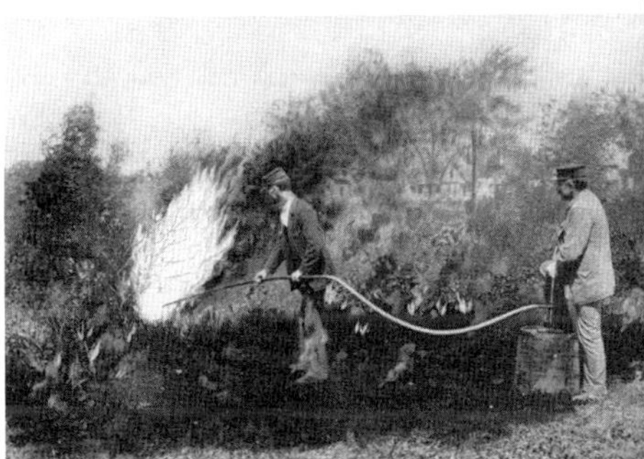

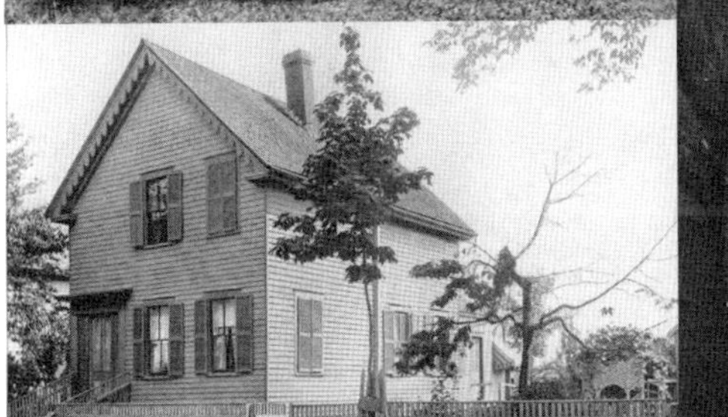

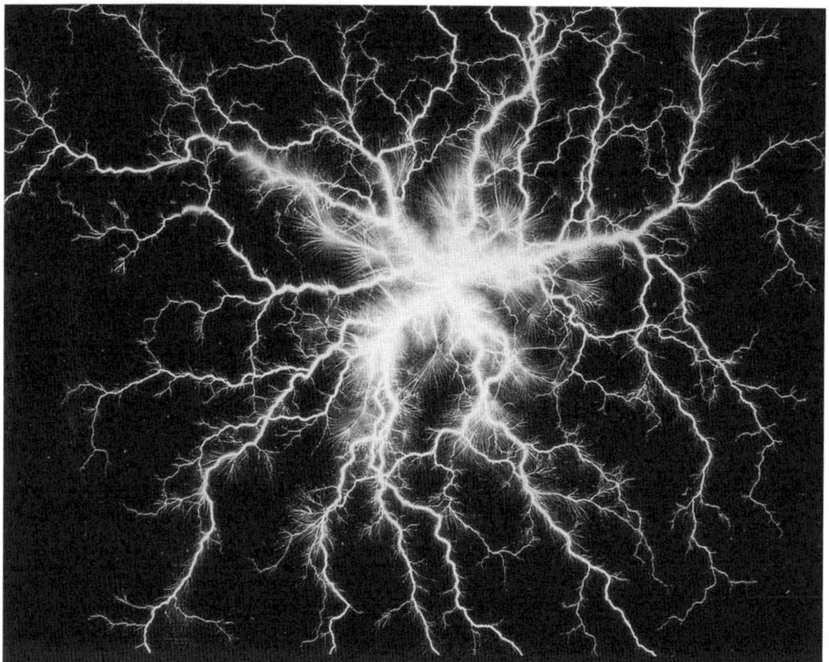

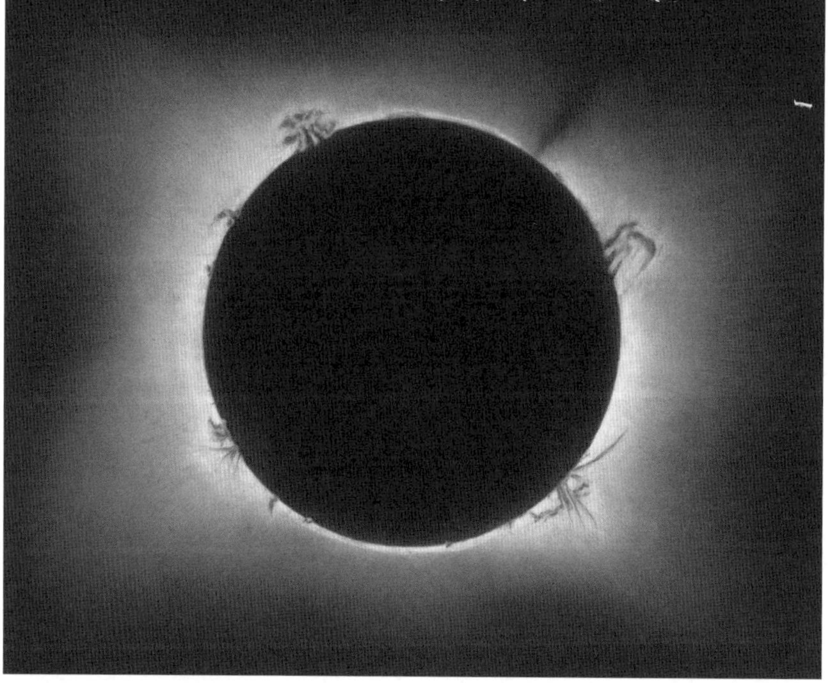

Top: Étienne Léopold Trouvelot, *Direct Electric Spark*, 1885
Bottom: Étienne Léopold Trouvelot, *Total Eclipse of the Sun*, May 6, 1883

The Viewer as a Scientist

A conversation with
Jimena Canales,
Sarah Demeuse,
and Christoph Keller

Sarah Demeuse

I think we should start by going right at the title of this conversation: "The Viewer as a Scientist." I think it's necessary, Christoph, that you unpack this phrase. For instance: Who is viewing? What kind of scientist do you have in mind?

Christoph Keller

In general, I think that titles are meant to trigger the imagination. "The Viewer as a Scientist" juxtaposes two elements, of which one is the viewer and the other is the scientist. The two are almost mythical figures: the scientist refers to scientific observation and thereby to the famous external observer in science. The viewer is also a mythical figure in the arts, as the beholder and contemplator of an artwork. I wanted to bring together not only these two figures, but also the places they inhabit. The scientific observer, on one hand, is connected to an architecture like the observatory or the laboratory. The viewer in the field of art, on the other hand, is related to a museum, or to an exhibition space. Intersecting these spaces of science and art is a recurring feature of my work. I'm interested in the superposition of these two fields, and in finding out how this quasi-complementary relation that I, at least, assign to them plays out.

SDM

While "The Viewer as a Scientist" at first sounded grammatically odd to me, I was also very much called in by it, because it broke down this idea of there being one general scientist, as if built according to a prototype, and that all scientists followed this formula.

JIMENA CANALES

There's no single essence or quality that turns someone into a scientist. Being a scientist, according to the philosopher Mary Hesse, involves "the decision to enter a certain form of life." Today a scientist is an expert with proper university diplomas and degrees who participates in the scientific community as such. But Thomas Kuhn in his *The Structure of Scientific Revolutions*[1] reminds us of the fragility of such a job in times of change: "The man who continues to resist after his whole profession has been converted [to a new paradigm] has ipso facto ceased to be a scientist." This is something that many other sociologists have written about. But even if we understand the complexities behind the category of scientist, the idea that there's a particular scientific "form of life," which entails becoming a certain type of person, engaging in a certain form of rational discourse (think of Jürgen Habermas), going to certain places, and even wearing certain kinds of clothes, is prevalent. It is a "form of life" that is frequently confused with particular cognitive abilities (having powerful or enlarged brains) and particular beliefs (such as secularism, materialism, and reductionism) and which is commonly seen as resulting in the discovery of transcendental universals. It's a social position that, I believe, has a great authority in our contemporary world—a monopoly on knowledge, in many respects. Your title, I think, can help us rethink it.

CK

To whom one speaks, both in the arts and in the sciences, is a question that I am very interested in. Who is the abstract other? The opposite of what you describe as the "general public" would be something like an acknowledged spectatorship, where instead of seeing the other as an amorphous mass, one perceives the other similar to oneself, as a counterpart. This reminds me of what the documentary filmmaker Johan van der Keuken once taught us as students: to assume the same amount of consciousness behind the eyes of another person as that that you assume for yourself. That means to address everybody else—not only in front of the camera, while shooting documentary film, but also off-camera and in real life—as persons, not as props. And this is something that really changes one's dialogue with an audience. This is likely the case in science, but it's especially true in the arts. You can observe how a given work of art approaches its audience—if it understands its viewers to be conscious beings or if it addresses them as a mass. And this is where something ethical or political comes in, both in the arts and in contemporary sciences: in the question of how an audience is addressed.

SDM

So an artwork that assumes the other's consciousness instead of numbing her—it acknowledges her as an active viewer and not as a passive spectator. What do you specifically think about, Christoph, when you think of the art viewer as scientist?

CK

Paradoxically, "The Viewer as a Scientist" first makes me think of a reversal of the direction of the view, and of the attention being directed towards oneself as a viewer rather than that being directed towards an object. The idea that a viewer becomes aware of being an instrument of his own perception, a sensorium if you like. This is something that is, for example, present in my installation *Wünschelruten Testfeld* (Divining rod test field, Kunstverein Hannover, 2004), where visitors were asked to sense the course of water pipes that I had installed beneath the floor. The drawings of their assessments were later photocopied and bound. Using a divining rod is almost a form of meditation, for which you have to relax, focus on nothing in particular, and trust your own inner impulses.

Also I think about Robert Smithson and Mel Bochner's magazine insert *The Domain of the Great Bear* (1966) in which a text describes the artists' experience wandering around the Hayden Planetarium in New York, joking about a sign that says, "Solar System & Rest Rooms," with an image of a pointed finger showing the way. This artwork is also formally important, because it was very consciously conceived as an artists' insert in a magazine and not as a museum piece. The work hints to the fact that museums were educational places at the beginning of modernity, where members of bourgeois society were initiated in rituals of culture. Some remnants of these rituals and regimes of viewing still exist in exhibition displays today.

JC

The observatory, the museum, and the laboratory are three institutions that are as central to modern science as the legislative, judicial, and executive branches are for modern government. A lot of people have a certain view of modernity tied to science, tied to technology, tied to objectivity. But this is a caricature; it's ideology. I've studied the history of how these associations were set in place, and no longer take them for granted. It is common to think that science is more tightly aligned with knowledge than with the arts and crafts and that science is what made us modern. But many others have considered technology as emerging more closely from the arts and crafts, and have found that truth is distilled and in a purer form in fiction or poetry than in math. Since the seventeenth century, thousands of scientists have dedicated themselves to promoting a particular view of their profession in public lectures and publications. That kind of promotion has been as much a part of their job as actually doing science.

It is important to remember that the opposition between the sciences and the arts is quite new. The sciences and the humanities were engaged in a friendly dialogue for a long time, but after the Albert Einstein/Henri Bergson debate of 1922 (which is the subject of my recent book)[2] and especially since the "Science Wars" of the 1990s, the competition has gotten ugly. One side has won out. It's shocking to realize how important science is in our world and yet there is almost nobody watching it from outside, with a critical distance, and with the authority to discuss what's going on.

CK

I'd like to add a few words about this dichotomy of art versus science, or science versus art. I think it's rather interesting to look at their interrelations. In my early essay "Physics of Images—Images of Physics" (which is also included in this book) I stated that you actually cannot think of science as something separate from the rest of culture and I try to elaborate a sort of "complementarity principle" between the two. Scientific developments would most certainly have been impossible without the parallel developments of philosophy, of psychology, and also without the advancements of literature and of the arts. If you think of all the breakthroughs and paradigm shifts in science, they never came completely out of the blue, or because of one single genius scientist, even though this is how it is sometimes portrayed or mythologized. In fact, scientific advances are often made possible by a cultural, social, and political development that accompanies or precedes them. To say it more provocatively: without the rest of culture, without philosophy, and without art, science simply wouldn't be there.

SDM

What you say outlines a role for the arts as intertwined with the rest of society. Can you give an example of how this entanglement plays out in your own work—for example in your Æther project at Centre Pompidou in Paris in 2011?

CK

This interrelation of art, science, and other fields is something that I have always been interested in. When I worked on "Æther—from Cosmology to Consciousness," for instance, which I conceived as an artist-curator, I began by proposing a "quasi-historiography" of the twentieth century, with a large selection of artworks with an emphasis on photography hung in a fictitious timeline. All the works dealt with the notion of the *medium*, either as addressing mediality or referring to the person who embodies spirits in trance seances. The exhibition was very dense and also featured books, video installations, and a film program. Every day we invited a philosopher, a scientist, or an artist to give a talk around the notion of the aether. It was almost like a public exhibition-conference centered on the question of the void. I purposely chose the aether as a topic because it's so broad and essential—the aether is the substance which constitutes the void. This subject inevitably leads us to the question of space, and, at the far end, to the question of the existence of god. These philosophical and theological tangents are still encapsulated in our current conception of space-time, as described by the theory of relativity. And contemporary physics is now bypassing this concept with newer models of space and time, which revisit previous ideas about the qualities of space, sometimes conspicuously echoing the concept of aether. The broad topic allowed me to invite a lot of people from very different fields and disciplines, and to create a conference around an elusive substance and discourse, about which we would otherwise not have been able to speak with each other.

SDM

For me, the clearest example of fields "touching" in your work is in *Go with the flow* (photo documentation of a performance that took place in Tone River, Japan, in 2001), where you leave it up to the river for your raft to go down the scientific or artistic route. Here, you're presenting yourself as someone who is not willingly steering everything himself—you are subject to other forces, too. It reminds me of the kayak Bruno Latour mentions in his essay "Why Has Critique Run Out of Steam." In it, rather than being moored to one side, a kayak moves between two—between humanist critique and scientific fact, or, to translate it a bit closer to our case, between culture and nature.[3]

CK

For sure, but it is also very important to see how the standards of a particular age can shape our categories. Paul Feyerabend's 1984 book *Wissenschaft als Kunst* (Science as a form of art), for instance, has been formative for me.[4] In this book, Feyerabend compares the history of science to the history of art, especially to the work of Alois Riegl, the renowned Austrian art historian. In the late nineteenth century, Riegl eliminated the still-present categories of "blossoming" and "decaying" phases from art historical discourse, and thus also a system of absolute value of higher and lower art. Similarly, Feyerabend's history of art lent the history of science the idea that each epoch has different references, different contexts, and even different epistemologies. This also means that there is no absolute hierarchy in the advancement of the science of humankind. And that science as a culture is not advancing towards a presumed culmination point, but rather that each epoch defines its own standards for evaluating scientific progress. I think you can find this throughout the history of science: that the proclaimed standards of objectivity of a discipline and its respective views on history are correlated with the construction of its own identity.

JC

Then there is Feyerabend's groundbreaking book *Against Method* (1975) that finally put an end to the fantasy of a single scientific method that could work like an efficient algorithm.[5] But although many of us no longer believe in that fantasy, we still do not have a good picture of how science works and how it has led to so many discoveries and advances. But to further my point about the need to dismantle cherished and long-held ideas about what science is, it's important for me to bring to light what is not talked about when we usually talk about science. You just have to look at the way that it is described in the public sphere to realize that questions of labor, diversity, inclusivity, gender, and technology are just not there. Agonistics, competition, and secrecy are similarly whitewashed from it. It's almost as if we're living in a universe full of planets, stars, nebulae, and black holes but with no place for our complex selves, with our identities and narratives, our desires, motivations and dreams, rituals and tools, all that makes us laugh and cry, and the reasons why we remember and why we forget. Those are the real "missing masses" of our universe.

With Foucault, we made some inroads by starting to consider the very concept of "human" as it is used in psychology and the social sciences as historically determined and epistemologically constrained, but there is much more work to do.

Where are our particular non-generic bodies? I'm now working on a project with the cosmologist Lee Smolin on the recent detection of gravity waves. Scientists transformed a ripple in spacetime (which is not perceptible) into sound. The media glossed over the thousands of workers, and their expensive tools and complex negotiations; there's a whole technological framework that translated something that occurred 1.3 billion years ago to something that we could perceive today. Lee and I are interested in exploring how "the universe" has become something so different from "our universe." As an awareness-raising exercise, we're developing a way to taste a gravity wave. It's a silly thing to do, and a provocative one.

SDM

This is a good segue, I think, into the question of research, which we can discuss before we come back to the bigger question of knowledge. Jimena often studies projects that are considered "fringe" for academia. Christoph highlights interconnectivity. There are preset ideas of how the academic conducts research and how the artist does, and I think it's important in this case to actually talk about how you, as a practicing person, make decisions and choices in your projects. Research, in the most general of terms, is about looking for materials, finding them, and about bringing them together in a certain order, framework, and form—giving a voice to matter, almost. None of this, of course, is possible without some sort of drive or curiosity.

CK

I am glad that you mention the notion of "fringe" sciences in the context of knowledge, because this leads to the question of the center and the periphery. In my experience, there is usually a transfer of knowledge from "the fringes" towards the center, simply because new developments tend to come from somewhere outside. In many cases, knowledge is not created in institutional laboratories, as one would design entirely new products, but is rather the result of a transferral of concepts from other, sometimes remote, abandoned, and contested fields and thereby of course a reformulation and transformation of these ideas. In my view the art field may serve as a valid place for temporarily reintroducing some of these ideas from the history of thought into an environment where they are not immediately rebuked with scorn or ridicule. From this perspective, some of my work could be seen as an attempt to reactivate modes of subjectivity and of existence that have been displaced or marginalized by mainstream science.

SDM

If I may, Christoph, I think *Cloudbuster* (2003–2011) is a very relevant case to talk about here. You learn about Wilhelm Reich's orgone theory, you build a rain-making machine based on his stipulations, and you place it in an art context where you also make it operate. You also make it at a time when people are acutely sensitive to questions of climate, draughts, and floods. Your *Cloudbuster* is not a readymade refabricated just to be seen. It has been tested and it worked stunningly on several occasions: first in New York, when you installed it on the roof of MoMA PS1, where it seemingly instigated record rainfalls, but also later as part of a project in a small village, suffering from draught, in the Atlas mountains in Morocco—I don't really know how to describe it. A marvelous accident, a coincidence perhaps. But that event connected non-mainstream or invalidated theory to actual possibility.

CK

When I first proposed the *Cloudbuster* project for PS1 in 2003, one of my starting points was that museums and exhibitions are places where "invalidated theories," as you say, those roads not taken by mainstream science, could be reactivated experimentally. Art, literature, theater, and so on have historically often been fields where transgressive experiences, which would have been not tolerated anywhere outside, could be played out within a cultural environment. The *Cloudbuster* project in Morocco was later and different, because there the initial idea was not just to come and make rain, but rather to collaborate with friends I had made there before. One of them, Hicham Afif, later became the mayor of the village. The project was more about forming a dialogue within the community of how to actively deal with the draught and adverse weather conditions that they have been facing in recent years. We wanted to instigate a form of narration about the scarcity of water in this region, which has long since been characterized by the cohabitation of different cultures with very old and strong ties to oral culture. The fact that the project actually resulted in these heavy and (at this time of the year) not at all to be expected rainfalls was magic for everybody, especially for all the kids in the villages.

JC

Sometimes by following fringe scientists we can learn more about science than just by looking at those in the mainstream. Christoph and I have both been fascinated by the astronomer and artist Étienne Léopold Trouvelot. He is the author of some of the most beautiful lithographs of astronomical phenomena known to us. We both have learned by following his failures. In the process, certain imaging techniques became orthodox in science, such as fixed single-lens cameras, mechanically reproducible photography, and filmstrip-based cinematographic cameras and projectors. In terms of art, his failures show a connection between scientific developments and the rise of the art for art's sake movement of the late nineteenth century. We see how standard boundaries between science and art were frequently contested and how they shifted during this period. For Trouvelot, "scrupulous fidelity and accuracy" in his drawings would "preserve the natural elegance and the delicate outlines peculiar to the objects depicted" as well as "the majestic beauty and radiance of the celestial objects."[6] According to this logic, any ugly images of astronomical phenomena would not be accurate depictions of the celestial vault. Today it would be ridiculous to consider beauty as a criterion for scientific images, but that was not always the case.

In my research on the history of the strobe light, I focused on researchers who decided to use a strong source of illumination in a radically new way—not for investigating nature, but for exploring previously inaccessible areas of their own psyche. These investigators learned a lot by employing this instrument in non-standard ways—they valiantly stared directly into the shining light. Their research was key for neurophysiology and cybernetics (John R. Smythies, William Grey Walter, etc.) and for art. Some of the most revolutionary artistic and literary experiments by Aldous Huxley, William S. Burroughs, Ken Kesey, and Tony Conrad arose from their experiences of staring directly into a strobe light.

SDM

The terms "knowledge" and "knowledge production" have come up a bit and, deep down, the question of art's relation to science and vice versa really has to do with knowledge—where does it reside, who owns it, how does it circulate, how does it live, how does it affect and have an effect? It's a question worth pondering especially at a time when knowledge has become a commodity—think of education, but also of increasing concerns about accessing information, with the resources for knowledge production becoming privatized, made scarce. I'm going on a tangent here, but that's because the place of knowledge and knowledge production you both circle around has, I think, a lot to do with how you envision the future practitioner, whether she is called a viewer, researcher, or artist.

CK

To get to the first part of what you said, Sarah, looking at the relationality of science from the point of view of an artist has to do with figuring out where we really stand today, but from a transcultural or perspectivist viewpoint. Take, for an example of an extreme perspective, the viewpoint of an interstellar traveller who is looking with anthropological interest at the earthlings' expertise from outer space. This is the question of "xenoscience," which means being aware of the peculiarity of science as a particular human or humanoid perspective. In response to your question about knowledge production, I would repeat that knowledge should be open and as comprehensible as possible. If you take my *Inverse Observatories* series (2007), for example, observatories are literally inverted in terms of how knowledge is transmitted. Normally the gaze in an observatory is directed outside towards the stars and one tries to receive information from the borders of the cosmos. I tried to reverse the view, changing the direction of the entire setup. One of the *Inverse Observatoriums* is called *Message to the Extraterrestrials* (2007). It consists of a Dobson telescope whose viewfinder has been replaced by a projector that sends images to outer space rather than receiving them. So instead of taking images in from outer space, you send images from this world to the borders of the universe. And what's important here is not whether the extraterrestrials, if they happen to exist, can really receive the images. The main source of knowledge production in this installation is the change of perspective, the mirror that the addressed extraterrestrials hold back toward us.

JC

It is amazing how much we have changed our environment on Earth through our attempts to explore and observe outer space. Consider wireless image transmission technologies, such as television. I doubt we would have improved them so much and as early as we did were it not for space exploration. Without it, it would be nearly impossible to get photographs from space satellites as astronauts would have to go back to space periodically to fetch and replace film canisters from satellites. Scientists tested various designs to return the film from camera space-rockets and satellites, but there was little point in funding missions that would not result in images. Consider the moon landing. President Kennedy was convinced the event had to be *televised* live to make a full political and national security impact. Television was a central element of space exploration. In 1979 astronomers mounted selenium-sulphur vidicon cameras on Voyager 1 and 2. Our entire system of satellite-based communications, starting with TVs in space and later cell phones and GPS, would not be in place were it not for these precedents.

Should we just consider these and many other innovations as technological offshoots of basic science research? Would we now have them available for civilian use? Would we have the bandwidths necessary for transmitting baby and puppy pics across the internet and the capacity for storing and processing them if it had not been for these government-backed initiatives? Space exploration and astronomical observatories have no doubt increased our knowledge of the universe, but more importantly they have changed our world back here on Earth.

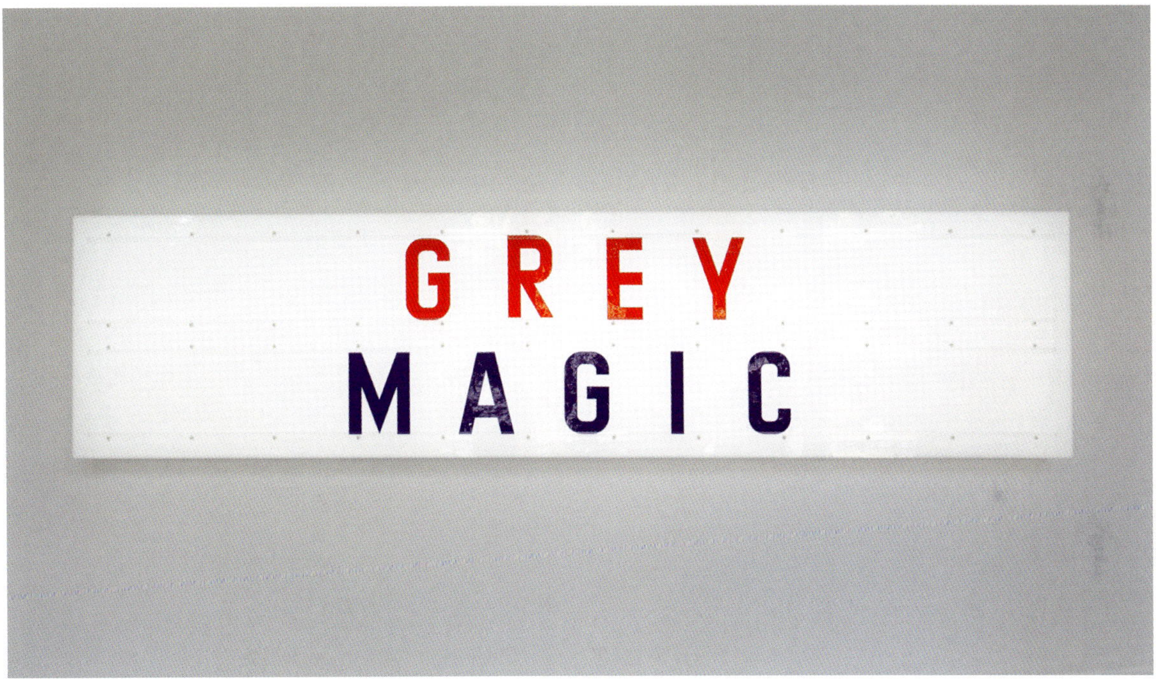
GREY
MAGIC

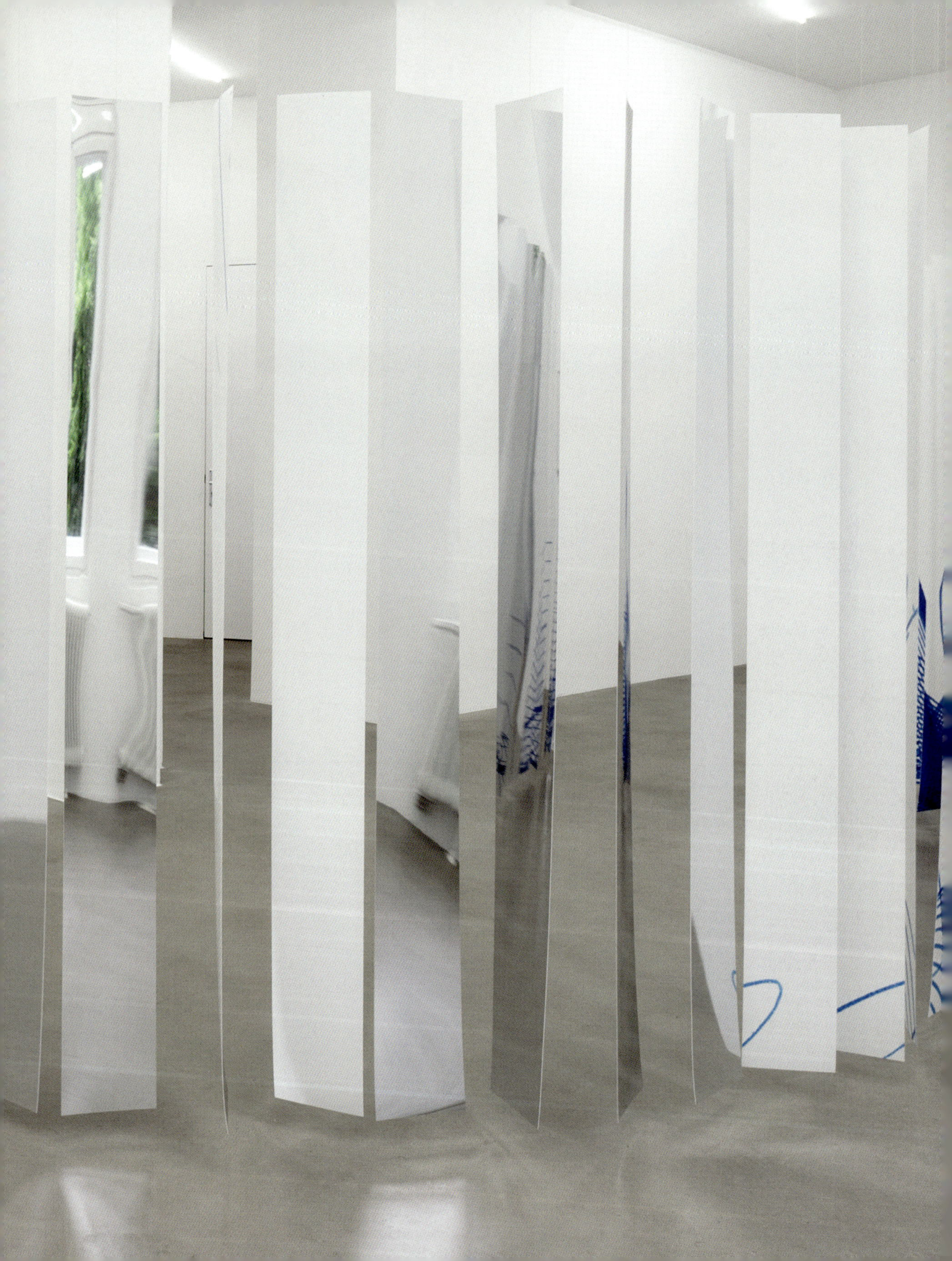

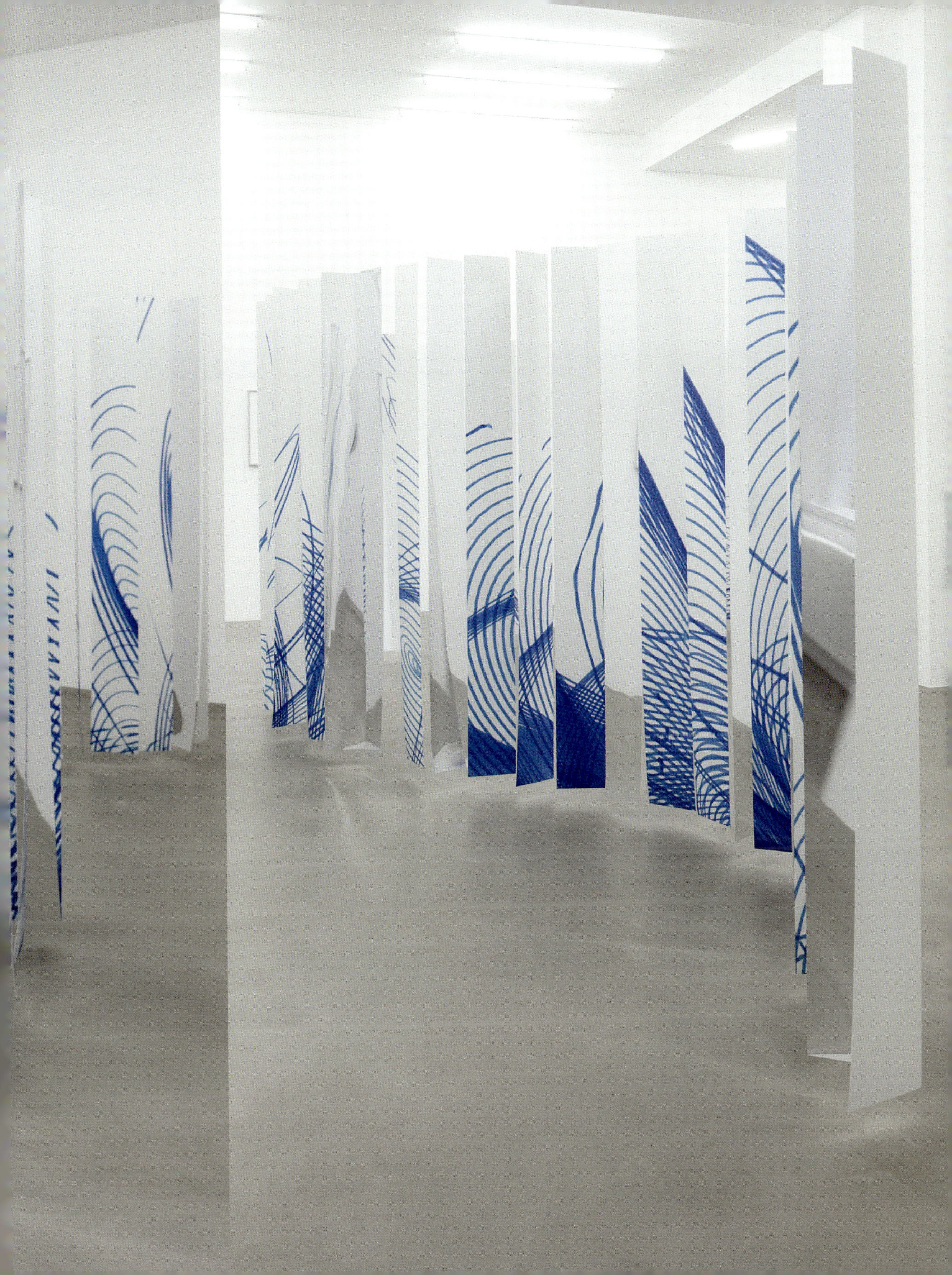

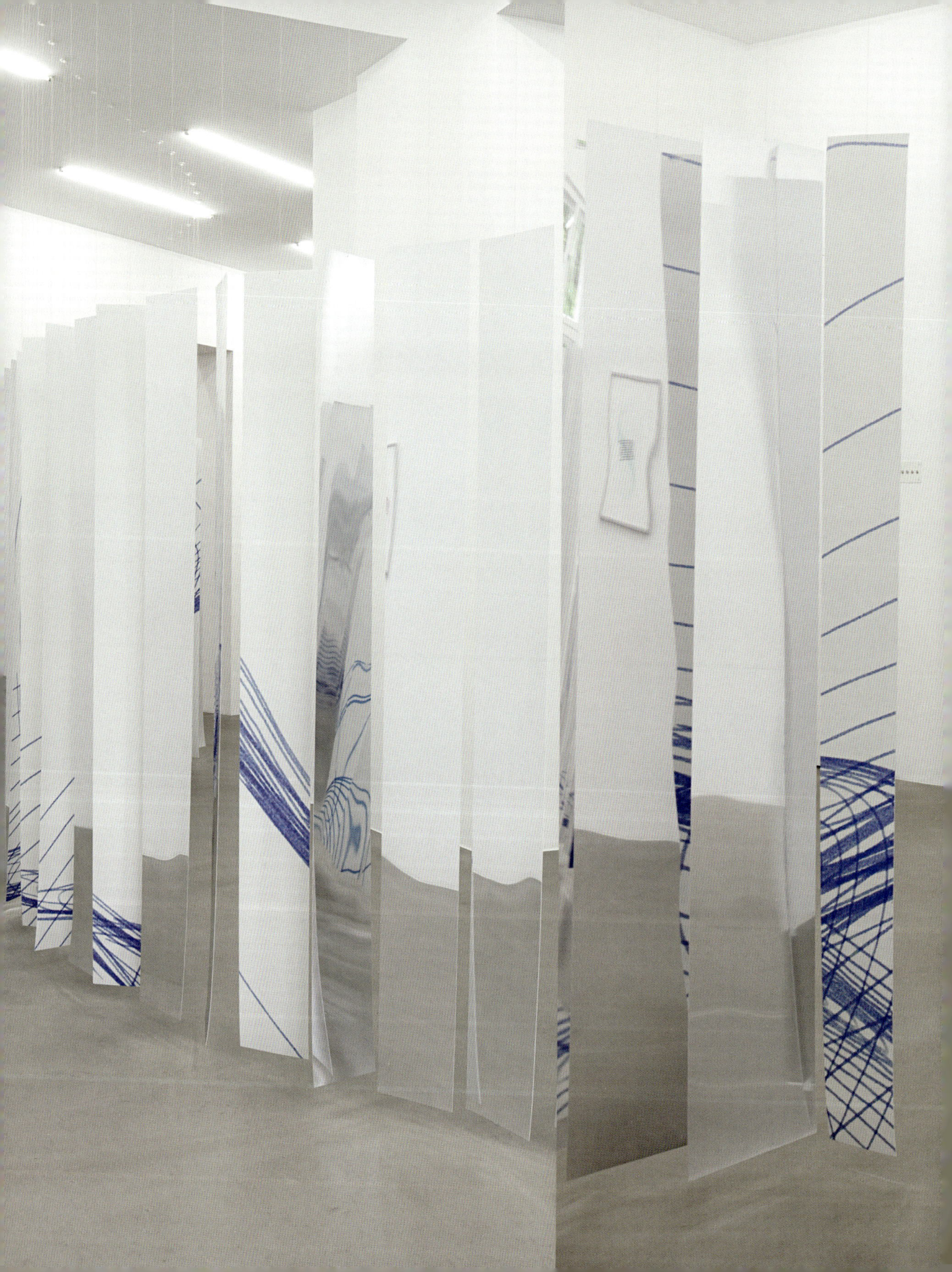

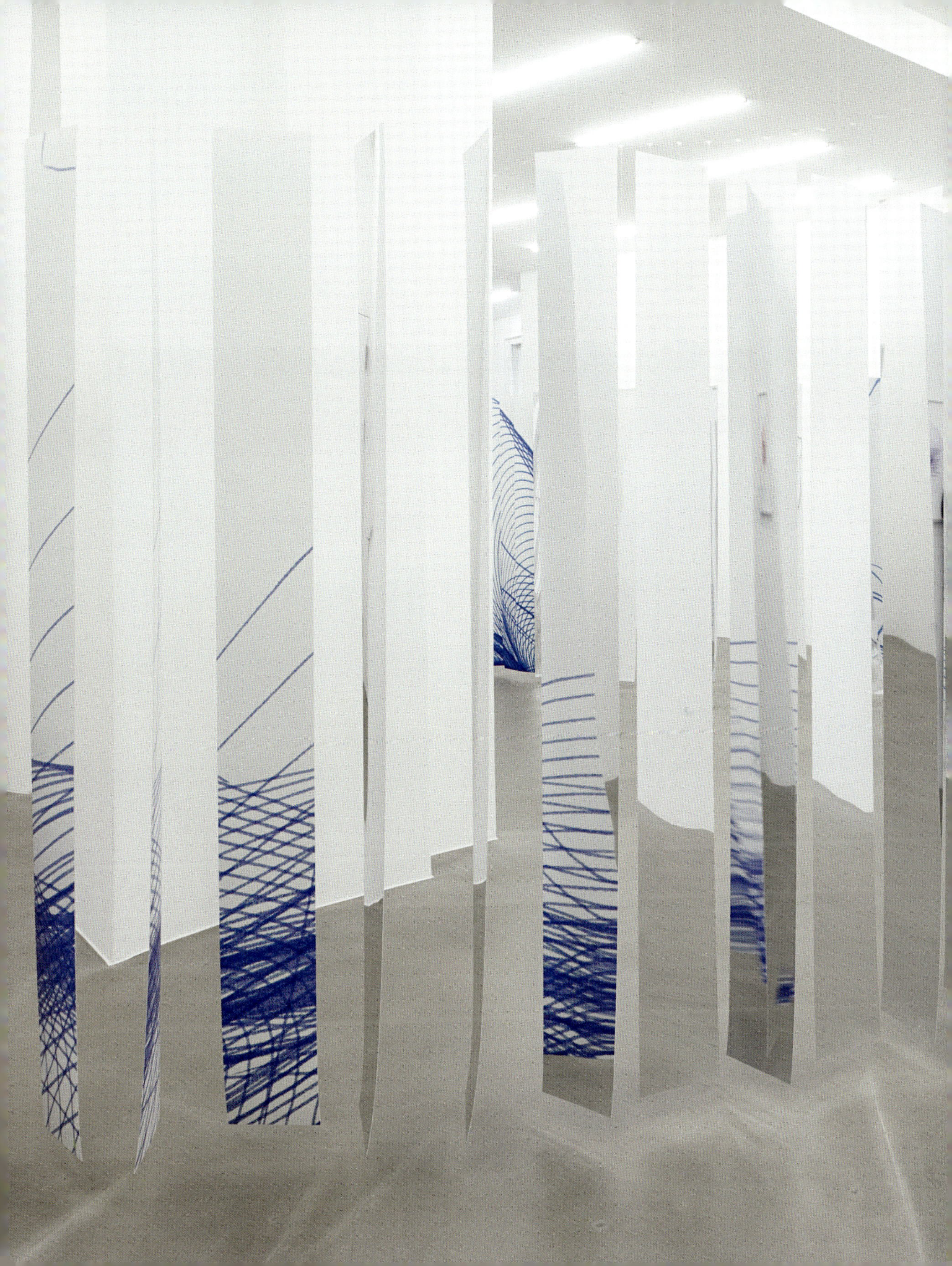

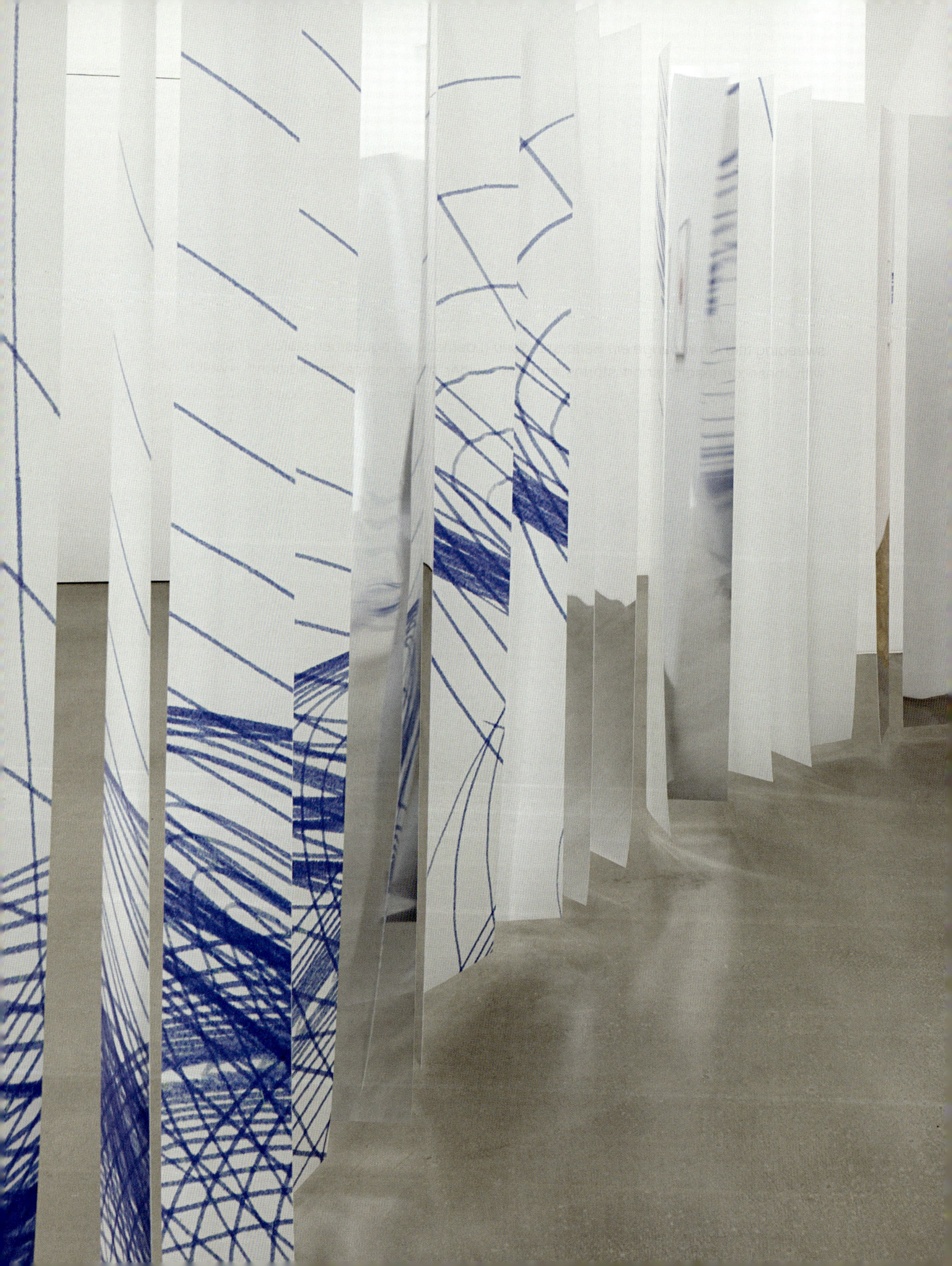

ECCENTRIC SENSATION

On the Aether Theory of Perception in Ernst Marcus and Salomo Friedlaender / Mynona
By Christoph Keller

When I first encountered the grotesques written by Salomo Friedlaender, also known as Mynona, I was still a teenager. More specifically, a friend recommended that I read an anthology of his work edited by Hartmut Geerken and published by *edition text+kritik* with the sweeping title *Ich verlange ein Reiterstandbild* (I demand an equestrian statue). The encounter with these grotesque short stories and their wider philosophical background—which only gradually became accessible to me—was a kind of initiation into the literature and arts of the early twentieth century in Berlin for me. Actually it was more of a portal: its many connections to contemporary authors, philosophers, anarchists, antimilitarists, and the artistic avant-garde (represented by Paul Scheerbart, Martin Buber, Alfred Kubin, Hannah Höch, Raoul Hausmann, Otto Gross, Erich Mühsam, Hugo Ball, George Grosz, Walter Benjamin, and many more), whose capricious biographies intersected with Mynona's life and work, constitute a pre-history of the fine arts, philosophy, literature, and science of the late nineteenth and early twentieth centuries in Berlin, extending beyond the realm of Expressionism and preceding the advent of Berlin Dada. The fact that the traces of this adventurous and in no way marginal scene and its work hardly continue to be felt today may be due in part to their ostracism and destruction during the Third Reich. More recently, however, neither the Federal Republic of Germany, the GDR, nor, later the reunified country until now have shown an interest in recognizing the cultural impact of this socially progressive and, in part, migrant bohemian group of artists who mocked bourgeois society.

Ernst Moses Marcus was a teacher and friend of Mynona, who honored him as the "heir of Kant" (the title was simultaneously a dig at Schopenhauer, who had claimed this crown for himself). Since 1898 Marcus had been working intensely with the aether theory of Kant's *Opus postumum*, from which he developed a scientific and philosophical theory of cognition that he termed *the eccentric sensation*, which he continued to expand until his death in 1928. According to Marcus's theory, we do not perceive objects themselves; rather we perceive an optical impulse led through the eye to the brain, causing an immediate emanation of aether waves through the cranium. The visual object that is perceived within the brain is then materialized in the form of an aether emanation in precisely the direction of the optical impulse. Accordingly, what we actually perceive is an aether world—which is nonetheless real.

Marcus lived and worked as a philosopher and lawyer in Essen, where Mynona visited him regularly, at least once in the company of his friend, the "Dadasoph" Raoul Hausmann, in 1915. The theory of eccentric sensation (i.e. the aether theory of cognition) meandered through many of Mynona's publications into Berlin's cultural scene. In 1918, Mynona facilitated the publication of Marcus's essay "Das Problem der exzentrischen Empfindung und seine Lösung" (The problem of eccentric sensation and its solution) by Herwarth Walden's publishing house

Der Sturm, one of the central publishers of Berlin's avant-garde of the time. Mynona's most important novel *Graue Magie: Ein Berliner Nachschlüsselroman* (Grey magic: a skeleton key novel from Berlin) was published four years later, in 1922. It is an homage to Marcus's theory of eccentric sensation and an elaboration of ethereal and rational magic in the form of a novel. Berlin and its bohemian circles form the background of the fantastical narrative, and Marcus makes an appearance as "Dr. Sucram," his name spelled backwards much like "Mynona" reads backwards as "anonym." Hausmann, too, advanced Marcus's theory (or at least those parts that he found interesting) in his later Dada philosophical work *Sensorialité excentrique* (Eccentric sensoriality) from 1970.

Marcus rejected the localization of sensations in the brain, anticipating today's criticism of imaging technologies within brain research and neuropsychology, which localize cognitive processes primarily in the brain. The concept of the organ of the brain as an apparatus and as the black box of the mind seems increasingly limited and obsolete. In a mediatized world, the ego no longer resides in the body, but exceeds it into media space. As Mynona writes in 1922 in *Graue Magie*: "Our body reaches ethereally into the cosmos, its skin is not its real boundary." We can draw definite parallels between the mediatized space of the present day and the aether-filled space of eccentric sensation that Marcus postulated. Consequently, literature and media scholar Friedrich Kittler, in his 1986 work *Gramophone, Film, Typewriter*, published two of Mynona's grotesque stories in full. To this day, the English edition of Kittler's book contains one of the rare English translations of Mynona's work.

This media aether, encompassing everything without exception (and therefore also art), is not static but in permanent flux. Marcus and, after him, Mynona imagined the world as a magical cinema which could only be materialized from the aether through sensation (following Kant). Marcus saw his theory of eccentric sensation as part of the groundbreaking discoveries of the turn of the twentieth century within neurophysiology and field theory, alongside the discoveries of x-rays and radioactivity—and the theory of relativity, against whose concept of space-time he argues with Kant. The experimental concept described within the theory of eccentric sensation—of a connecting medium between the perceived object and the observer, between matter and consciousness, and therefore also between the world and its linguistic and pictorial access—remains an inspiration even today. As our experience of reality is increasingly shaped by interconnected technological media, our worlds become completely immersed in and entangled with a data cloud or vortex, up to the point where reality itself becomes just a temporal emanation within this "new aether."

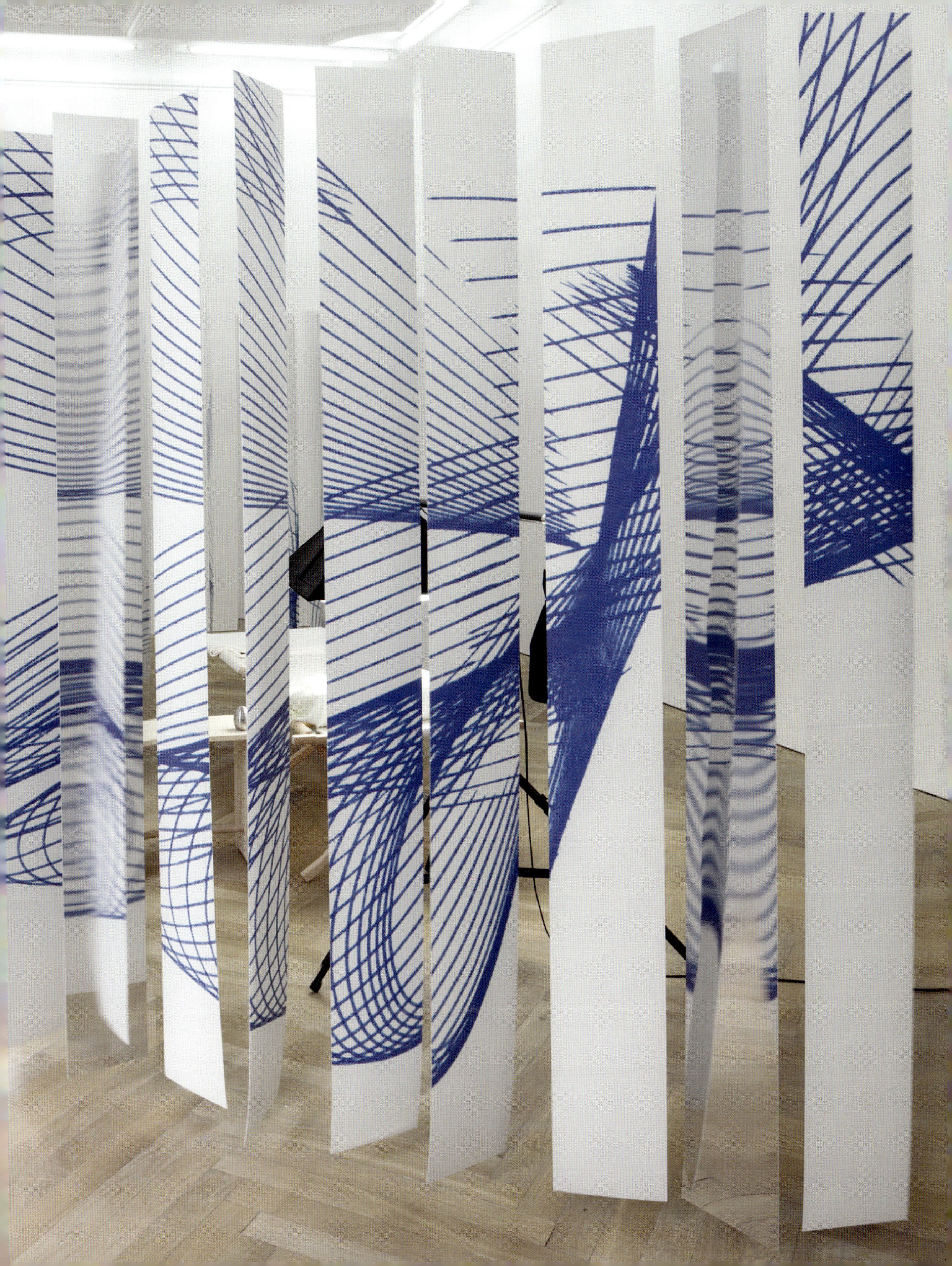

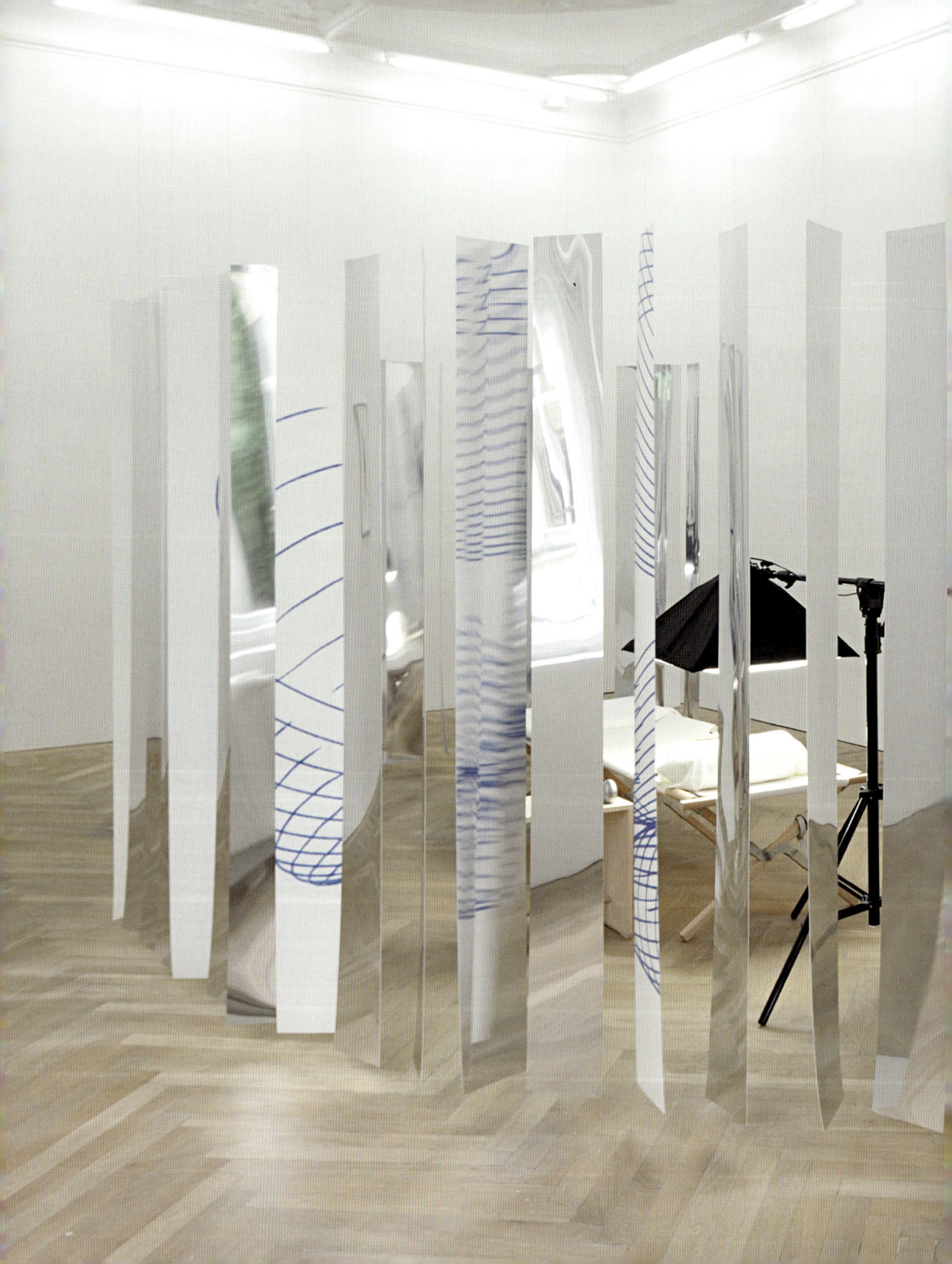

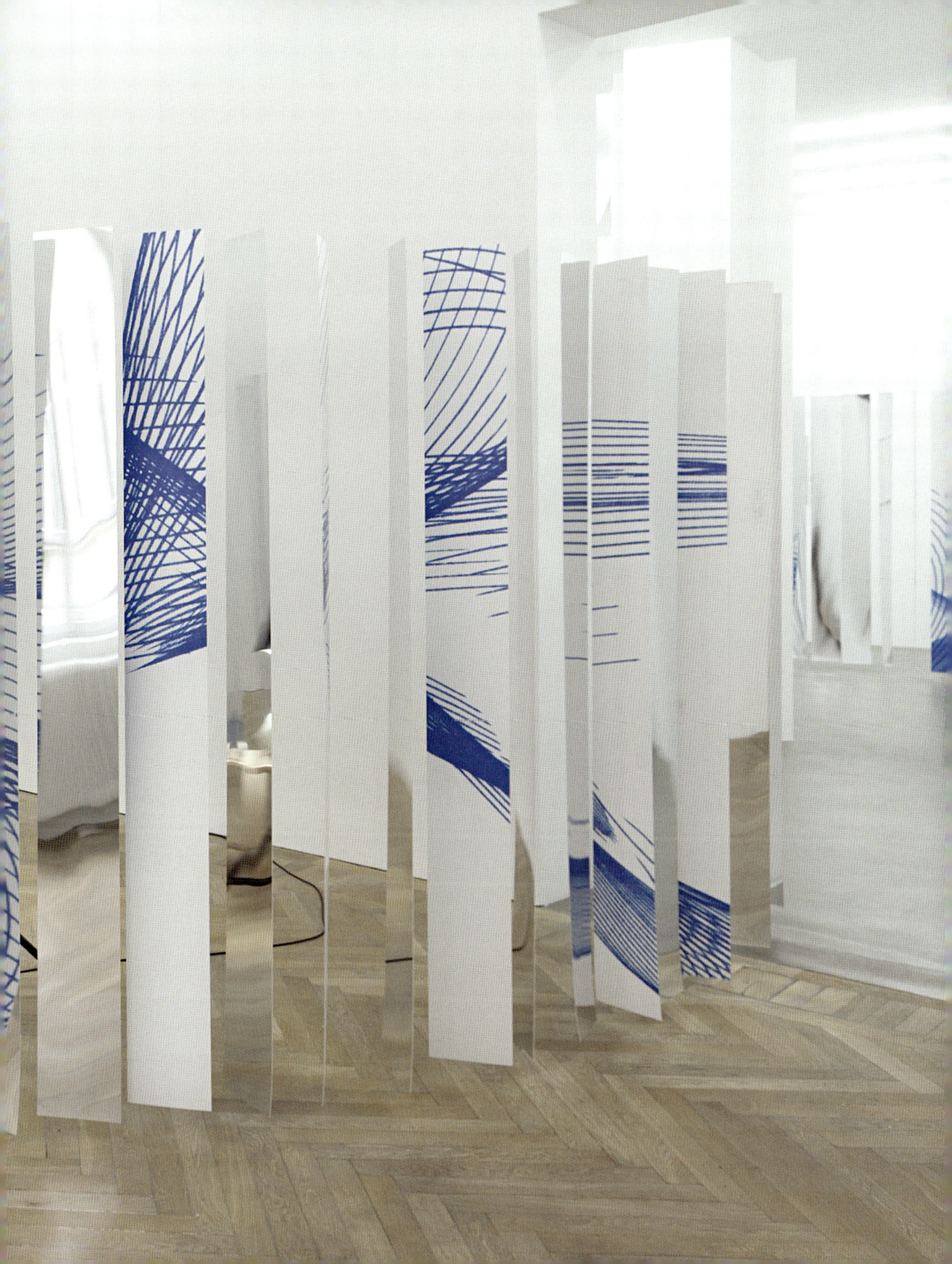

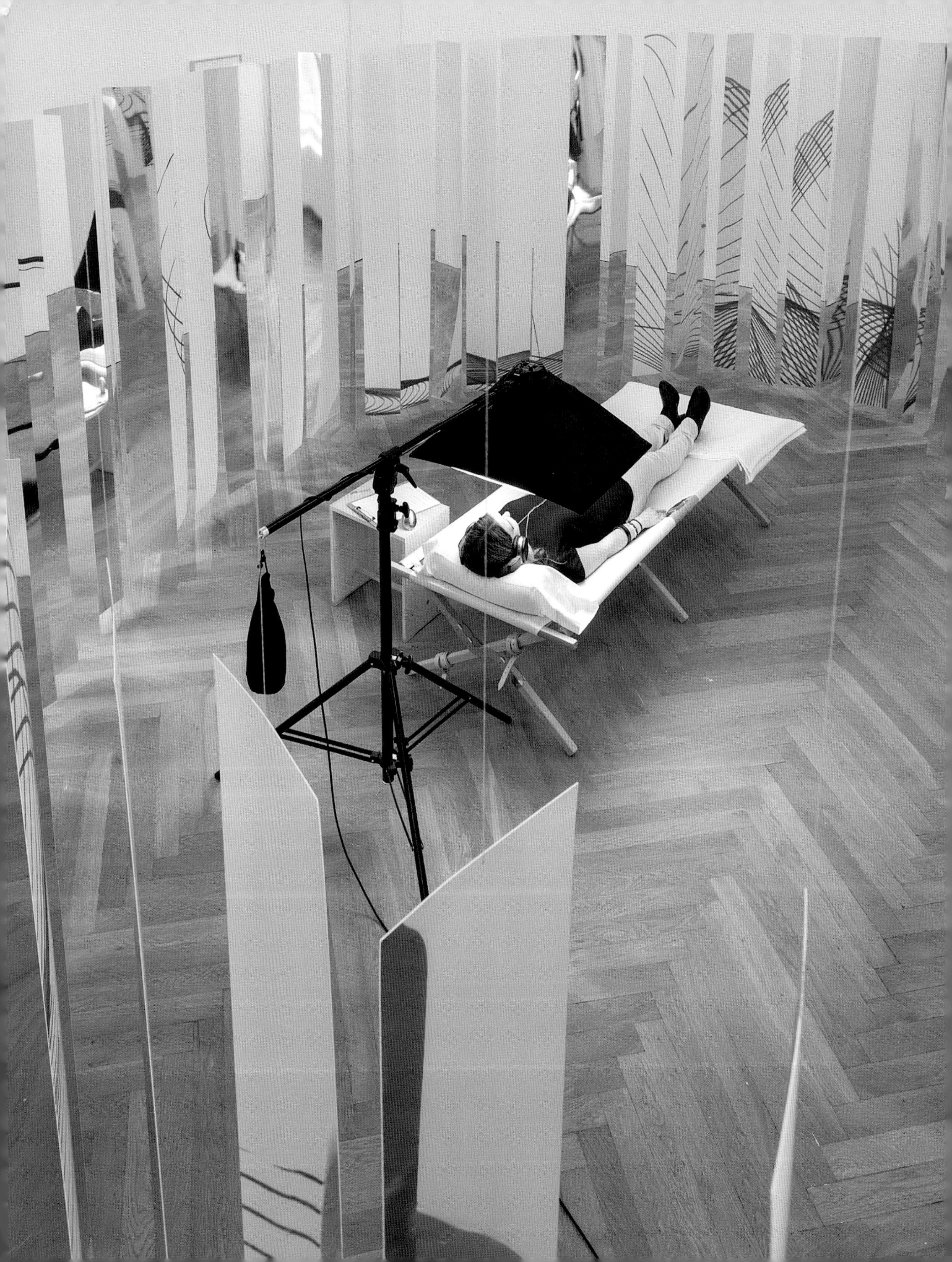

CONVERSATION ON ERNST MARCUS

From a conversation between Christoph Keller and Detlef Thiel on Ernst Marcus's *Exzentrische Empfindung*, Salomo Friedlaender / Mynona, and others

Detlef Thiel In 1920, Ernst Marcus started the whole anti-Einstein campaign. And this here is *Kant und der Äther*, Marcus's review of the publication by Erich Adickes, an 850-page tome, considered to this day to be the standard work on Kant's *Opus postumum*. Adickes tried for the first time to discern its various structures and to date them and all that. And Marcus railed against him, as he formulated his aether theory for the first time. Marcus found his material in Adickes's work, but put it together in a totally different way.

When Kant died, the 500 or so pages of the manuscript were found on his desk. And then "tourists" kept coming, so to speak: curious people who came and leafed through it. That's the state in which it was found—all mixed up—and that's how it was first printed.

Christoph Keller At the time, Ernst Marcus was already in pursuit of the aether theory—or that of the world aether. He must have developed it at an earlier date. When did Marcus begin with this?

DT It's actually a fundamental idea in Marcus's work. He said he had the idea in 1892. He stated this precisely in *Problem der exzentrischen Empfindung*—that's where he dates it. I believe he had the idea in March of 1892. At the time, he was still immersed in Schopenhauer, who is a very important source for this.

How do we arrive at perceptions of things residing outside our direct environment? When I look outside and see leaves, for instance, what exactly is happening? It's this eccentric form of sensation. The brain is the center. The "central organ"—this was the old term. And for Marcus, this was the fundamental problem. He developed this in various steps and phases over the course of his life.

And the issue he had with Erich Adickes and the *Opus postumum* was one of his last major work phases. After that, he unraveled, developed, and refined his aether theory. This carried on to the very last book of 1927, one year before he died. The final chapter constitutes the definitive version of the aether theory, where he talks about primary and secondary aether...

CK Primary aether is a priori aether?

DT Yes, practically everything is a priori. The aether is the precondition for the possibility of experience. When I experience something, it has to come from the outside somehow. From

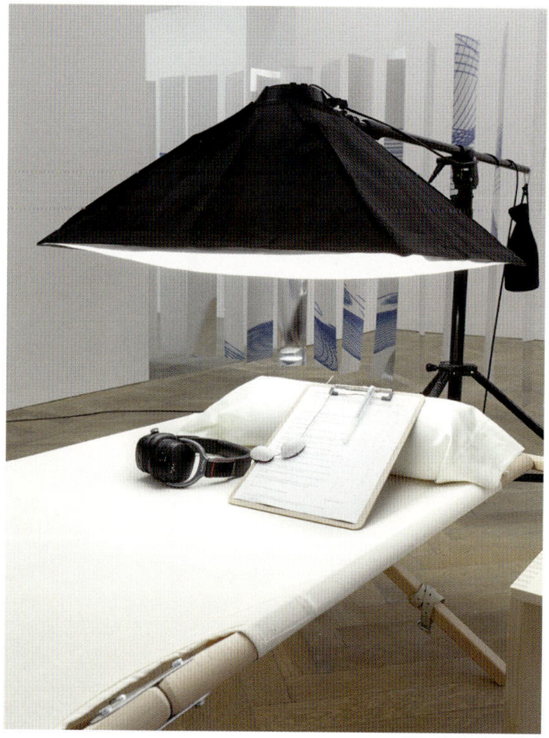

outside my body. Even my body still belongs to the outside world. And you can readily observe this: that you can transplant a heart, for instance—in other words, the body's parts are replaceable. Where does the self reside? It's immaterial, this is the center. Kant was concerned with the unity of nature and its recognizability. He laid the foundation for the physical sciences; he aspired to this, and this is the transition from the purely metaphysical considerations—the writing desk—to actual praxis and what physicists do in a concrete sense. And this should go for today's physicists as well. The rest is details. The aether is everywhere and in constant motion. Kant said that the aether is in a constant state of attraction/repulsion, that these are its basic movements. And that, as Mynona would say, is a polarity. The aether itself does not change its location; rather, changes in location always take place *in* the aether. The aether is fixed, and when we arrive at the aether's boundaries—if we were able to arrive there—then we'd be at the edge of the universe. More or less.

CK But he also says, "The aether is all-moving," doesn't he? This means that all matter comes from the aether. Can you explain this?

DT Yes, Marcus says this—that's his continuation. He states that there is this primary

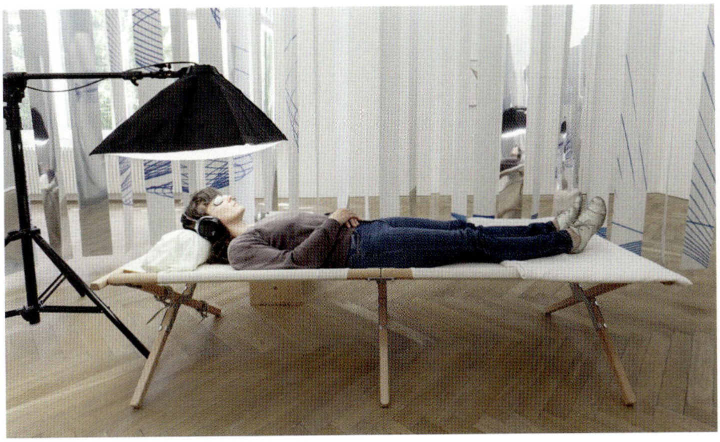

aether. And that there's a secondary aether that consists in the embodied objects. Whether this is living or dead matter is beside the point. A stone is already as though congealed. Now and again he uses the word "congealed"—in other words, compressed. The aether is in constant motion, and when this compresses somewhat…

CK … as a "vortex," so to speak?

DT Yes. This is all hypothesis—you have to try to imagine something out of this. All bodies and living beings and everything else arise out of this aether. And the special thing about Marcus is that there's only one entity that is not affected by the aether, and that's the self, or the will. And if you don't accept this, then all of Marcus falls flat. The will is a substance that is not material, and consequently, it's not a part of the aether and hence not "coordinated," but rather "superordinated," as he says. And for this reason, by using my will, and by cultivating it, I can influence the aether.

CK But he goes even further in his theory, I believe—he goes so far as to say that one could actually influence the entire universe with one's will, with a kind of "natural magic."

DT Yes, these are those "fantasies of omnipotence"—but this is far too severe, too rough a way of describing this—it isn't clear in Marcus's writing, but it is with Mynona, who lived in a different time, exiled in Paris. He tried to mobilize counterforces in himself in order to compen-

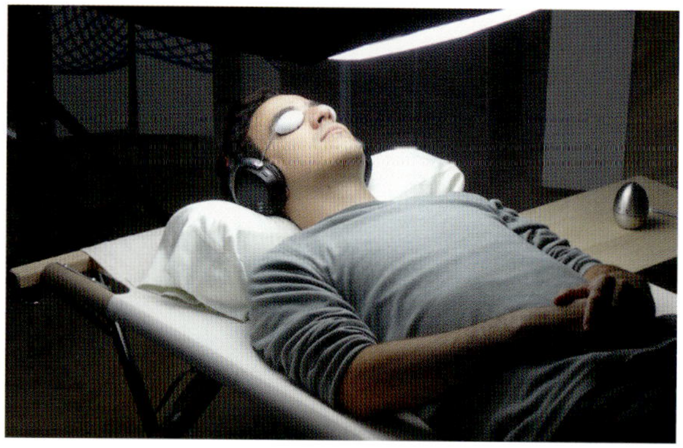

sate the external insanity—World War II and all that, his personal situation. And as a result, of course, he tended to take these fantasies of power further. But I don't think he was so naïve as to dream of this just like that. He was too critical for that.

CK What Mynona wanted to do with the aether was more of a kind of literary wish, he isn't deadly serious, of course—there's always an ironic point to it all.

DT He played out something similar with the radio towers in *Der antibabylonische Turm*, where the will of certain individuals—Kantians, Socrates-Kantians, Socratic Kantians—is inculcated in people via radio waves, "repurposing" them by degrees. These were the measures he took against Nazi indoctrination, which worked with similar means, radio broadcasting and television. Not so much TV as radio, however. All media were polarized in one direction. And he tried to reverse the polarity of this.

There's that funny book by Upton Sinclair, *Mental Radio* (1930), that he mentions again and again. There's a German edition that was published later, *Radar der Psyche*, with an introduction by Albert Einstein. It wasn't translated until 1973. So perhaps Mynona had a copy of the American edition of *Mental Radio*—I don't know if he read it. At any rate, he talks about it again and again. Sinclair was a Pulitzer Prize winner, he was a socially critical writer, very critical, a muckraker, committed to social change in the United States. But in this book, he merely describes experiments he conducted with his wife. She was lying in a room with her eyes closed, and he was in another room of the house. He drew certain figures on a piece of paper—they're all printed in the book—and she redrew them. And then he compared the two. These experiments went on for years, ten years I believe. It was an attempt to make a crazy phenomenon plausible.

CK And she was able to “see” these drawings?

DT Yes, apparently she was that telepathic, or given to being a medium, and so they played it out. It was about mental and psychic influence, using very simple means: shapes, line drawings, words. Words are already complicated.

CK When was this published?

DT The American edition was published in 1930. In my opinion, Mynona didn’t read the English version, otherwise he wouldn’t have been as enthusiastic. Because the book really does go in the direction of telepathy. He was interested in something else, and was inspired by the title *Mental Radio*, which gets bungled in the German title. It’s about the mind, mental radio. The mind, the brain is also a broadcasting station. It doesn’t only take in impressions, but transmits them, too. The activity of the self: this is also one of Kant’s thoughts. And Marcus picked up on this.

CK And so that’s the basis for what he termed the “eccentric sensation”?

DT “Sensorialité excentrique,” I think that’s how they translated it into French. There’s this late book by Raoul Hausmann, in which Marcus was mentioned once or twice “by mistake.” Other than that, it’s all Hausmann’s own stuff. That’s typical for him.

He probably arrived at Marcus through Mynona, whom he met at the very latest in 1915. And so he heard of Marcus, and Hausmann was such an impulsive guy that always wanted to do everything himself. And he said: “OK, he told me there’s this crazy philosopher in Essen, let’s go there right away.” And the painter Otto Freundlich too, by the way. They both visited Marcus at the same time, and read this manuscript that Marcus had lying there, the *Exzentrische Empfindung*, that is, read it through, and then “bang”—the rest was all their own speculation.

CK Also Emmy Hennings could have met Mynona in Berlin…

DT At least she knew who he was. Prior to Dada Zurich, in the summer before the Cabaret Voltaire was founded, Hugo Ball and Emmy Hennings held literary evenings, occasionally in hotels on Lake Zurich and nearby, and texts by Mynona were also read there.

CK But then there is also a connection between Mynona and the Cabaret Voltaire?

DT Hugo Ball.

CK Did Ball integrate Mynona in Zurich, in the Spiegelgasse? Do you know anything about that?

DT He himself didn't, but Olli Jacques recited texts by him at the opening.

CK In the Cabaret Voltaire?

DT Yes, that's definitely known. It happened in March 1916 or thereabouts. Ball knew who Mynona was, and on the other hand, ten years later, Mynona reviewed Ball's autobiography, *Die Flucht aus der Zeit*. And at the beginning he says: "Hugo Ball claims to have invented Dadaism." You can hear from the way he phrases it that it's not entirely true.

Whoever invented Dadaism is another question. We say that Mynona laid the philosophical cornerstone for Dada: Dada Berlin. Dada Berlin was a bit later than Dada Zurich. You know, quarrels over priority.

CK And a completely different Dada than Dada Paris, for instance...

DT Yes, and from there it spread further, via Cologne, to Max Ernst, Baargeld, and all the others. Otto Freundlich had a studio near Cologne. And it went from there to this group of artists on the Rhine. Freundlich also digested his reading of Marcus's manuscript in various texts. But then he turned away from Kant. Mystical communism, cosmic stuff and so on. In *Graue Magie*, Otto Freundlich appears under the name "Dodo Würdig."

CK Würdig, as in worthy?

DT Yes, Würdig. And his cousin was Edwin, Edwin Freundlich (as in friendly), who worked with Einstein. In the novel he turns up as "Edwin Feindlich" (which means hostile). And Freundlich's paintings are called "Darmverschlingungsbilder," or "intestinal loop paintings."

CK He fit the whole avant-garde scene in the book, it can't even all be reconstructed. But is there more information about who else Mynona was connected to at the time, between 1906 and 1919, roughly, before Dada Berlin emerged?

DT Through Herwarth Walden he knew various different people from *Der Sturm*, he was a part of that. He also knew Franz Pfemfert, although it wasn't a close contact, and there's no evidence of correspondence. But he was also a part of that, since he published in *Die Aktion* from the very beginning. He knew Arthur Segal, and that goes back to 1914, if not earlier. And Segal was the "philosophical painter," as Mynona confirmed to him in writing: "You are a Kantian philosophical painter because you translate the concept of polarity."

CK Wasn't Mynona also friends with Martin Buber?

DT The early Mynona had a casual contact to Martin Buber that carried on throughout their lives. Buber was seven years younger, one mustn't forget. From 1906, they lived close to one another in Berlin, so they must have seen each other frequently. And it was Buber who was impressed, not the other way around.

CK Did he have any contact with Gershom Scholem?

DT Scholem got to know Mynona through Walter Benjamin, otherwise Scholem would have probably ignored Mynona. There are quotes from Scholem in which he says: "When I read *Rosa die schöne Schutzmannsfrau* from 1913, I fell off my chair laughing, and today"—he was writing this in the 1960s—"when I read this today, it leaves me cold." Scholem didn't have many good things to say about Mynona, but he acknowledged that his friend, Benjamin, was very keen on him. He recounted: "Walter was visiting again today and raved about Mynona." Benjamin and Mynona met several times, that much is clear.

CK What did Benjamin write about Mynona? Are there any records of that?

DT He appropriated the term, "creative indifference," at least five or six times in his own writing. But it took a long time for him to mention the names Mynona or Friedlaender.

When Benjamin wanted to work out his political theory, which is lost now, or only exists in fragments, in 1920/21, Mynona blew Bloch away, the *Geist der Utopie*. And Benjamin especially liked this, and used it against Bloch for his own political theory. And so when Mynona reproaches Bloch: "Bloch, cut out the preaching! Become sober and profane!"—then this "profane" became a catchword for Benjamin.

1) Paranormal ideation questionnaire[*]

Please place a tick in one of the four boxes for each of the below statements, according to how true you believe it to be: 0=Definitely True 1=Somewhat True 2=Somewhat false 3=Definitely False

	Definitely True 0	1	2	Definitely False 3
1) I have had at least one telepathic experience with another person.	( )	( )	( )	( )
2) I never had any extrasensory perceptions.	( )	( )	( )	( )
3) I have had at least once a premonition that came true and I thought this was not due to chance.	( )	( )	( )	( )
4) I think telepathy exists.	( )	( )	( )	( )
5) Some dreams refer to future incidences, which cannot be known before.	( )	( )	( )	( )
6) I have had at least one dream that referred to the future and it was fulfilled so exactly that I think it was not due to chance.	( )	( )	( )	( )
7) I think there is something such as a spirit, soul or ghost that may continue to exist after a person has died.	( )	( )	( )	( )
8) I think that it is possible to communicate with the dead.	( )	( )	( )	( )
9) I have had at least one experience in which I was aware of the spirit, soul or ghost of someone who was not physically alive.	( )	( )	( )	( )
10) I think beings exist that are divine/godly and not of the physical world.	( )	( )	( )	( )
11) I think that prayers or wishes are sometimes heard and granted by divine/godly beings.	( )	( )	( )	( )
12) I think certain mythical creatures (e.g. elves, dragons, fairies) exist which human beings are not easily aware of.	( )	( )	( )	( )
13) I believe that intelligent life-forms from other planets have visited our planet.	( )	( )	( )	( )
14) I have had at least one experience in which I witnessed a flying object or life-form which I think was not from this planet.	( )	( )	( )	( )

Thank you for completing this assessment.

Subject Number:

[*] from "Ganzfeld-induced hallucinatory experience, its phenomenology and cerebral electrophysiology" by Jiri Wackermann, Peter Pütz and Carsten Allefeld, Cortex, 44: 1364–1378, 2008.

2) Visual imagination record (ganzfeld experiment)

After completing the questionnaire you are asked to put on headphones and goggles. Please lie down, look into the diffusion lamp above your head and listen to the white noise for 10 min.
Let your mind flow and allow images to emerge in front of your eyes. Just be open to what appears.

When the relaxation phase ends, please make a sketch of the images or forms that have appeared in your mind during the experience on the drawing area below. If you would like to add comments, you may do so.

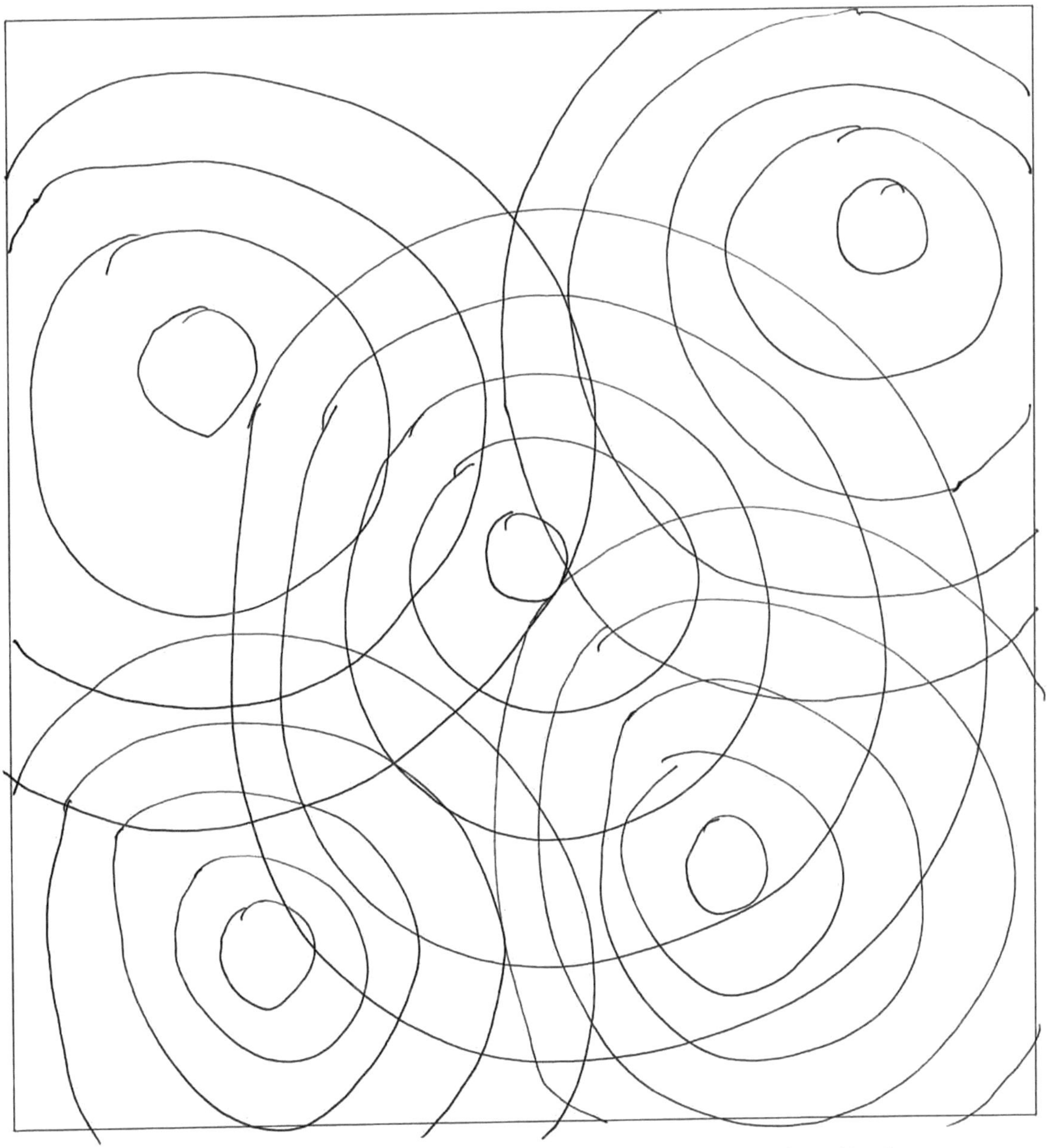

Please submit the form after completion to a staff member.
Thank you for your participation.*

Subject Number:

---

* The participation in the experiment is anonymous and at the users' own responsibility. The questionnaires may be evaluated and published in the process of this research project.

1) Paranormal ideation questionnaire*

Please place a tick in one of the four boxes for each of the below statements, according to how true you believe it to be: 0=Definitely True 1=Somewhat True 2=Somewhat false 3=Definitely False

	Definitely True 0	1	2	Definitely False 3
1) I havc had at least one telepathic experience with another person.	( )	( )	( )	( )
2) I never had any extrasensory perceptions.	( )	( )	( )	( )
3) I have had at least once a premonition that came true and I thought this was not due to chance.	( )	( )	( )	( )
4) I think telepathy exists.	( )	( )	( )	( )
5) Some dreams refer to future incidences, which cannot be known before.	( )	( )	( )	( )
6) I have had at least one dream that referred to the future and it was fulfilled so exactly that I think it was not due to chance.	( )	( )	( )	( )
7) I think there is something such as a spirit, soul or ghost that may continue to exist after a person has died.	( )	( )	( )	( )
8) I think that it is possible to communicate with the dead.	( )	( )	( )	( )
9) I have had at least one experience in which I was aware of the spirit, soul or ghost of someone who was not physically alive.	( )	( )	( )	( )
10) I think beings exist that are divine/godly and not of the physical world.	( )	( )	( )	( )
11) I think that prayers or wishes are sometimes heard and granted by divine/godly beings.	( )	( )	( )	( )
12) I think certain mythical creatures (e.g. elves, dragons, fairies) exist which human beings are not easily aware of.	( )	( )	( )	( )
13) I believe that intelligent life-forms from other planets have visited our planet.	( )	( )	( )	( )
14) I have had at least one experience in which I witnessed a flying object or life-form which I think was not from this planet.	( )	( )	( )	( )

Thank you for completing this assessment. Subject Number:

* from "Ganzfeld-induced hallucinatory experience, its phenomenology and cerebral electrophysiology" by Jiri Wackermann, Peter Pütz and Carsten Allefeld, Cortex, 44: 1364–1378, 2008.

2) Visual imagination record (ganzfeld experiment)

After completing the questionnaire you are asked to put on headphones and goggles. Please lie down, look into the diffusion lamp above your head and listen to the white noise for 10 min.
Let your mind flow and allow images to emerge in front of your eyes. Just be open to what appears.

When the relaxation phase ends, please make a sketch of the images or forms that have appeared in your mind during the experience on the drawing area below. If you would like to add comments, you may do so.

I didn't see anything

Please submit the form after completion to a staff member.
Thank you for your participation.*

Subject Number:

* The participation in the experiment is anonymous and at the users' own responsibility. The questionnaires may be evaluated and published in the process of this research project.

1) Paranormal ideation questionnaire[*]

Please place a tick in one of the four boxes for each of the below statements, according to how true you believe it to be: 0=Definitely True 1=Somewhat True 2=Somewhat false 3=Definitely False

	Definitely True 0	1	2	Definitely False 3
1) I have had at least one telepathic experience with another person.	( )	( )	( )	(✓)
2) I never had any extrasensory perceptions.	( )	( )	( )	(✓)
3) I have had at least once a premonition that came true and I thought this was not due to chance.	(✓)	( )	( )	( )
4) I think telepathy exists.	(✓)	( )	( )	( )
5) Some dreams refer to future incidences, which cannot be known before.	(✓)	( )	( )	( )
6) I have had at least one dream that referred to the future and it was fulfilled so exactly that I think it was not due to chance.	( )	(✓)	( )	( )
7) I think there is something such as a spirit, soul or ghost that may continue to exist after a person has died.	( )	( )	(✓)	( )
8) I think that it is possible to communicate with the dead.	( )	( )	(✓)	( )
9) I have had at least one experience in which I was aware of the spirit, soul or ghost of someone who was not physically alive.	( )	( )	(✓)	( )
10) I think beings exist that are divine/godly and not of the physical world.	( )	(✓)	( )	( )
11) I think that prayers or wishes are sometimes heard and granted by divine/godly beings.	( )	(✓)	( )	( )
12) I think certain mythical creatures (e.g. elves, dragons, fairies) exist which human beings are not easily aware of.	( )	( )	(✓)	( )
13) I believe that intelligent life-forms from other planets have visited our planet.	( )	( )	(✓)	( )
14) I have had at least one experience in which I witnessed a flying object or life-form which I think was not from this planet.	( )	( )	( )	(✓)

Thank you for completing this assessment.

Subject Number: 12

[*] from "Ganzfeld-induced hallucinatory experience, its phenomenology and cerebral electrophysiology" by Jiri Wackermann, Peter Pütz and Carsten Allefeld, Cortex, 44: 1364–1378, 2008.

2) Visual imagination record (ganzfeld experiment)

After completing the questionnaire you are asked to put on headphones and goggles. Please lie down, look into the diffusion lamp above your head and listen to the white noise for 10 min.
Let your mind flow and allow images to emerge in front of your eyes. Just be open to what appears.

When the relaxation phase ends, please make a sketch of the images or forms that have appeared in your mind during the experience on the drawing area below. If you would like to add comments, you may do so.

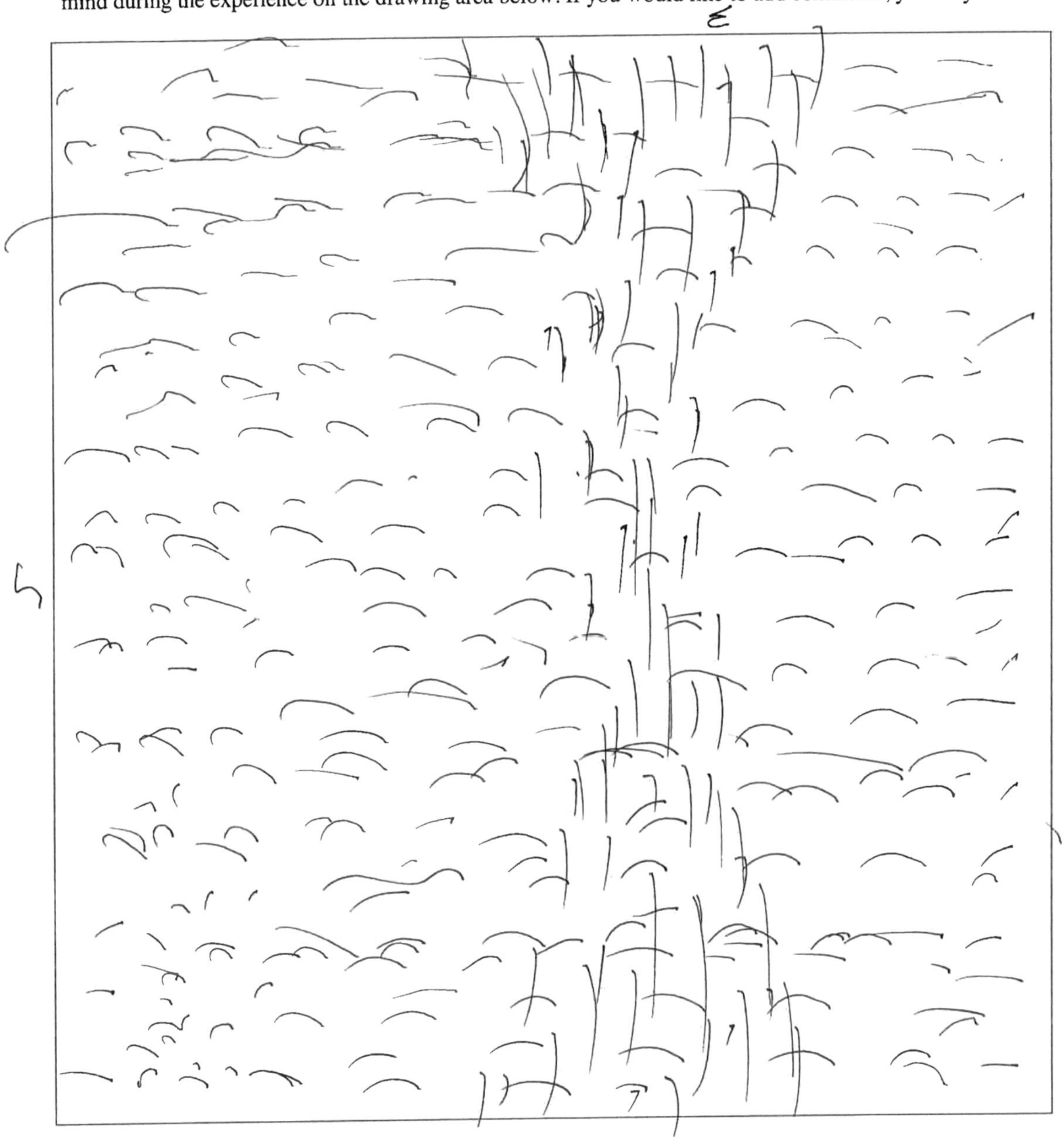

Please submit the form after completion to a staff member. Subject Number:
Thank you for your participation.*

* The participation in the experiment is anonymous and at the users' own responsibility.
The questionnaires may be evaluated and published in the process of this research project.

1) Paranormal ideation questionnaire*

Please place a tick in one of the four boxes for each of the below statements, according to how true you believe it to be: 0=Definitely True 1=Somewhat True 2=Somewhat false 3=Definitely False

	Definitely True 0	1	2	Definitely False 3
1) I have had at least one telepathic experience with another person.	(X)	()	()	(X)
2) I never had any extrasensory perceptions.	()	()	()	(X)
3) I have had at least once a premonition that came true and I thought this was not due to chance.	()	(X)	()	()
4) I think telepathy exists.	(X)	()	()	()
5) Some dreams refer to future incidences, which cannot be known before.	()	(X)	()	()
6) I have had at least one dream that referred to the future and it was fulfilled so exactly that I think it was not due to chance.	()	()	(X)	()
7) I think there is something such as a spirit, soul or ghost that may continue to exist after a person has died.	(X)	()	()	()
8) I think that it is possible to communicate with the dead.	()	()	(X)	()
9) I have had at least one experience in which I was aware of the spirit, soul or ghost of someone who was not physically alive.	()	()	()	(X)
10) I think beings exist that are divine/godly and not of the physical world.	()	()	(X)	()
11) I think that prayers or wishes are sometimes heard and granted by divine/godly beings.	()	()	()	(X)
12) I think certain mythical creatures (e.g. elves, dragons, fairies) exist which human beings are not easily aware of.	()	()	()	(X)
13) I believe that intelligent life-forms from other planets have visited our planet.	(X)	()	()	()
14) I have had at least one experience in which I witnessed a flying object or life-form which I think was not from this planet.	()	()	()	(X)

Thank you for completing this assessment.

Subject Number:

* from "Ganzfeld-induced hallucinatory experience, its phenomenology and cerebral electrophysiology" by Jiri Wackermann, Peter Pütz and Carsten Allefeld, Cortex, 44: 1364–1378, 2008.

2) Visual imagination record (ganzfeld experiment)

After completing the questionnaire you are asked to put on headphones and goggles. Please lie down, look into the diffusion lamp above your head and listen to the white noise for 10 min.
Let your mind flow and allow images to emerge in front of your eyes. Just be open to what appears.

When the relaxation phase ends, please make a sketch of the images or forms that have appeared in your mind during the experience on the drawing area below. If you would like to add comments, you may do so.

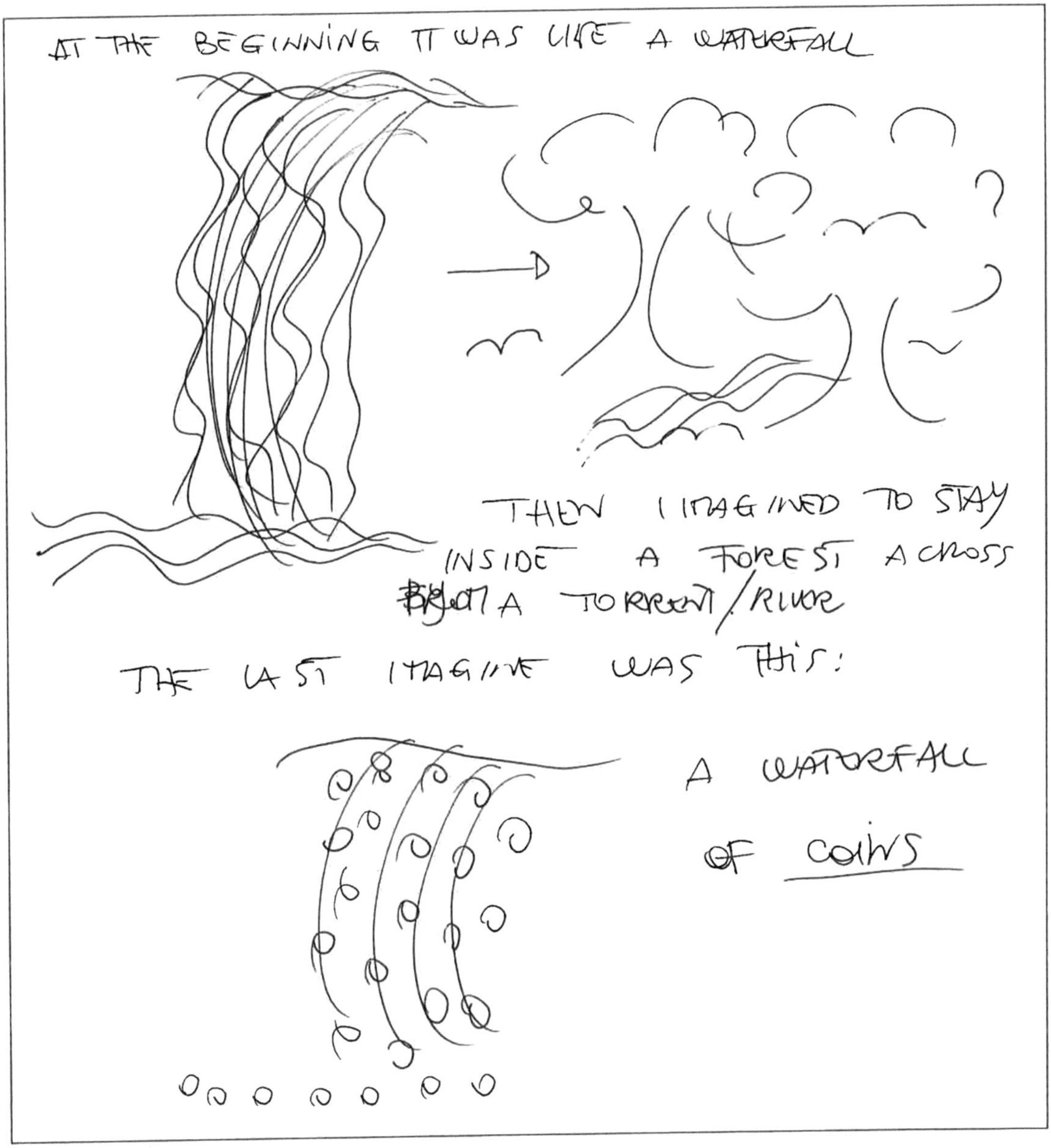

Please submit the form after completion to a staff member.
Thank you for your participation.*

Subject Number:

* The participation in the experiment is anonymous and at the users' own responsibility. The questionnaires may be evaluated and published in the process of this research project.

1) Paranormal ideation questionnaire*

Please place a tick in one of the four boxes for each of the below statements, according to how true you believe it to be: 0=Definitely True 1=Somewhat True 2=Somewhat false 3=Definitely False

	Definitely True 0	1	2	Definitely False 3
1) I have had at least one telepathic experience with another person.	(X)	( )	( )	( )
2) I never had any extrasensory perceptions.	( )	( )	( )	(X)
3) I have had at least once a premonition that came true and I thought this was not due to chance.	( )	(X)	( )	( )
4) I think telepathy exists.	( )	(X)	( )	( )
5) Some dreams refer to future incidences, which cannot be known before.	(X)	( )	( )	( )
6) I have had at least one dream that referred to the future and it was fulfilled so exactly that I think it was not due to chance.	( )	(X)	( )	( )
7) I think there is something such as a spirit, soul or ghost that may continue to exist after a person has died.	(X)	( )	( )	( )
8) I think that it is possible to communicate with the dead.	( )	( )	( )	(X)
9) I have had at least one experience in which I was aware of the spirit, soul or ghost of someone who was not physically alive.	( )	(X)	( )	( )
10) I think beings exist that are divine/godly and not of the physical world.	( )	( )	(X)	( )
11) I think that prayers or wishes are sometimes heard and granted by divine/godly beings.	( )	( )	( )	(X)
12) I think certain mythical creatures (e.g. elves, dragons, fairies) exist which human beings are not easily aware of.	( )	( )	( )	(X)
13) I believe that intelligent life-forms from other planets have visited our planet.	( )	(X)	( )	( )
14) I have had at least one experience in which I witnessed a flying object or life-form which I think was not from this planet.	( )	( )	( )	(X)

Thank you for completing this assessment. Subject Number:

* from "Ganzfeld-induced hallucinatory experience, its phenomenology and cerebral electrophysiology" by Jiri Wackermann, Peter Pütz and Carsten Allefeld, Cortex, 44: 1364–1378, 2008.

2) Visual imagination record (ganzfeld experiment)

After completing the questionnaire you are asked to put on headphones and goggles. Please lie down, look into the diffusion lamp above your head and listen to the white noise for 10 min.
Let your mind flow and allow images to emerge in front of your eyes. Just be open to what appears.

When the relaxation phase ends, please make a sketch of the images or forms that have appeared in your mind during the experience on the drawing area below. If you would like to add comments, you may do so.

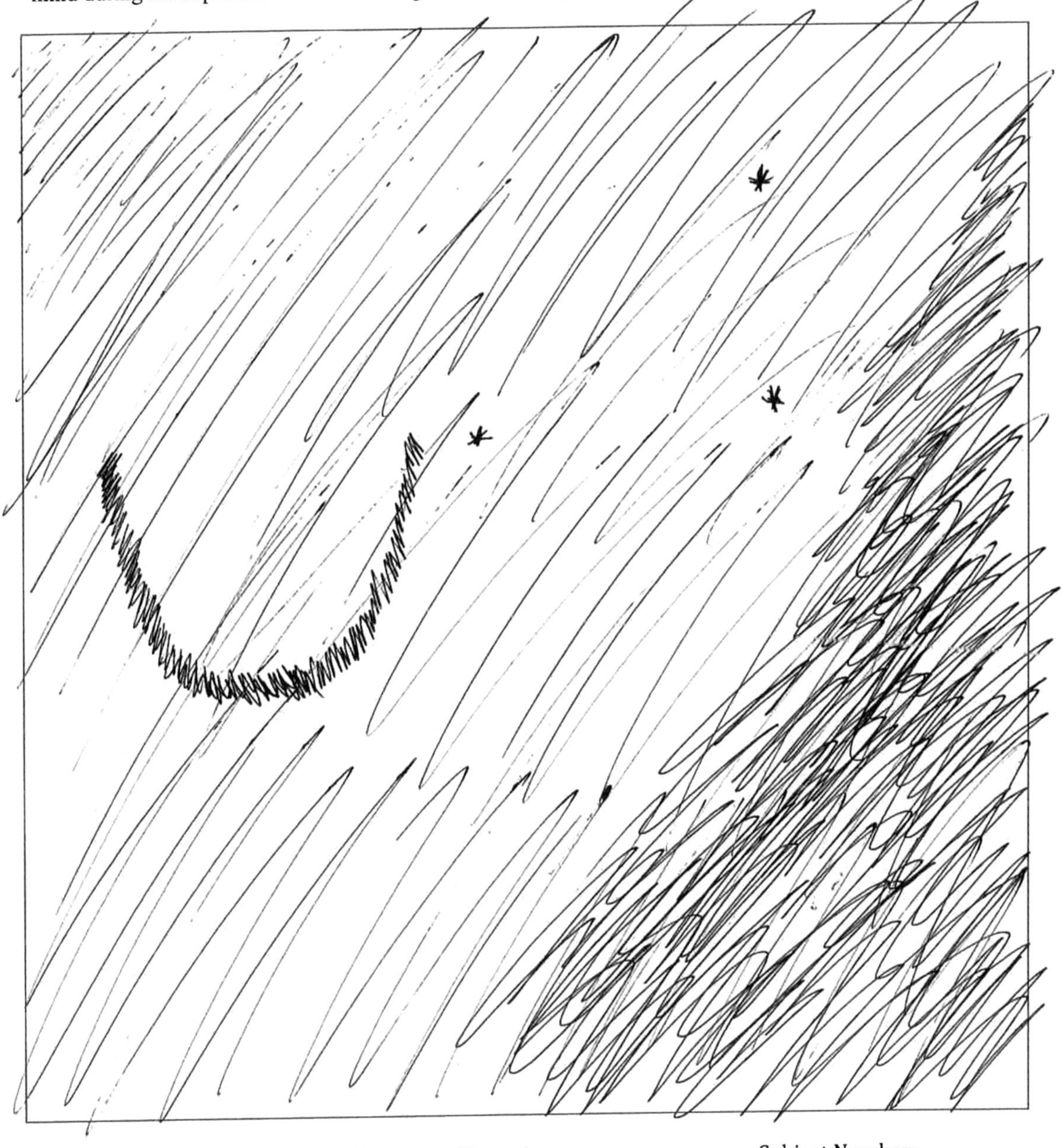

Please submit the form after completion to a staff member.
Thank you for your participation.*

Subject Number:

* The participation in the experiment is anonymous and at the users' own responsibility. The questionnaires may be evaluated and published in the process of this research project.

1) Paranormal ideation questionnaire*

Please place a tick in one of the four boxes for each of the below statements, according to how true you believe it to be: 0=Definitely True 1=Somewhat True 2=Somewhat false 3=Definitely False

	Definitely True 0	1	2	Definitely False 3
1) I have had at least one telepathic experience with another person.	( )	( )	(X)	( )
2) I never had any extrasensory perceptions.	( )	( )	(X)	( )
3) I have had at least once a premonition that came true and I thought this was not due to chance.	( )	(X)	( )	( )
4) I think telepathy exists.	( )	( )	(X)	( )
5) Some dreams refer to future incidences, which cannot be known before.	( )	(X)	( )	( )
6) I have had at least one dream that referred to the future and it was fulfilled so exactly that I think it was not due to chance.	( )	( )	(X)	( )
7) I think there is something such as a spirit, soul or ghost that may continue to exist after a person has died.	( )	( )	(X)	( )
8) I think that it is possible to communicate with the dead.	( )	( )	( )	(X)
9) I have had at least one experience in which I was aware of the spirit, soul or ghost of someone who was not physically alive.	( )	( )	( )	(X)
10) I think beings exist that are divine/godly and not of the physical world.	( )	( )	(X)	( )
11) I think that prayers or wishes are sometimes heard and granted by divine/godly beings.	( )	( )	( )	(X)
12) I think certain mythical creatures (e.g. elves, dragons, fairies) exist which human beings are not easily aware of.	( )	( )	( )	(X)
13) I believe that intelligent life-forms from other planets have visited our planet.	( )	( )	(X)	( )
14) I have had at least one experience in which I witnessed a flying object or life-form which I think was not from this planet.	( )	( )	( )	(X)

Thank you for completing this assessment. Subject Number:

* from "Ganzfeld-induced hallucinatory experience, its phenomenology and cerebral electrophysiology" by Jiri Wackermann, Peter Pütz and Carsten Allefeld, Cortex, 44: 1364–1378, 2008.

2) Visual imagination record (ganzfeld experiment)

After completing the questionnaire you are asked to put on headphones and goggles. Please lie down, look into the diffusion lamp above your head and listen to the white noise for 10 min.
Let your mind flow and allow images to emerge in front of your eyes. Just be open to what appears.

When the relaxation phase ends, please make a sketch of the images or forms that have appeared in your mind during the experience on the drawing area below. If you would like to add comments, you may do so.

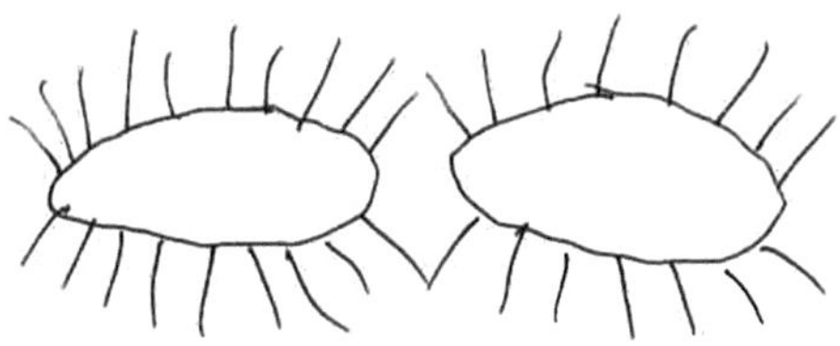

Please submit the form after completion to a staff member.
Thank you for your participation.*

Subject Number:

* The participation in the experiment is anonymous and at the users' own responsibility. The questionnaires may be evaluated and published in the process of this research project.

1) Paranormal ideation questionnaire*

Please place a tick in one of the four boxes for each of the below statements, according to how true you believe it to be: 0=Definitely True 1=Somewhat True 2=Somewhat false 3=Definitely False

	Definitely True 0	1	2	Definitely False 3
1) I have had at least one telepathic experience with another person.	( )	( )	(X)	( )
2) I never had any extrasensory perceptions.	( )	( )	( )	(X)
3) I have had at least once a premonition that came true and I thought this was not due to chance.	( )	(X)	( )	( )
4) I think telepathy exists.	( )	( )	(X)	( )
5) Some dreams refer to future incidences, which cannot be known before.	( )	(X)	( )	( )
6) I have had at least one dream that referred to the future and it was fulfilled so exactly that I think it was not due to chance.	( )	(X)	( )	( )
7) I think there is something such as a spirit, soul or ghost that may continue to exist after a person has died.	( )	(X)	( )	( )
8) I think that it is possible to communicate with the dead.	( )	( )	( )	(X)
9) I have had at least one experience in which I was aware of the spirit, soul or ghost of someone who was not physically alive.	( )	( )	( )	(X)
10) I think beings exist that are divine/godly and not of the physical world.	( )	( )	( )	(X)
11) I think that prayers or wishes are sometimes heard and granted by divine/godly beings.	( )	( )	( )	(X)
12) I think certain mythical creatures (e.g. elves, dragons, fairies) exist which human beings are not easily aware of.	( )	( )	( )	(X)
13) I believe that intelligent life-forms from other planets have visited our planet.	( )	( )	( )	(X)
14) I have had at least one experience in which I witnessed a flying object or life-form which I think was not from this planet.	( )	( )	( )	(X)

Thank you for completing this assessment.

Subject Number:

* from "Ganzfeld-induced hallucinatory experience, its phenomenology and cerebral electrophysiology" by Jiri Wackermann, Peter Pütz and Carsten Allefeld, Cortex, 44: 1364–1378, 2008.

2) Visual imagination record (ganzfeld experiment)

After completing the questionnaire you are asked to put on headphones and goggles. Please lie down, look into the diffusion lamp above your head and listen to the white noise for 10 min.
Let your mind flow and allow images to emerge in front of your eyes. Just be open to what appears.

When the relaxation phase ends, please make a sketch of the images or forms that have appeared in your mind during the experience on the drawing area below. If you would like to add comments, you may do so.

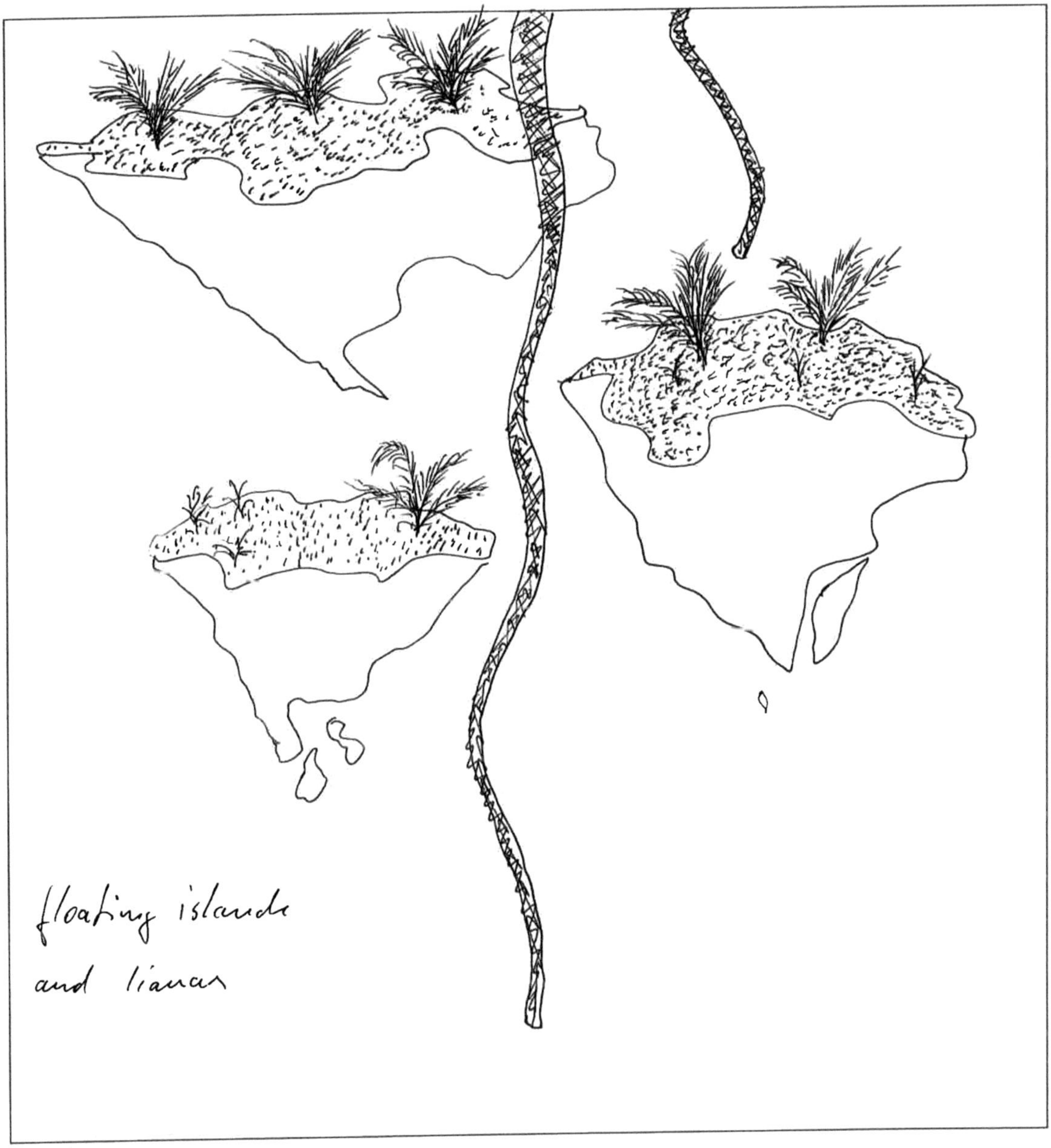

Please submit the form after completion to a staff member.
Thank you for your participation.*

Subject Number:

* The participation in the experiment is anonymous and at the users' own responsibility. The questionnaires may be evaluated and published in the process of this research project.

1) Paranormal ideation questionnaire*

Please place a tick in one of the four boxes for each of the below statements, according to how true you believe it to be: 0=Definitely True 1=Somewhat True 2=Somewhat false 3=Definitely False

	Definitely True 0	1	2	Definitely Falsc 3
1) I havc had at least one telepathic experience with another person.	( )	(X)	( )	( )
2) I never had any extrasensory perceptions.	( )	( )	(X)	( )
3) I have had at least once a premonition that came true and I thought this was not due to chance.	( )	(X)	( )	( )
4) I think telepathy exists.	( )	( )	(X)	( )
5) Some dreams refer to future incidences, which cannot be known before.	( )	( )	(X)	( )
6) I have had at least one dream that referred to the future and it was fulfilled so exactly that I think it was not due to chance.	(X)	( )	( )	( )
7) I think there is something such as a spirit, soul or ghost that may continue to exist after a person has died.	( )	( )	( )	(X)
8) I think that it is possible to communicate with the dead.	( )	( )	( )	(X)
9) I have had at least one experience in which I was aware of the spirit, soul or ghost of someone who was not physically alive.	( )	( )	( )	(X)
10) I think beings exist that are divine/godly and not of the physical world.	( )	( )	( )	(X)
11) I think that prayers or wishes are sometimes heard and granted by divine/godly beings.	( )	( )	( )	(X)
12) I think certain mythical creatures (e.g. elves, dragons, fairies) exist which human beings are not easily aware of.	( )	( )	(X)	( )
13) I believe that intelligent life-forms from other planets have visited our planet.	( )	(X)	( )	( )
14) I have had at least one experience in which I witnessed a flying object or life-form which I think was not from this planet.	( )	( )	( )	(X)

Thank you for completing this assessment.

Subject Number:

* from "Ganzfeld-induced hallucinatory experience, its phenomenology and cerebral electrophysiology" by Jiri Wackermann, Peter Pütz and Carsten Allefeld, Cortex, 44: 1364–1378, 2008.

2) Visual imagination record (ganzfeld experiment)

After completing the questionnaire you are asked to put on headphones and goggles. Please lie down, look into the diffusion lamp above your head and listen to the white noise for 10 min.
Let your mind flow and allow images to emerge in front of your eyes. Just be open to what appears.

When the relaxation phase ends, please make a sketch of the images or forms that have appeared in your mind during the experience on the drawing area below. If you would like to add comments, you may do so.

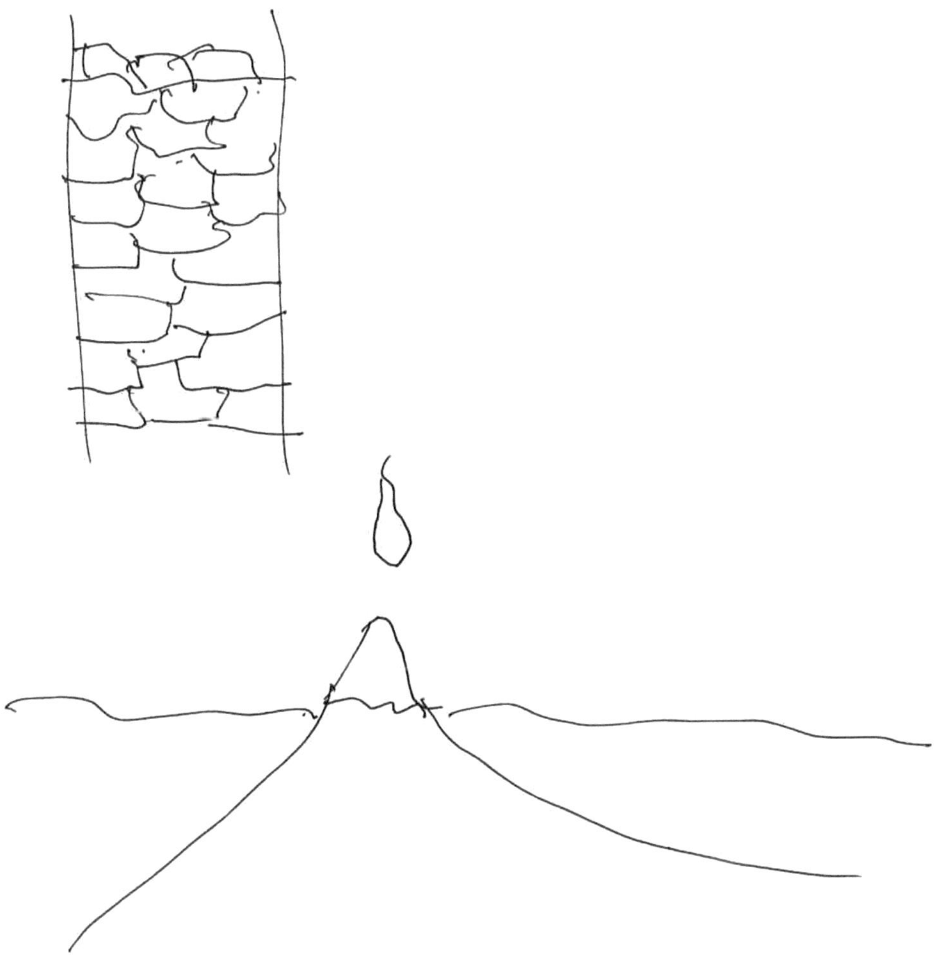

Please submit the form after completion to a staff member.

Thank you for your participation.*

Subject Number:

* The participation in the experiment is anonymous and at the users' own responsibility.
The questionnaires may be evaluated and published in the process of this research project.

1) Paranormal ideation questionnaire*

Please place a tick in one of the four boxes for each of the below statements, according to how true you believe it to be: 0=Definitely True 1=Somewhat True 2=Somewhat false 3=Definitely False

	Definitely True 0	1	2	Definitely False 3
1) I have had at least one telepathic experience with another person.	( )	(✓)	( )	( )
2) I never had any extrasensory perceptions.	( )	( )	( )	(✓)
3) I have had at least once a premonition that came true and I thought this was not due to chance.	(✓)	( )	( )	( )
4) I think telepathy exists.	(✓)	( )	( )	( )
5) Some dreams refer to future incidences, which cannot be known before.	( )	(✓)	( )	( )
6) I have had at least one dream that referred to the future and it was fulfilled so exactly that I think it was not due to chance.	(✓)	( )	( )	( )
7) I think there is something such as a spirit, soul or ghost that may continue to exist after a person has died.	(✓)	( )	( )	( )
8) I think that it is possible to communicate with the dead.	(✓)	( )	( )	( )
9) I have had at least one experience in which I was aware of the spirit, soul or ghost of someone who was not physically alive.	( )	( )	( )	(✓)
10) I think beings exist that are divine/godly and not of the physical world.	( )	(✓)	( )	( )
11) I think that prayers or wishes are sometimes heard and granted by divine/godly beings.	(✓)	( )	( )	( )
12) I think certain mythical creatures (e.g. elves, dragons, fairies) exist which human beings are not easily aware of.	( )	( )	( )	(✓)
13) I believe that intelligent life-forms from other planets have visited our planet.	( )	(✓)	( )	( )
14) I have had at least one experience in which I witnessed a flying object or life-form which I think was not from this planet.	( )	(✓)	( )	( )

Thank you for completing this assessment.

Subject Number:

* from "Ganzfeld-induced hallucinatory experience, its phenomenology and cerebral electrophysiology" by Jiri Wackermann, Peter Pütz and Carsten Allefeld, Cortex, 44: 1364–1378, 2008.

2) Visual imagination record (ganzfeld experiment)

After completing the questionnaire you are asked to put on headphones and goggles. Please lie down, look into the diffusion lamp above your head and listen to the white noise for 10 min.
Let your mind flow and allow images to emerge in front of your eyes. Just be open to what appears.

When the relaxation phase ends, please make a sketch of the images or forms that have appeared in your mind during the experience on the drawing area below. If you would like to add comments, you may do so.

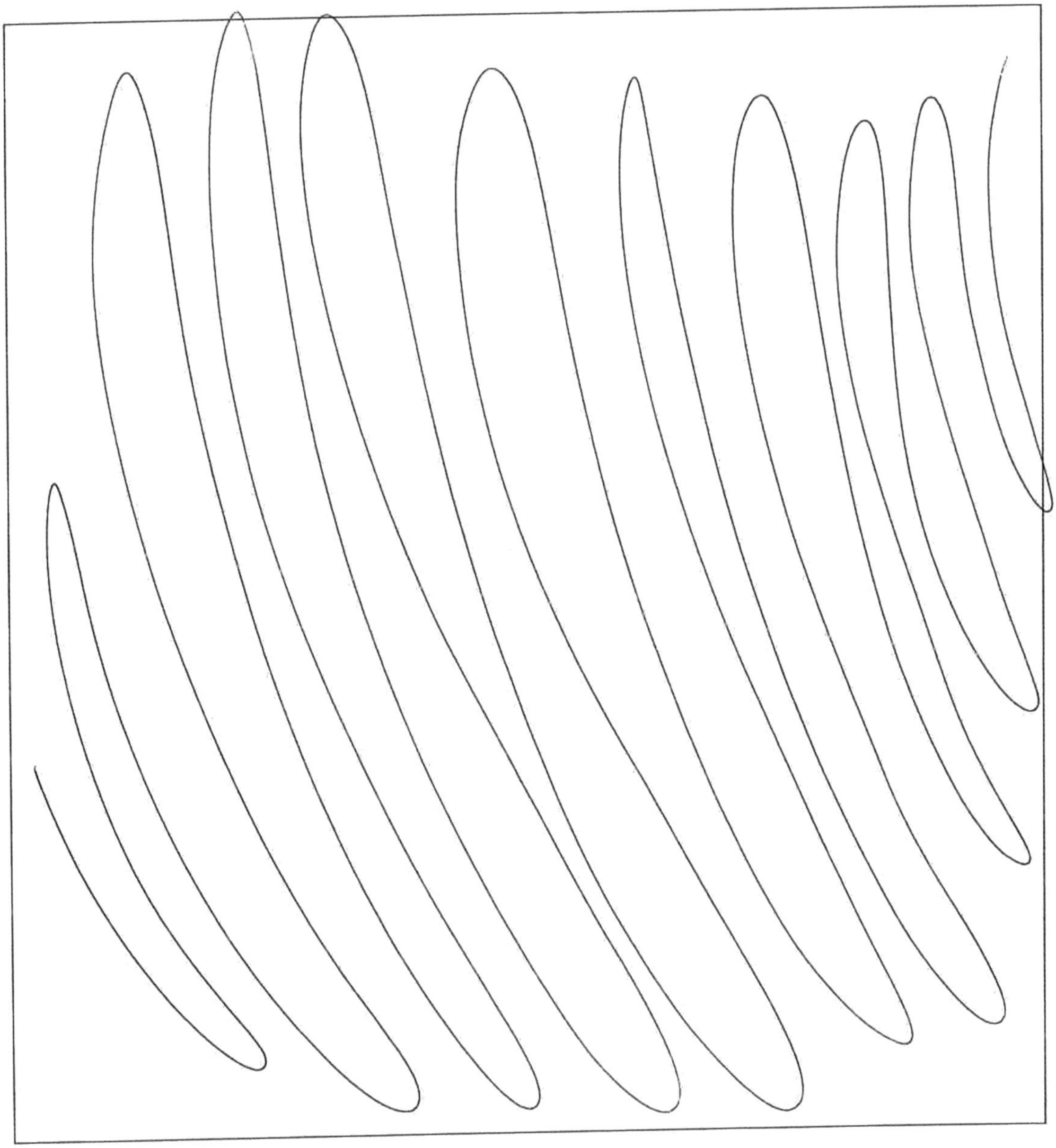

Please submit the form after completion to a staff member.
Thank you for your participation.*

Subject Number:

* The participation in the experiment is anonymous and at the users' own responsibility. The questionnaires may be evaluated and published in the process of this research project.

1) Paranormal ideation questionnaire[*]

Please place a tick in one of the four boxes for each of the below statements, according to how true you believe it to be: 0=Definitely True 1=Somewhat True 2=Somewhat false 3=Definitely False

	Definitely True 0	1	2	Definitely False 3
1) I have had at least one telepathic experience with another person.	(X)	()	()	()
2) I never had any extrasensory perceptions.	()	()	()	(X)
3) I have had at least once a premonition that came true and I thought this was not due to chance.	(X)	()	()	()
4) I think telepathy exists.	(X)	()	()	()
5) Some dreams refer to future incidences, which cannot be known before.	(X)	()	()	()
6) I have had at least one dream that referred to the future and it was fulfilled so exactly that I think it was not due to chance.	()	(X)	()	()
7) I think there is something such as a spirit, soul or ghost that may continue to exist after a person has died.	()	(X)	()	()
8) I think that it is possible to communicate with the dead.	()	(X)	()	()
9) I have had at least one experience in which I was aware of the spirit, soul or ghost of someone who was not physically alive.	(X)	()	()	()
10) I think beings exist that are divine/godly and not of the physical world.	()	(X)	()	()
11) I think that prayers or wishes are sometimes heard and granted by divine/godly beings.	()	()	()	(X)
12) I think certain mythical creatures (e.g. elves, dragons, fairies) exist which human beings are not easily aware of.	()	()	()	(X)
13) I believe that intelligent life-forms from other planets have visited our planet.	()	()	(X)	()
14) I have had at least one experience in which I witnessed a flying object or life-form which I think was not from this planet.	()	(X)	()	()

Thank you for completing this assessment.

Subject Number:

[*] from "Ganzfeld-induced hallucinatory experience, its phenomenology and cerebral electrophysiology" by Jiri Wackermann, Peter Pütz and Carsten Allefeld, Cortex, 44: 1364–1378, 2008.

2) Visual imagination record (ganzfeld experiment)

After completing the questionnaire you are asked to put on headphones and goggles. Please lie down, look into the diffusion lamp above your head and listen to the white noise for 10 min.
Let your mind flow and allow images to emerge in front of your eyes. Just be open to what appears.

When the relaxation phase ends, please make a sketch of the images or forms that have appeared in your mind during the experience on the drawing area below. If you would like to add comments, you may do so.

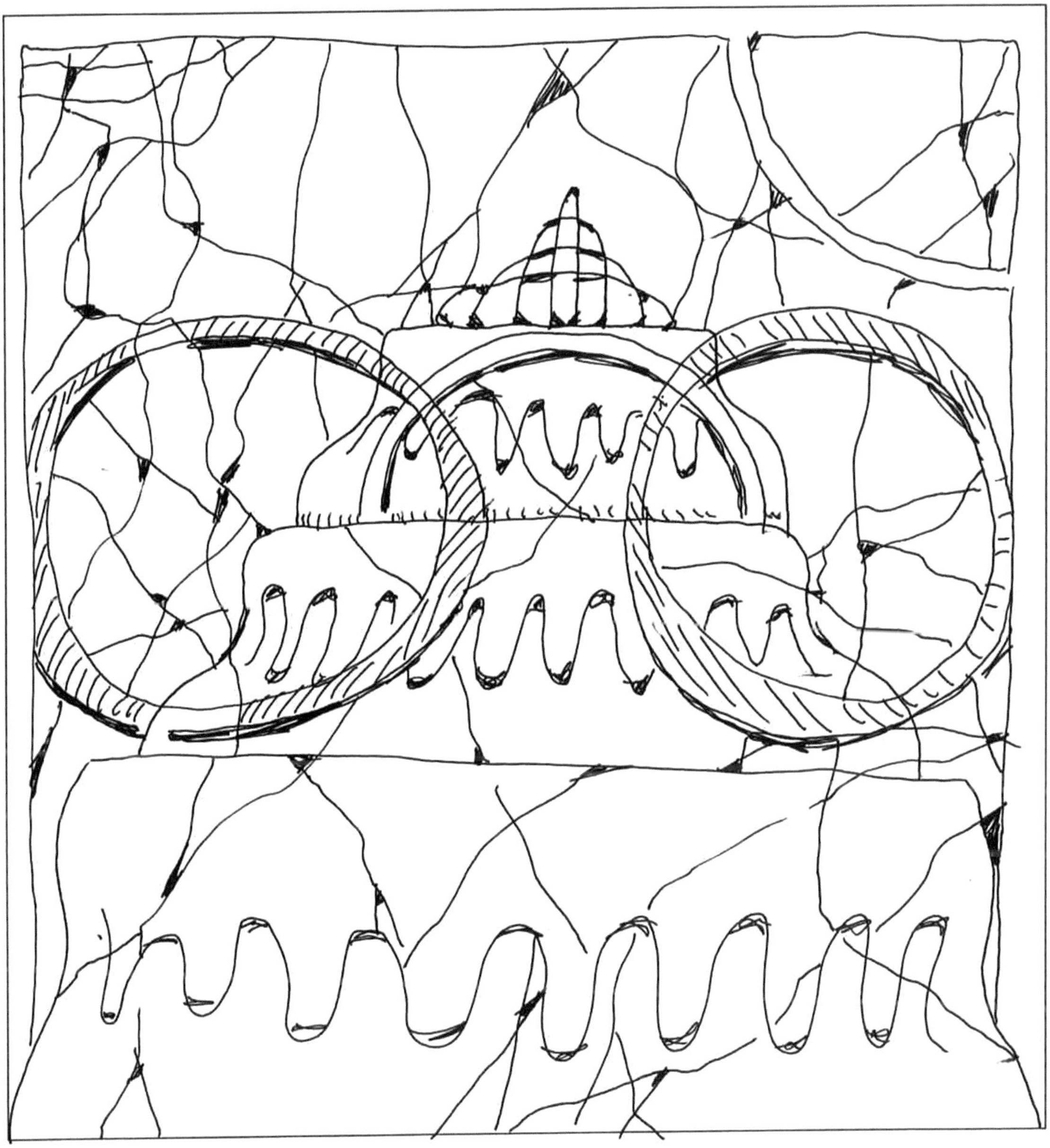

Please submit the form after completion to a staff member. Subject Number:
Thank you for your participation.*

* The participation in the experiment is anonymous and at the users' own responsibility. The questionnaires may be evaluated and published in the process of this research project.

Æther

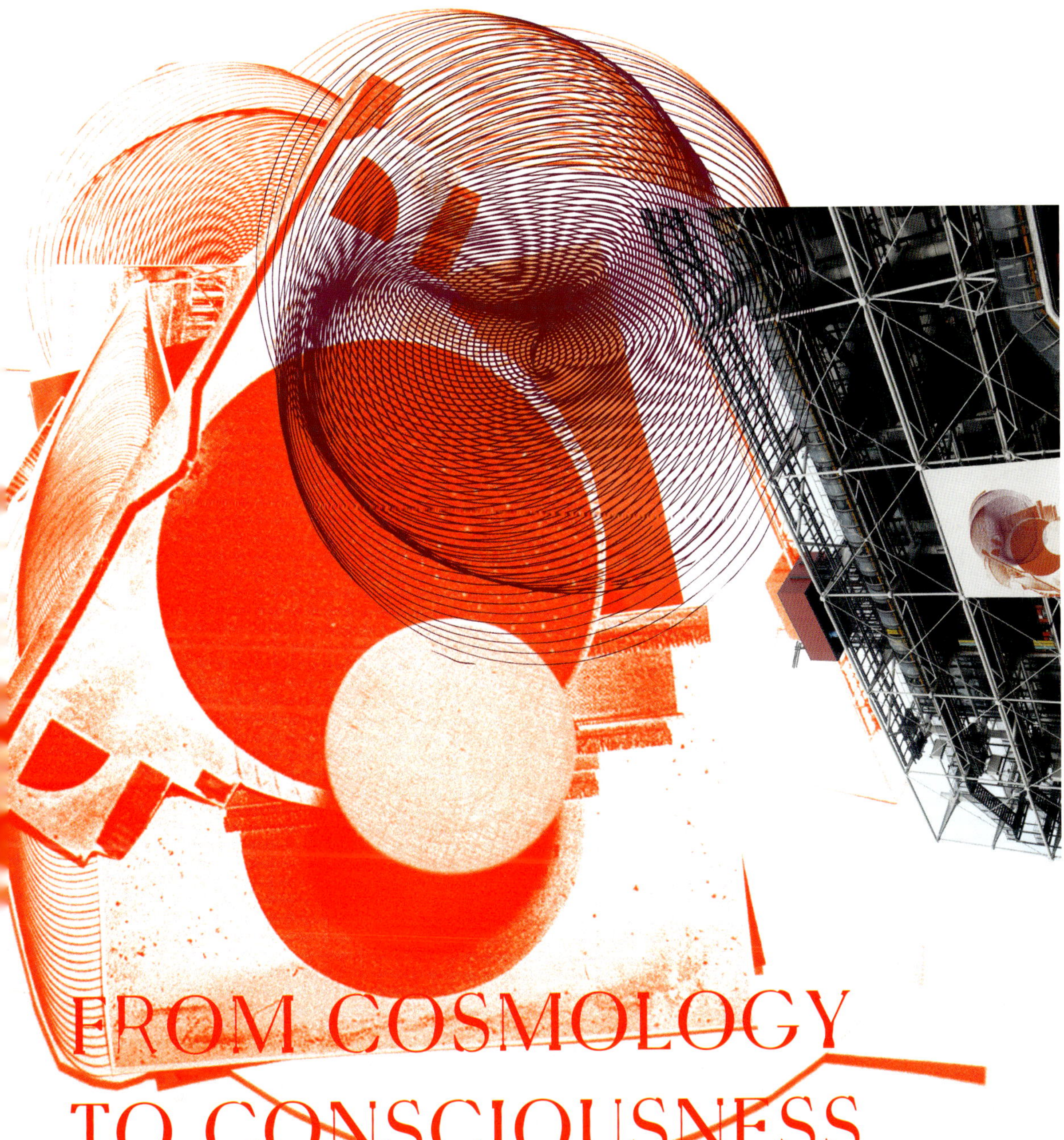

FROM COSMOLOGY TO CONSCIOUSNESS

Æther

A PROPOSITION BY CHRISTOPH KELLER

FROM COSMOLOGY TO CONSCIOUSNESS

Espace 315, Nouveau Festival du Centre Pompidou

Aether is an elusive concept, both a classical element and a substance. In philosophy it represents the absence of absence; that is, the impossibility of conceiving the void. In science it represents an element and a medium, incapable of change and subtler than light. The aether is also the fifth element, which had no qualities and per definition could never be exactly conceived nor physically proven.

However ancient its roots, the aether is, notwithstanding, the medium of modernity. Its dismissal as a scientific concept — in the aftermath of Einstein's theory of relativity — marked the moment when the natural sciences finally broke free from the pervasive occultism that still besieged nineteenth century research. This territory left vacant by science was soon reoccupied by art. Thus the fall of the aether corresponds to the rise of the modern scientific condition and its rational worldview, the obverse of which is the sublimatory function thereafter assigned to cultural expression. That is, the death of the aether is the birth of modern art, together with all the irrational powers it unleashes.

By electing aether as its central concept, the project tackles the ambivalent relation between art and science, with art both adhering to scientific models as well as offering an experience that transcends its sheer materiality.

Aether, one could say, is the unknown.

But how can the unconceivable be conceived?

The answer is multifold: From Plato's fifth element to Descartes, one can find a multitude of philosophical-theological and scientific theories of aether. Several natural philosophers, like Giordano Bruno, Christiaan Huygens, and Isaac Newton, whose works are fundamental for today's science, based their theories on the assumption that aether was a given.

Parallel to the rise of the enlightenment an abundance of esoteric theories of aethers appear. In pre-revolutionary Paris the healer Franz Anton Mesmer posited an ethereal "fluidum" which supposedly served as the medium for his psycho-physical "Animal

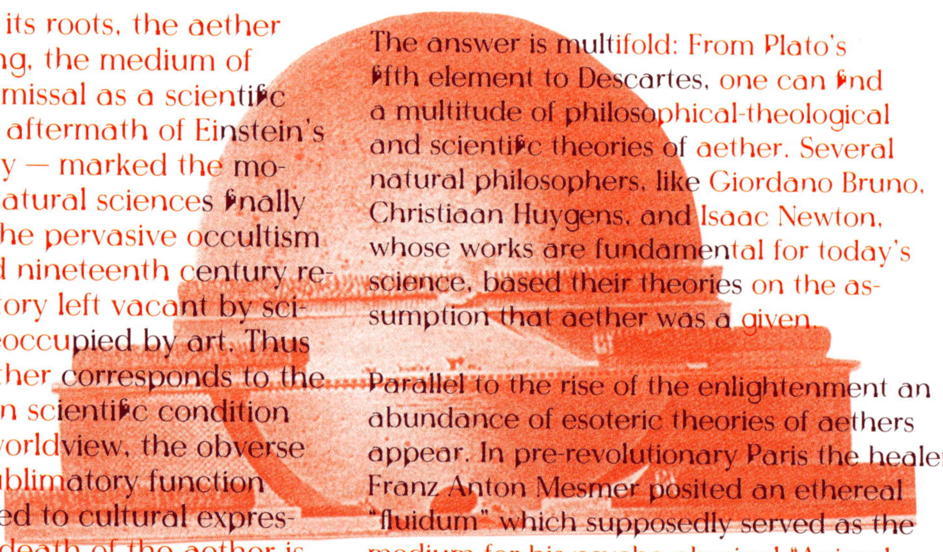

Magnetism." Further, many scientific circles and literary salons had strong affinities with remote and alchemist aether-conceptions and speculations. The French artist and passionate astronomer Étienne Léopold Trouvelot made stunning interpretative drawings of what powerful telescopes revealed from outer space, before photography was developed enough to do the job in the late nineteenth century.

Likewise, the romantic writers Edgar Allen Poe and Friedrich Hölderlin, as well as Immanuel Kant, were aetherists who wrote lengthy poems and treatises about it.

Then of course there is the concept of the "luminiferous aether," a concrete subtle matter, whose existence was heavily disputed throughout the nineteenth century yet defended by prominent scientists like James Clerk Maxwell, Henri Poincaré, and Nikola Tesla until finally disproved by the "experimentum crucis" of Michelson and Morley in 1887.

Yet, however often banished and disproved, the aether kept reappearing and reemerging as a concept of continuity or contingency, which binds together the microcosmic and the universal. Be it in Wilhelm Reich's orgone physics, new age esotericism or even—as some claim—in today's dark-matter or unified field theory, despite their careful avoidance of the term "aether."

Last but not least, there was also the early anesthetic substance, an easily obtained drug, called ether, popularly consumed by members of the avant-garde to enhance perception and to escape reality, whose usage was popular when the battle over the aether was still at its height. Some notable artistic experiments, which allude to altered states of consciousness were done by Henri Michaux, Gisèle Freund, and Brassaï, as well as the experimental photograms and abstractions of Étienne-Jules Marey.

These explorations lead in the exhibition "Æther" at Centre Pompidou quasi-chronologically, to the contemporary works of Evariste Richer, Claude Lévêque, Thomas Ruff, Ugo Rondinone, and Wolfgang Tillmans. Or more loosely to a vast experimental field, consisting of contemporary art videos and films that relate to the notion of the aether, such as the works of John Smith, Mariana Castillo Deball, Joachim Koester, Adolf Wölfli/Daniel Baumann, David Maljkovic, and Cyprien Gaillard.

The Æther project places the question of the aether into a contemporary discourse, asking where we stand now, at the beginning of the twenty-first century, having bypassed the modern condition yet with the fundamental questions of science, reality, transcendence, and art still left open.

The mental world (...) is liable to be imagined as gaseous, or rather, aethereal. But let me remind you here of the queer role which the gaseous and the aethereal play in philosophy, — when we perceive that a substantive is not used as what in general we should call the name of an object, and when therefore we can't help saying to ourselves that it is the name of an aethereal object.

Ludwig Wittgenstein, The Blue and Brown Books

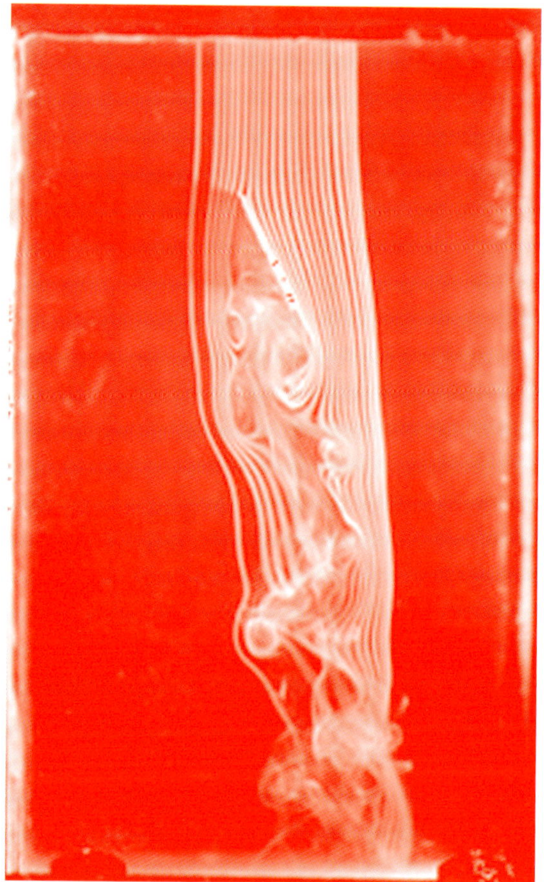

Destroy the idea of the atomic constitution and we should no longer be able to regard the ether as an entity, or at least as matter. For want of a better word we might term it spirit.

Edgar Allan Poe, Mesmeric Revelation

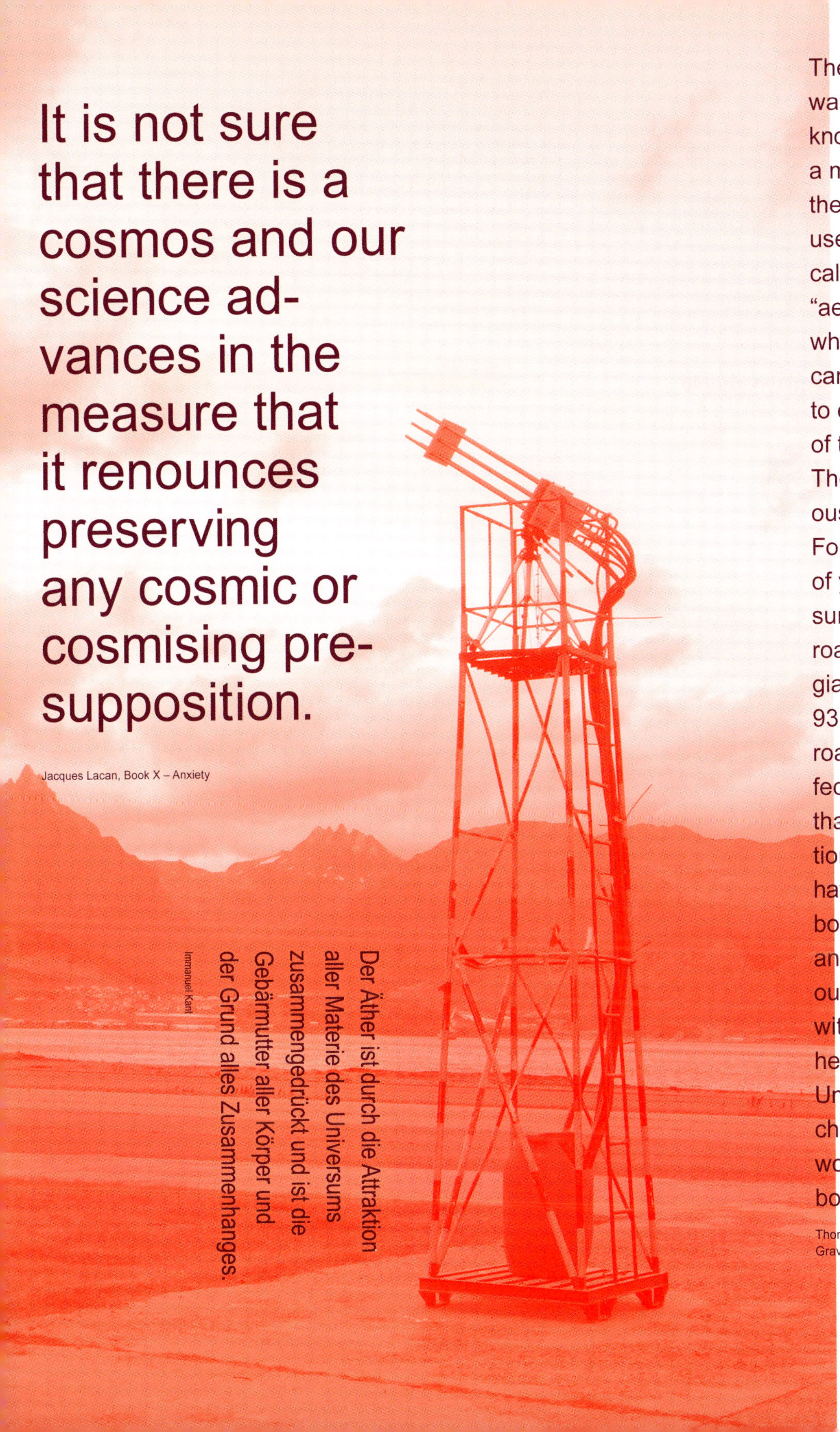

It is not sure that there is a cosmos and our science advances in the measure that it renounces preserving any cosmic or cosmising presupposition.

Jacques Lacan, Book X – Anxiety

Der Äther ist durch die Attraktion aller Materie des Universums zusammengedrückt und ist die Gebärmutter aller Körper und der Grund alles Zusammenhanges.

Immanuel Kant

They don't want us to know there is a medium there, what used to be called an "aether," which can carry sound to every part of the Earth. The Soniferous Aether. For millions of years, the sun has been roaring, a giant, furnace, 93 millionmile roar, so perfectly steady that generations of men have been born into it and passed out of it again, without ever hearing it. Unless it changed, how would anybody know?

Thomas Pynchon, Gravity's Rainbow

On Æther – Œuvre parlée

A conversation between **Christoph Keller** and **Bernard Blistène**
English/French, français/anglais

Bernard Blistène Christoph, pour cette deuxième édition du Nouveau festival du Centre Pompidou, je suis venu vers toi parce que je souhaitais explorer à partir de ton travail et de ton savoir, la relation complexe qui me semble aujourd'hui de nouveau se manifester entre arts plastiques et science.

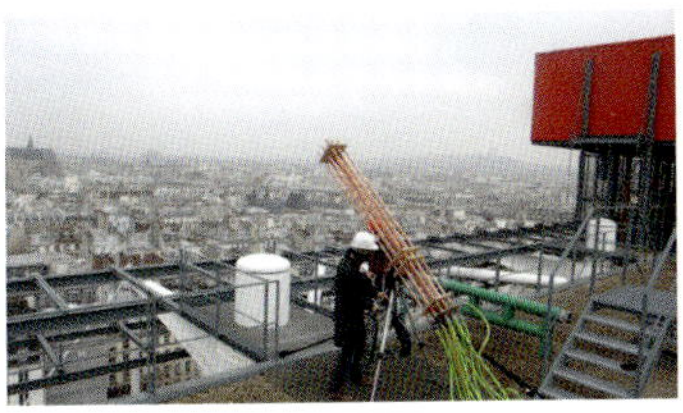

Christoph Keller I think there has been a very strong link between science and art throughout the twentieth century and throughout the whole of our culture. If you study science with an interest in philosophy, which I did, you will find yourself dealing with questions not so different from those that art also deals with today.

BB Christoph souligne que le lien est très profond entre art et science au vingtième siècle. Si vous étudiez la chose avec intensité, de fait, vous vous retrouvez sur les deux chemins à la fois.

CK Of course, in my work there are a lot of links to science, but my main interests — as well as the results of my work — are artistic. For example, two topics are present here that I have been working on in recent years, the first of which is "les états modifiés de la conscience," or altered states of consciousness...

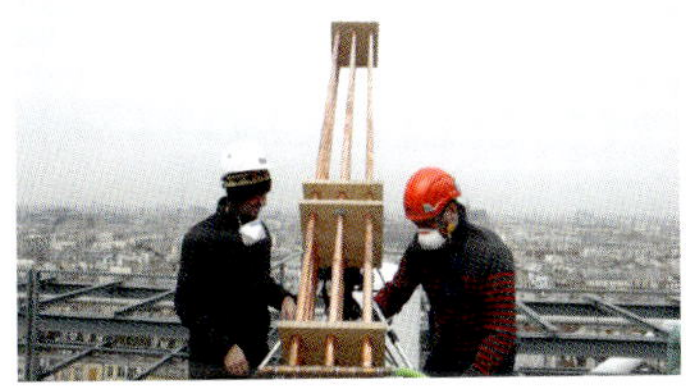

BB Attends, laisse-moi le temps de traduire ta pensée! Le travail de Christoph témoigne d'un intérêt majeur pour la science, mais ce que vous voyez dans son œuvre, c'est un résultat artistique, pas un résultat scientifique. Et ce projet ici témoigne de l'une de ses préoccupations entre art et science: ce que nous appelons les "états altérés de la conscience."

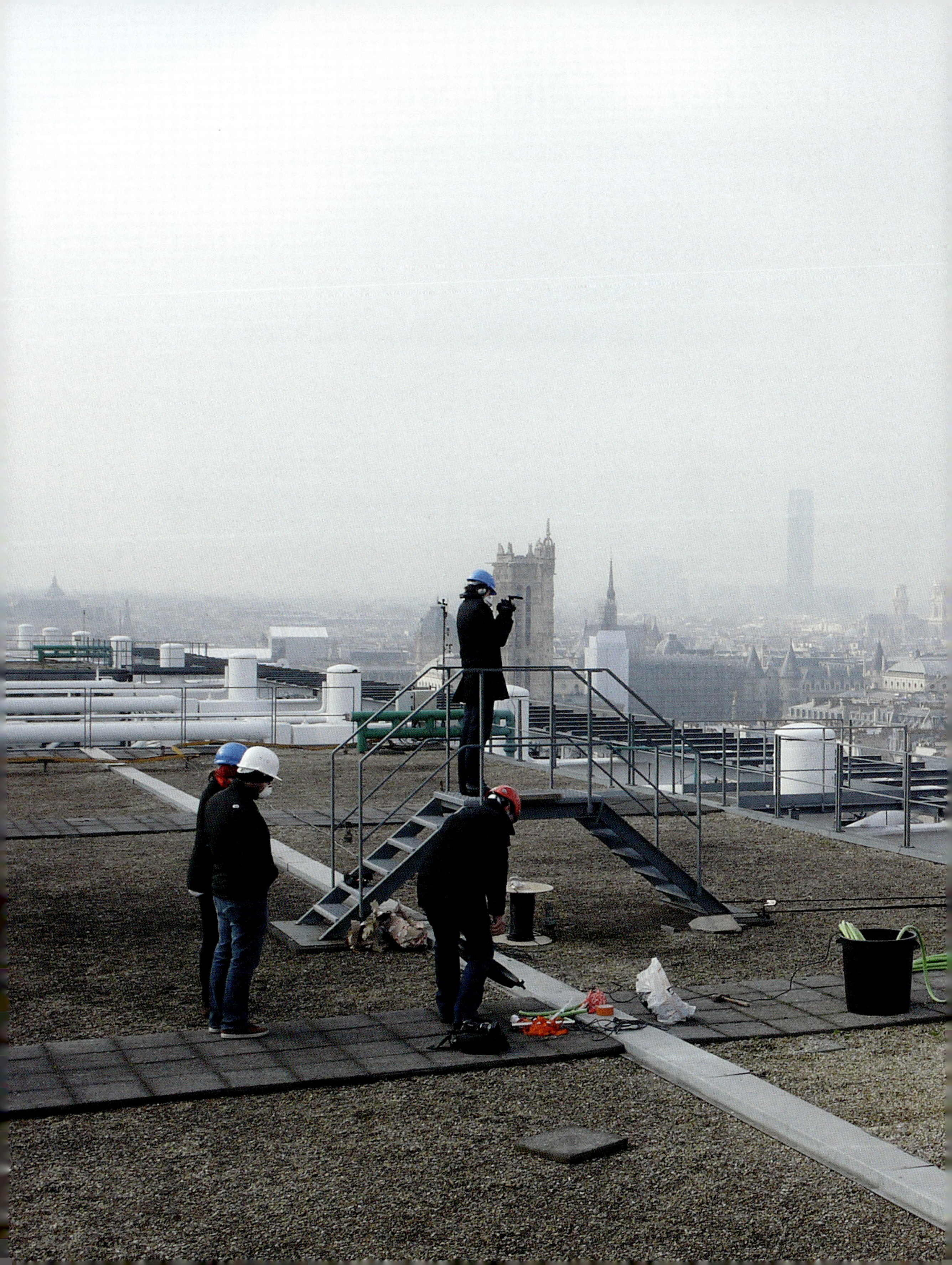

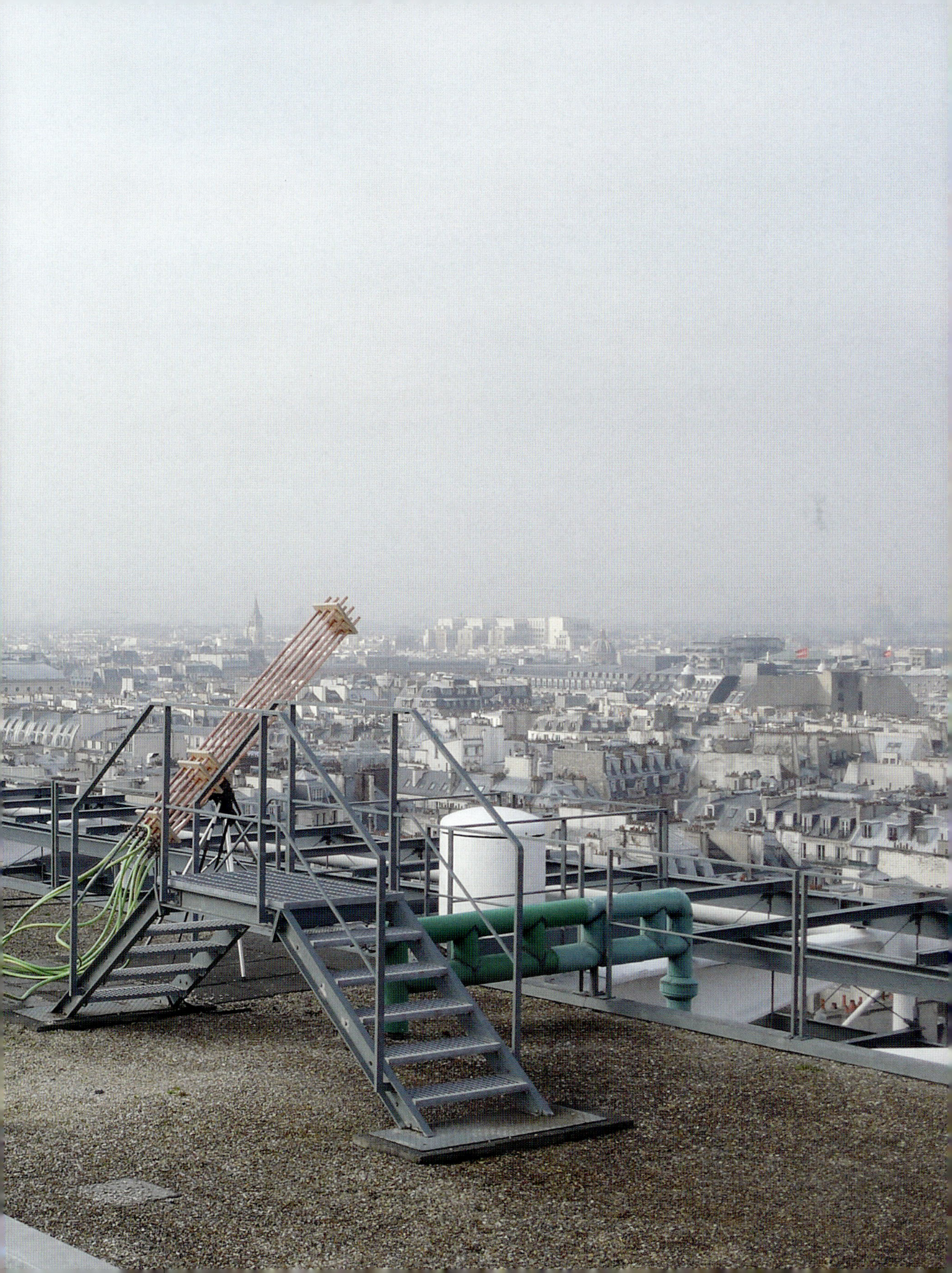

CK And the second topic is the relation between the material world and the immaterial world, which might even go in the direction of a world one could term spiritual. In the twentieth century, the more science stressed the "rational" dimension of its research, the more art embraced the "irrational." And at the junction of these two realms you have the concept of the aether. That's why I chose this topic for the exhibition. It is an elusive concept and it is also a substance. It is both. It is what links immateriality with materiality.

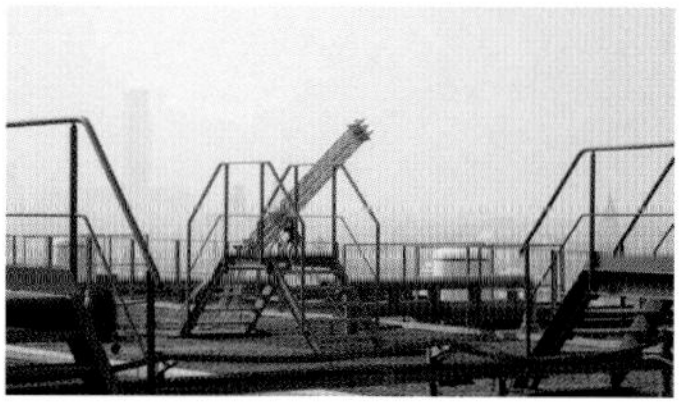

BB Ce que Christoph met en évidence — en me permettant d'édulcorer ici quelque peu sa pensée —, c'est à la fois la dimension de plus en plus rationnelle de la science en l'instant où nous entrons dans le vingtième siècle, et parallèlement, la dimension de plus en plus irrationnelle de l'expérience artistique. Et finalement, cette exposition est sans doute à la croisée de ces deux idées. Les œuvres choisies témoignent fondamentalement de cette entrée de la science dans la rationalité du tournant du vingtième siècle et en même temps, bien sûr, de cet intérêt de plus en plus croissant pour leur dimension proprement irrationnelle.

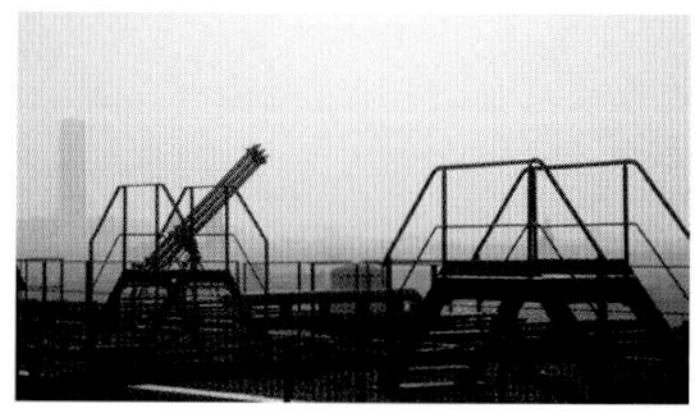

CK So, what is the aether? The aether is, in the old Greek tradition, the absence of the absence. "L'absence de l'absence, c'est l'éther." Then there is also the aether of the nineteenth century, which is the luminiferous aether. Here aether refers to a scientific concept, actually to a substance, subtler than any other substance. So, there are different notions of the aether, yet above all the aether is a medium of modernity. The modern era is essentially connected to the topic of the aether.

BB Alors, je ne traduis pas tout, mais vous l'avez compris, en choisissant l'éther, on choisit le médium par excellence, qui pose des questions à la modernité.

CK As an artist, I always ask myself what art is and where it comes from. From a historical viewpoint, I would say that the art that we are talking about today is roughly one hundred years old. It is still the art of modernity.

BB Fondamentalement, il s'agit d'interroger la modernité, de questionner la modernité, ses utopies comme ses attentes. Et finalement d'utiliser l'éther comme vecteur pour interroger ce qu'est notre modernité, ou ce qu'elle a été.

CK But, if you look further back into the nineteenth century, things were still quite different. Science was much more associated with occultism and spiritualism, and art was more tied to depicting an objective reality than it is today.

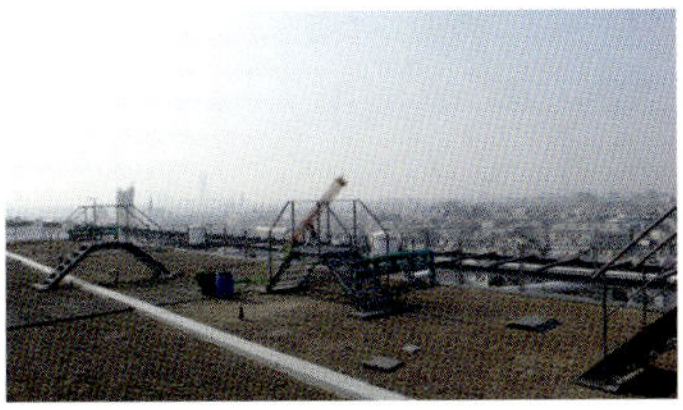

BB L'important, c'est ce croisement, ce chiasme en quelque sorte — le mot n'est sans doute pas adéquat: ce qui fait qu'au dix-neuvième siècle, l'intérêt pour les parasciences, l'intérêt pour l'occultisme était absolument essentiel, alors que les choses vont se retourner par la suite. C'est un peu ce que tu laisses entendre: les choses vont s'inverser dans la modernité.

CK Yes. The moment when the aether hypothesis was actually disproved and rejected by science marks also the time when science became "rational." It is a decisive moment for the following twentieth century, and it still determines the world we inhabit today. Not long after science discarded the concept of the aether, the terrain of the occult and the spiritual left behind was explored and taken over by the vanguard of the arts.

BB Le postulat, l'hypothèse de Christoph, en tant qu'artiste, c'est de dire que lorsque la dimension irrationnelle de la science a été rejetée par la pensée rationaliste du vingtième siècle, cette dimension est passée dans le champ des arts plastiques. Encore une fois, c'est une hypothèse. J'insiste, car je vois des scientifiques parmi vous!

CK It is a hypothesis, or a metaphor, one could say. Like the Titans, who once were exiled by the new Olympic gods, the aether was expelled from the domain of the scientific — and the new rational worldview of modern science became a condition of modernity.

BB La condition de la modernité c'est justement, vous l'avez compris, une condition soumise à la réalité du rationalisme scientifique.

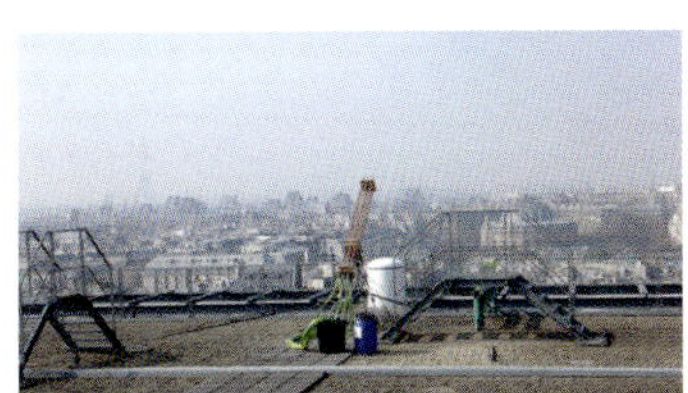

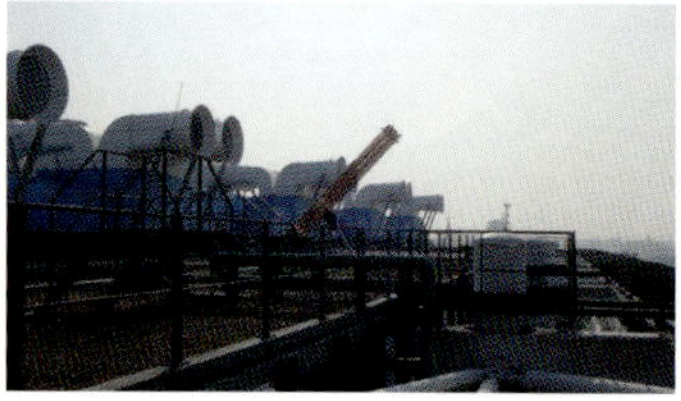

CK One of the basic, or most important tasks of art in the twentieth century is to conceive the unconceivable — to name the unnamable, as Barnett Newman puts it. Hence it is the role of modern science to describe reality as it is, and it is the role of art to address things that have no name.

BB Tandis que l'art s'attache à nommer l'innommable, ou à signifier l'insignifiable, la science de son côté, tend de plus en plus vers une vision rationaliste des choses.

CK Of course, the concept of an ethereal substance had various manifestations, like the nineteenth century luminiferous aether that we've talked about, or the all-pervasive "fluidum" suggested by the doctor Franz Anton Mesmer, who proclaimed his theory of the animal magnetism in Paris on the verge of the French Revolution, or later Wilhelm Reich, whose concept of orgone energy is also based on the assumption of an ethereal substance: a life-energy, actually.

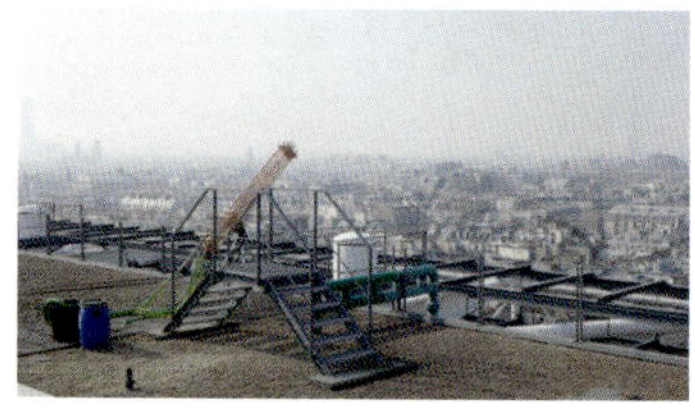

BB Chose importante: Christoph parle de Mesmer, de la fameuse "expérience de Mesmer." Mais il parle également de Wilhelm Reich. Or Wilhelm Reich joue un rôle crucial dans l'élaboration du projet de Christoph, puisque nous avons mis en place avec lui le projet du *Cloudbuster*, cette machine à faire pleuvoir pour le dire vite, que nous photographions quotidiennement sur le toit du Centre Pompidou, avec l'idée de pouvoir vérifier si nous modifions ainsi le climat. L'idée tout à fait intéressante ici, c'est de voir que Wilhelm Reich est à la fois un chercheur, un scientifique, et un psychanalyste; un personnage tout à fait entre-deux, qui a joué un rôle absolument capital mais controversé sur la scène universitaire américaine. Peux-tu justement nous parler de ton rapport à Wilhelm Reich?

CK Well, Wilhelm Reich is one of the figures who embodies the dilemma of the nineteenth century scientist — someone who tried to overcome science with the means of science. Predictably, the scientific community

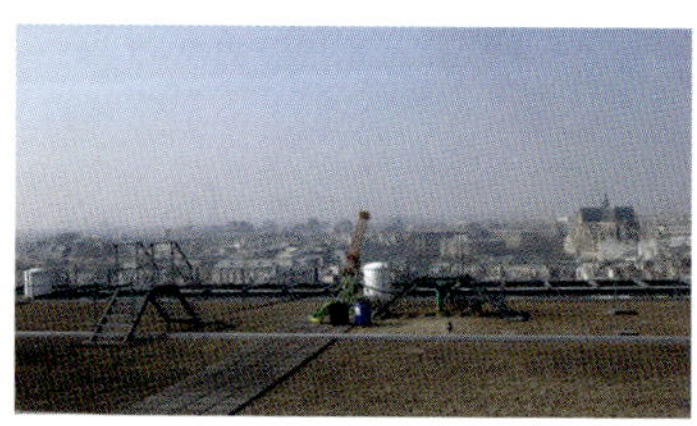

rejected him and today he is still widely considered a charlatan. Any scientist that deviates from science's main track, and turns torwards a speculative mode, maybe even towards the arts, will be consequently rejected by mainstream science — and, from science's point of view, for good reason. In the exhibition you can see examples of this in Nick Laessing's video on Alessandro Cruto, where these men are trying to invent machines that produce free energy. Of course, none of the men work for an official research project at a university — they are all private researchers.

BB Un point intéressant, que vous pourrez d'ailleurs voir à travers les quelques vidéos qui sont présentées sur les écrans de l'exposition, c'est qu'évidemment, on peut assimiler la pensée de Reich à la pensée d'un charlatan puisqu'il a ouvert la voie à des pratiques qui ont été mises en place sur un mode parallèle, et qui sont aujourd'hui totalement hors du champ de la science. Car au fil du temps, tout cela a été proscrit comme finalement totalement anti-scientifique! Une question importante, outre la personnalité et les expériences de Wilhelm Reich, c'est qu'ici, sur le toit du Centre Pompidou, Christoph a souhaité "rejouer" l'expérience de Wilhelm Reich. C'est cette idée très contemporaine du "re-enactment," dont a parlé d'ailleurs Bruno Latour dans les rencontres que nous avons faites ici, de se réapproprier une expérience et de la rejouer dans un autre moment historique qui en fait également la pleine actualité. Outre l'expérience du Cloudbuster de Wilhelm Reich, vous avez aussi pu voir dans les vitrines à l'entrée, que nous avons choisi quelques reférents historiques importants qui sont Descartes, Newton, etc. Il y a aussi Étienne Trouvelot, que je ne connaissais pas, probablement parce que je ne suis pas un lecteur attentif du Minotaure, la revue d'André Breton... Pour Christoph, Étienne Léopold Trouvelot est une personnalité-clé, voire symptomatique de ce projet.

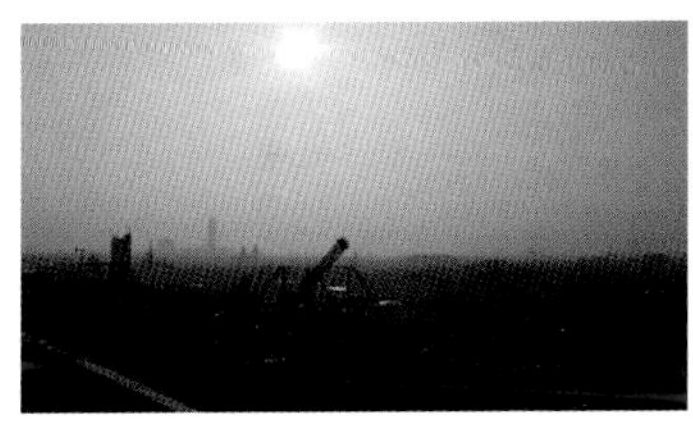

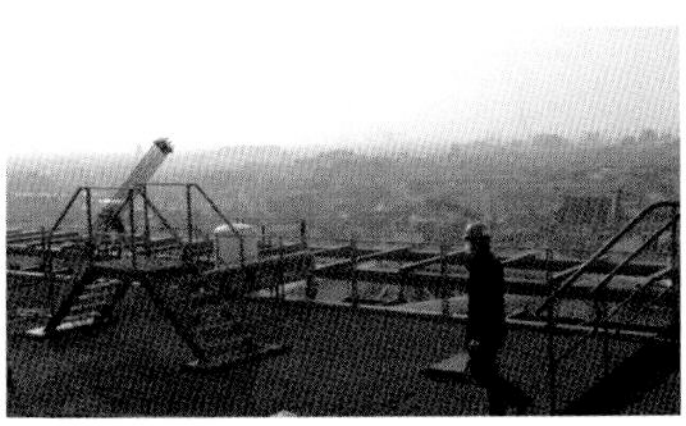

CK In the context of the exhibition Trouvelot represents a starting point — a gimmick, if you will. His photographic depictions of electrical flashes were featured in one of the editions of André Breton's *Minotaure* that we are showing in one of the vitrines near the entrance. From there I began to research this personage, who is at the same time both an amateur artist and an amateur scientist. And as it turns out, he had made spectacular drawings of the universe seen

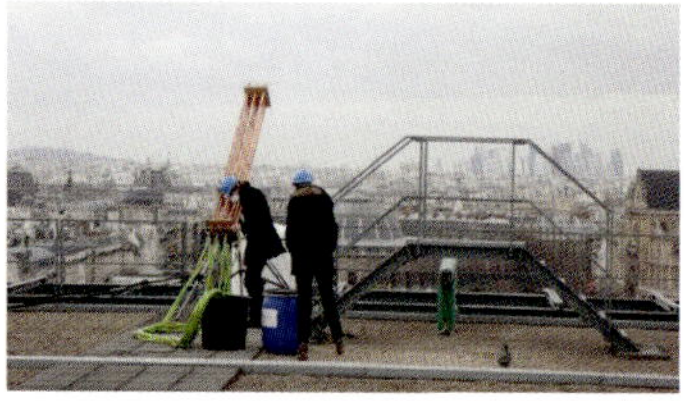

through large scientific telescopes in Paris and in Boston in the late nineteenth century, just before photography was able to capture these images automatically. Three of his works that were lent by the Observatoire de Paris are now on display at the beginning of the exhibition.

BB Trouvelot est de fait l'une des figures qu'André Breton avait publiées dans le numéro 5 du *Minotaure* en 1935, après ses investigations à l'Observatoire de Paris. Trouvelot était à la fois un entomologiste de formation, puis un astronome, qui observait avec les moyens du bord les astres, mais qui parallèlement avait une activité artistique. De telle sorte qu'il est l'être ambigu, ou le chiasme dont tu parlais par excellence: à la fois scientifique à sa façon, avec les instruments que l'on avait en 1870, et à la fois ce pastelliste qui observait puis notait dans des livres illustrés l'ensemble de ses observations. Il est un peu le modèle, le paradigme de cette exposition. D'ailleurs, vous l'avez vu, nous avons aussi souhaité présenter une toile magnifique d'Ugo Rondinone, qui est une grande œuvre ouvrant à son rapport à l'espace de l'art d'aujourd'hui. Vous avez également à l'entrée de l'exposition un ensemble de pièces de Trouvelot, pastels et carnets — nous remercions l'Observatoire de nous les avoir prêtés —,

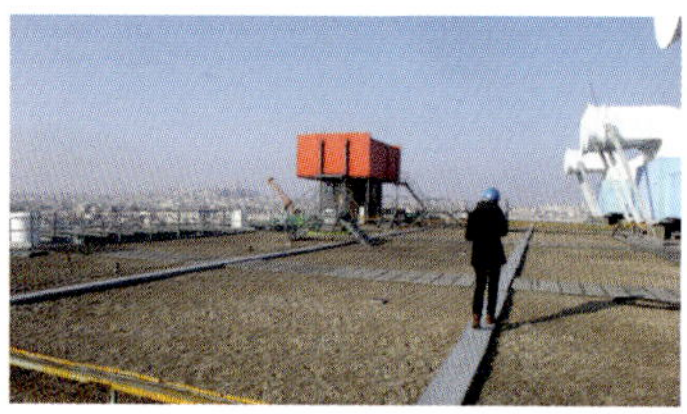

et l'expo se clôture, du moins en tant qu'exposition d'arts plastiques, puisque je ne parle pas des films et de tout ce qui va être montré ou activé, par l'image de Thomas Ruff que vous voyez, qui renvoie aussi à cette idée de l'espace vu par les artistes ou les appareils scientifiques. Je traduis tout en prenant quelques libertés avec la parole de Christoph Keller, vous voudrez bien m'en excuser! Une façon quelque peu "postmoderne."

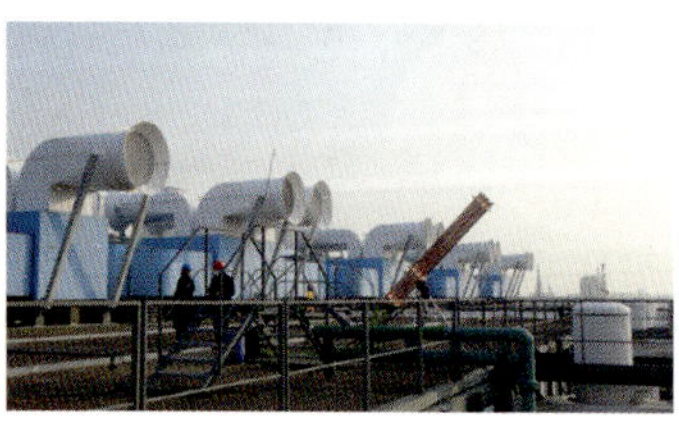

CK Oui, "Postmoderne," c'est une bonne transition… because Trouvelot is actually pre-modern, one of the last pre-modern figures as it were. In the historiography of this exhibition, he is therefore the starting point. After Trouvelot, we enter the era of technical representation through photography, when this kind of artist is no longer needed. He is not really a scientist, he is not really an artist, he is an almost tragic figure… no, he is just a late figure in his epoch. And ironically he became famous not for his paintings, nor for his science, but for accidentally introducing an insect, the European Gypsy Moth, which he used in his research, into the United States. It then spread over the whole American continent, producing one of the world's first well-documented ecological disasters.

BB Ce qui est absolument merveilleux, c'est que Trouvelot, un homme qui se rêvait artiste, qui se rêvait astronome, et qui n'est peut-être finalement ni complètement l'un ni complètement l'autre, cette figure un peu tardive, "fin de siècle" comme on dit, est aussi finalement le malheureux responsable de l'introduction aux États-Unis de ce Bombyx qui a décimé la moitié des fôrets d'Amérique du Nord dans les années mille neuf cent... c'était combien ?

CK C'était mille huit cent...

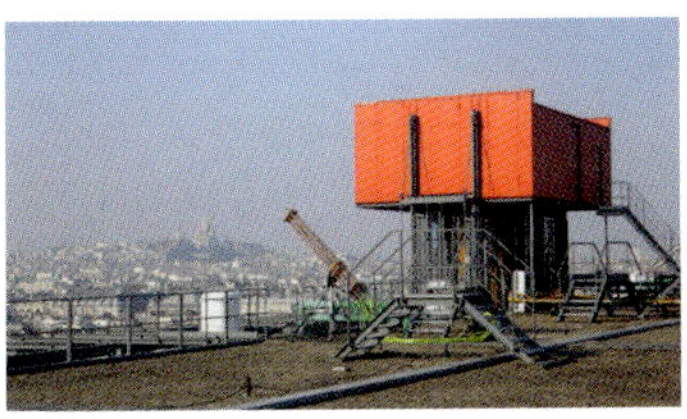

BB Soixante...

CK Trois ou sept...

BB C'est vraiment le savant dans tout ce que cela peut avoir de contradictoire. Voilà un homme qui rêve d'obtenir une vision parfaite du monde qui nous entoure, un homme qui, à défaut d'avoir les instruments scientifiques adaptés, dessine les choses et les inscrits dans ces merveilleux petits livres qu'il a réalisés, et finalement un homme qui sera connu chez les scientifiques pour avoir désastreusement introduit un parasite qui a décimé la moitié de la forêt américaine! Mon collaborateur Jean-Marie Gallais me racontait qu'à l'Observatoire, on le connaît aussi pour ça. On ne dit pas que c'est le grand observateur des astres ou de je ne sais trop quel anneau de Saturne, on dit "Ah oui, c'est celui qui a envoyé un parasite qui a dévasté la forêt américaine!"

CK All of which happens at roughly the same time when the Michelson-Morley experiment disproved, or actually failed to prove the existence of an aether wind.

BB Qui plus est, Trouvelot est apparu exactement au moment où l'expérience de Michelson-Morley a été mise au point, l'expérience qui voulait prouver l'existence d'un "vent d'éther" et qui finalement n'a pas pu le prouver! — une expérience que nous sommes allés filmer au Palais de la Découverte, qui a été réalisée pour l'exposition par Camille Fadel, un grand scientifique, et que nous projetons tous les matins en ouverture de la journée.

CK Now I would like to make a small jump to...

BB Attends, il y a une chose que je n'ai pas traduite tout à l'heure et qui est importante, c'est la question de la photographie. Le rôle évidemment crucial que la photographie joue dans l'histoire de la modernité — rôle que vous retrouvez au travers de l'ample sélection d'œuvres qui sont ici: vous avez remarqué qu'une grande part de celles-ci sont de nature photographique ou filmique. Ça n'est pas un hasard. Et, il y a par exemple une œuvre que j'aime beaucoup, qui est la petite photo de Joachim Koester, The Magic Mirror of John Dee, parce que c'est une œuvre tout à fait significative du pouvoir de la photographie. Qu'est-ce que c'est? C'est une pierre dure qu'il est allé photographier au British Museum et qu'il a grossie énormément. Cela montre que l'acte photographique d'une certaine façon, ne révèle pas tant la réalité qu'un "au-delà du visible." C'est un peu l'effet Blow Up, si vous voulez. Donc, ce que vous voyez ici, et qui n'est rien d'autre que l'agrandissement d'une petite pierre que les anciens utilisaient pour invoquer les esprits. Et bien, qu'est-ce que cela révèle? Cela révèle un au-delà du visible, un monde que les scientifiques avaient rêvé de trouver. C'est cette fonction de la photographie, cette fonction phatique de la photographie, que je trouve très importante dans l'ensemble de l'exposition. C'est peut-être aussi quelque chose qui intéresse Evariste Richer — l'auteur du grand diptyque qui est sur le mur là-bas — et avec qui nous converserons ici-même dans quelques jours.

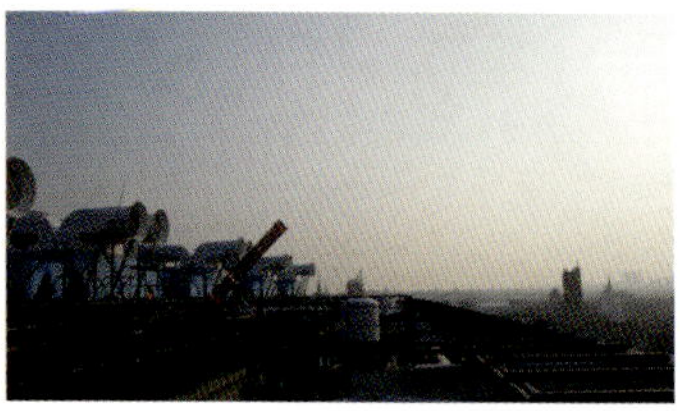

CK Alors...

BB Ma traduction est une traduction élastique!

CK Along the long wall we continue the quasi-chronological image sequence with the photographs of air turbulences by Étienne-Jules Marey. His task here was to capture the movement of the very fluid, almost ethereal flow of air streams. Next in the sequence is a series of chemigrams and photograms of the 1920s and '30s with works from Emeric Feher, Hannes Beckmann, and Willy

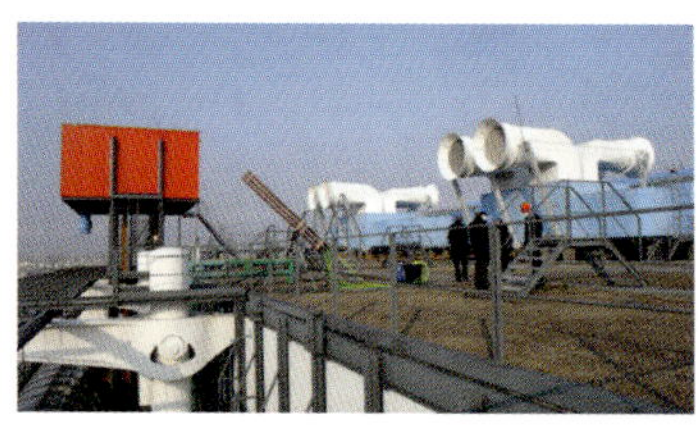

Kessels. In these works photography becomes the medium and the subject matter itself. Therefore they constitute a shift in the notion of mediality and materiality, which the artists reflect in their work. It's the medium that becomes interesting for the artists.

BB La photographie elle-même, parfois jusque dans sa matérialité, devient le médium. Et si vous suivez, après Trouvelot, les quelques images que nous avons réunies en séquence "quasi-chronologique," on trouve rapidement celles d'Etienne-Jules Marey par exemple, qui est évidemment connu pour le fameux fusil chronophotographique, qui a tant influencé Marcel Duchamp et nombre d'autres artistes se posant la question du temps et du mouvement dans la modernité, — Et bien, ces quatre photographies d'Etienne-Jules Marey, de 1901, visent à photographier les turbulences de l'air et les incidences de formes sur l'air. Parce qu'en fait, l'une des questions de l'exposition, c'est aussi la question du vide et de ses représentations, n'est-ce pas?

CK Absolutely, the question of the void is fundamental. If you ask about nonexistence, you ask about existence at the same time. So, this is certainly a very large question. Also I would like to say that there is a link between the notion of the medium and the notion of the transcendental. That is the reason why, in the medium of the photogram and the chemigram, there is always something "appearing." Even though these are just technical processes, something actually emerges. As we further proceed in the sequence of images we get to the second kind of "medium": the medium as in "états altérés," or altered states of consciousness.

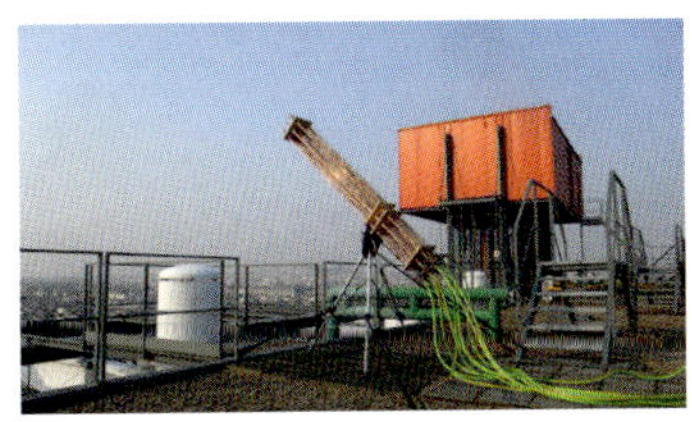

BB Dès lors que la photographie est le médium par excellence de la modernité, vous la retrouvez dans tout un ensemble d'expériences chimiques qui ont fasciné, entre autres, les surréalistes; les dadaistes aussi, mais d'une manière tout à fait différente. Marc Dachy viendra nous parler de ce rapport que les dadaistes et les surréalistes entretenaient à la chimie — aux chimies, disons. Car en fait, il de la chimie, mais également du chimique au sens des produits chimiques qui altèrent la conscience et qui à un moment donné, deviennent, à travers les expériences surréalistes, à travers les premières expériences faites aux États-Unis dans les années 40 par Brian Gysin, ou par la scène de San Francisco, des vecteurs d'expérimentation artistique. Vous en avez différents exemples réunis ici, de Gysin à Michaux. Elles deviennent des expériences absolument cruciales.

CK And their relations to alchemy…

BB Certes, certes. Au demeurant, c'est assez intéressant de voir que par exemple, dans le fameux ouvrage de László Moholy-Nagy, *Art et Photographie*, de 1926 que nous présentons ici, vous trouvez, reproduit dans ce livre qui traite évidemment de la photographie comme un au-delà de la peinture, comme une réfutation du pouvoir de la peinture, la fameuse image de la table tournante du film de Fritz Lang, qui nous ramène à un imaginaire tout à fait autre. Laquelle photographie va d'ailleurs servir Guillaume Désanges, dans ce photomontage là-bas, pour faire léviter le minimalisme, c'est à dire pour arracher le minimalisme à sa dimension purement objectale.

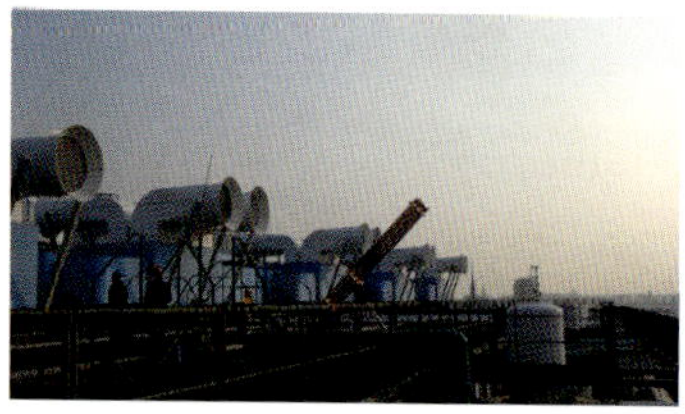

Ce qui est intéressant dans un projet comme celui que nous propose Christoph, c'est qu'il n'a pas dans le cadre modeste de notre festival, d'ambition scientifique: il s'agit d'éveiller les choses, de créer des magnétismes entre des choses qui viennent de territoires différents. Le magnétisme étant, si je veux aller plus loin, présent dans la pièce de Tunga, l'artiste brésilien, pièce qui est tout à fait extraordinaire. C'est d'ailleurs le seul objet, finalement, de l'exposition: une boîte à l'intérieur de laquelle il y a un cristal de roche tenu par des pierres aimantées, qui le retiennent et l'attirent.

CK Maybe here we need to emphasize that this exhibition is not a historical exhibition, even though we are showing a lot of historical works. Instead we tried to draft a journey through the twentieth century in order to find out where we stand now. There have been major changes in the role of science in society. Somehow we have bypassed modernity, and some of the fundamental questions that once seemed clarified or answered are suddenly back on the table. Like the relation between art and science, or the relation of the material world to the immaterial, to the vacuum

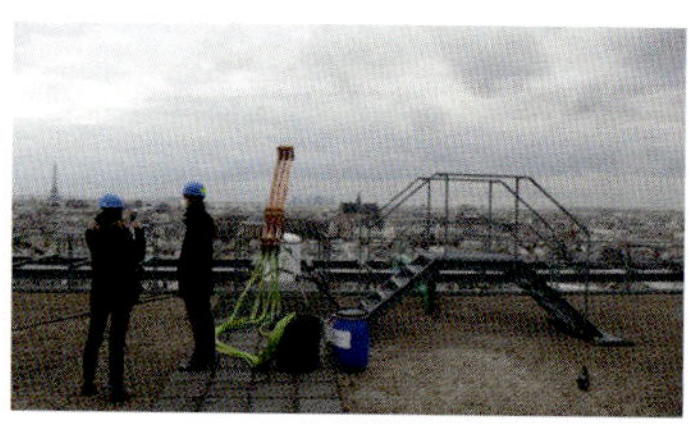

and the void — which touches on questions of the transcendental. There is a reappearance of spiritual topics in the arts, and in cinema, too. In this way, we are trying to draw a picture of where we are now.

BB C'est intéressant, parce que finalement, à travers ce projet, l'idée est de questionner le dépassement de la modernité. Il est clair que dans l'exposition, rien n'est pensé sur le mode de l'inventaire systématique, mais davantage sur le mode de l'indice. Ce sont des pistes, qui passent par le médium photographie, par le livre ou bien-sûr, par le médium cinéma.

Je pense qu'il serait bien aussi d'ouvrir les choses par des échanges et des questions avec le public. À moins que tu ne veuilles dire quelque chose de plus?

CK About the setup of the exhibition, one could say that it has three parts. The first one is the part with the sequence of images on the long wall in a quasi-chronological order that we've already talked about. Then, we have this zig-zag viewing structure in the middle of the room with contemporary videos displayed on identical plasma screens which we've dubbed "Champs Expérimentaux," or experimental field. And last there is the amphitheater, which we have built into the far end of the exhibition space where we are now. What interested me about the three different kinds of displays are the different modalities of viewing. The first one is the classical modality in which you look at an image or a painting from a distance. The second is the modality of an installation, where you are completely immersed in the works, which in this case are videos with audio over headphones. Lastly, you have the ritual ceremony of a science theater or a performing arts theater, where an audience collectively witnesses a live presentation — for example, a play or an "œuvre parlée" or a film on the screen.

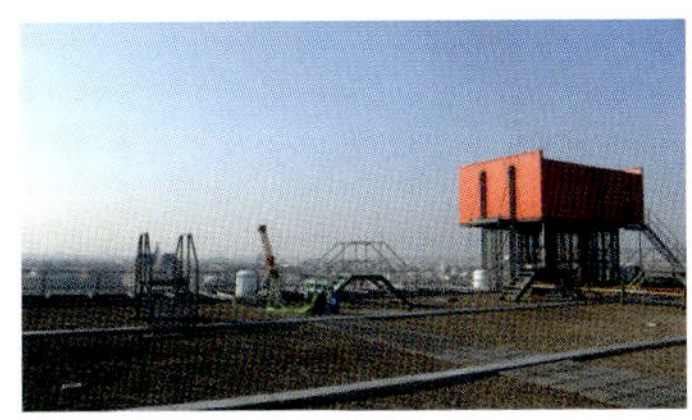

BB Le propre même du Nouveau festival du Centre Pompidou, c'est de camper des situations qui sont d'une certaine façon des situations inaccoutumées, ou du moins, c'est de confronter des situations de natures différentes: regarder des œuvres accrochées sur un mur, s'installer dans un rapport plus intime avec un casque pour voir des vidéos, ou bien se retrouver "comme à l'école" dans un mini amphithéâtre comme celui dans lequel vous vous trouvez. L'expérience de l'exposition en tant que telle devient un paradigme du projet général.

CK ...and here I would like to quickly jump to an anecdote from 1916, in Zurich, where the Cabaret Voltaire was founded by Hugo Ball and Emmy Hennings, among others. It could be called the cradle of modern art. And in the poster brochure that we've printed as a reader to this exhibition you will find as a reverence to Emmy Hennings, her poem "Äther" (Aether). The poem was written in the early years when she was consuming ether, the narcotic substance. A lot of avant-gardistes at that time were using ether as a drug to escape reality, because it was cheaper than alcohol... Maybe you can first translate that?

BB Vous connaissez l'histoire du Cabaret Voltaire, de la formation de Dada en 1916 et donc du rôle de Hugo Ball et aussi d'Emmy Hennings, qui était "addict" à l'éther, une substance moins chère que l'alcool, et qui a initié une réflexion sur la pratique artistique à partir de ces substances. Mais, toute l'exposition témoigne de cette expérience, les deux mescalines d'Henri Michaux par exemple. Au demeurant, nous projetterons ce film très rare que Michaux détestait, qui est une commande d'un laboratoire pharmaceutique, dans lequel il explique pourquoi il a inhalé de la mescaline pour réaliser ces dessins. Toute l'exposition est traversée de ces idées, d'autant plus que pour Christoph, elles refont vraiment surface aujourd'hui, à l'ère de la postmodernité, d'un certain retour de la dualité entre art et science.

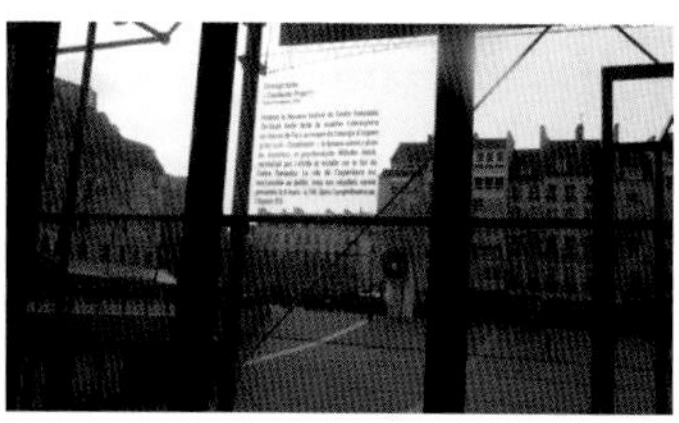

CK The connection between ether, the drug, and the aether is coincidental, you might say. Yet stunningly it all happens around the same time at almost the same place. If you imagine the Cabaret Voltaire in Zurich, you may realize that Albert Einstein lived in more or less the same neighborhood when working on the theory of general relativity. Ok, when the Cabaret Voltaire was founded, he was already in Berlin...

BB Et Lénine!

CK ...and Lenin also. But the man who actually finished off the aether was in the vicinity of the Cabaret Voltaire. And Lenin was there, as well as James Joyce. They were all there. You have the main influences of twentieth century literature, art, politics, and physics geographically all very close together at that crucial moment, when the aether was refuted.

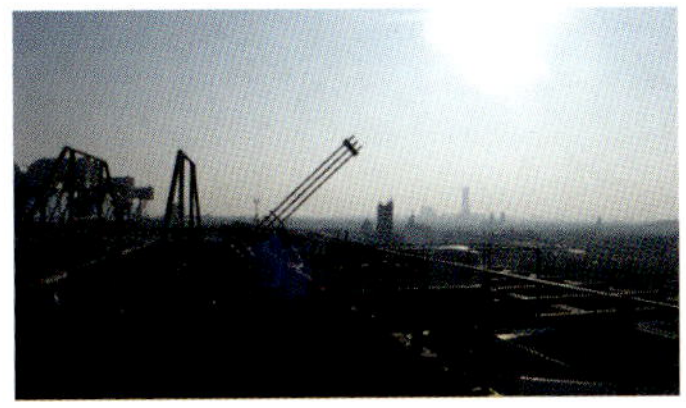

BB Ce qui intéresse Christoph, c'est cette proximité géographique du Cabaret Voltaire, lieu névralgique de Zurich, petit cabaret dans la vieille ville. D'ailleurs, "cabaret" est un mot impropre, c'est un bar finalement. Christoph s'amuse à noter la proximité d'artistes et de scientifiques là-bas. Moi, j'y ajoutais Lénine, parce que dans le genre, c'est quand même pas mal! Il aimait les bonnes choses aussi Lénine, il a été addict à pas mal de choses... Ce qui m'intéresse en tout cas, à travers ce que tu dis, ce qui est en question, ce n'est pas tant la production d'objets qu'une réflexion sur le corps. Il faut voir à mon avis Dada non pas comme une simple réflexion sur une production d'objets critiques ou d'objets qui visaient à prendre une position absolument violente contre la première guerre mondiale, mais aussi comme une réflexion sur le statut du corps et le statut du sujet dans la modernité...

Roger Rotmann D'abord, je voulais saluer le passage de Lénine dans cette discussion autour de l'éther! Ne trouvez-vous pas que ça change toute l'histoire du mouvement ouvrier! Ma question: ne pensez-vous pas que depuis ces dernières années, la science se tourne ou se retourne, peut-être pas vers l'irrationnel, mais du moins vers des interrogations philosophiques, plus poétiques, plus métaphysiques, dans ses formes les plus avancées? Et, est-ce que c'est un domaine qui vous intéresse, sur lequel vous travaillez aussi?

CK Yes, I think this is surely happening. Obviously! As I said before, the situation of science in the twenty-first century has changed. It is different from the nineteenth and early twentieth centuries, when the sciences were still mainly national endeavours, funded by the nation-state. Science is now integrated into a globalized economy of production. But as an artist, I am not just interested in what has happened in science, I am also very interested in what happens in the arts in relation to these changes in scientific practice. Because art is not completely autonomous from science; they are interdependent fields. These

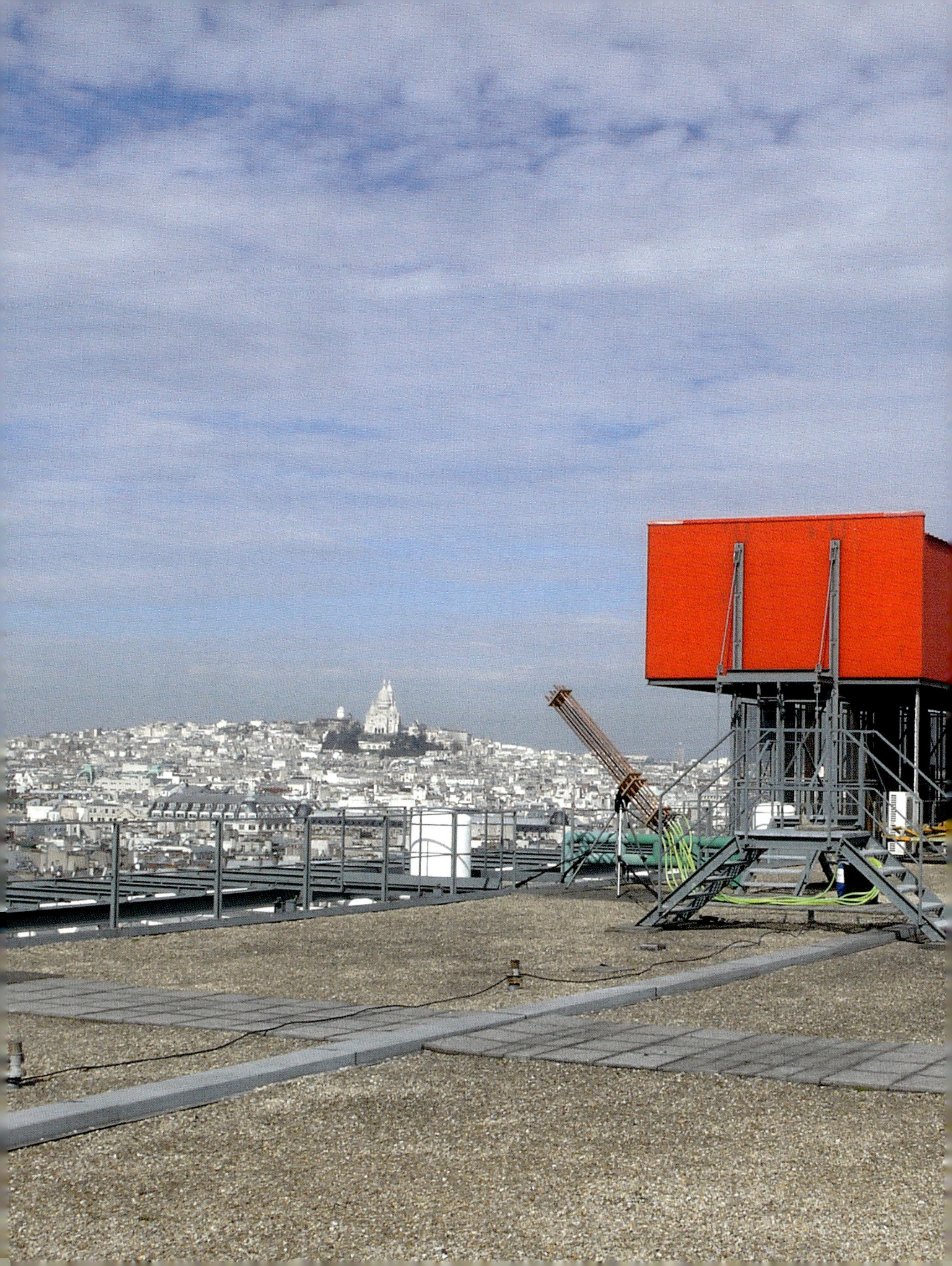

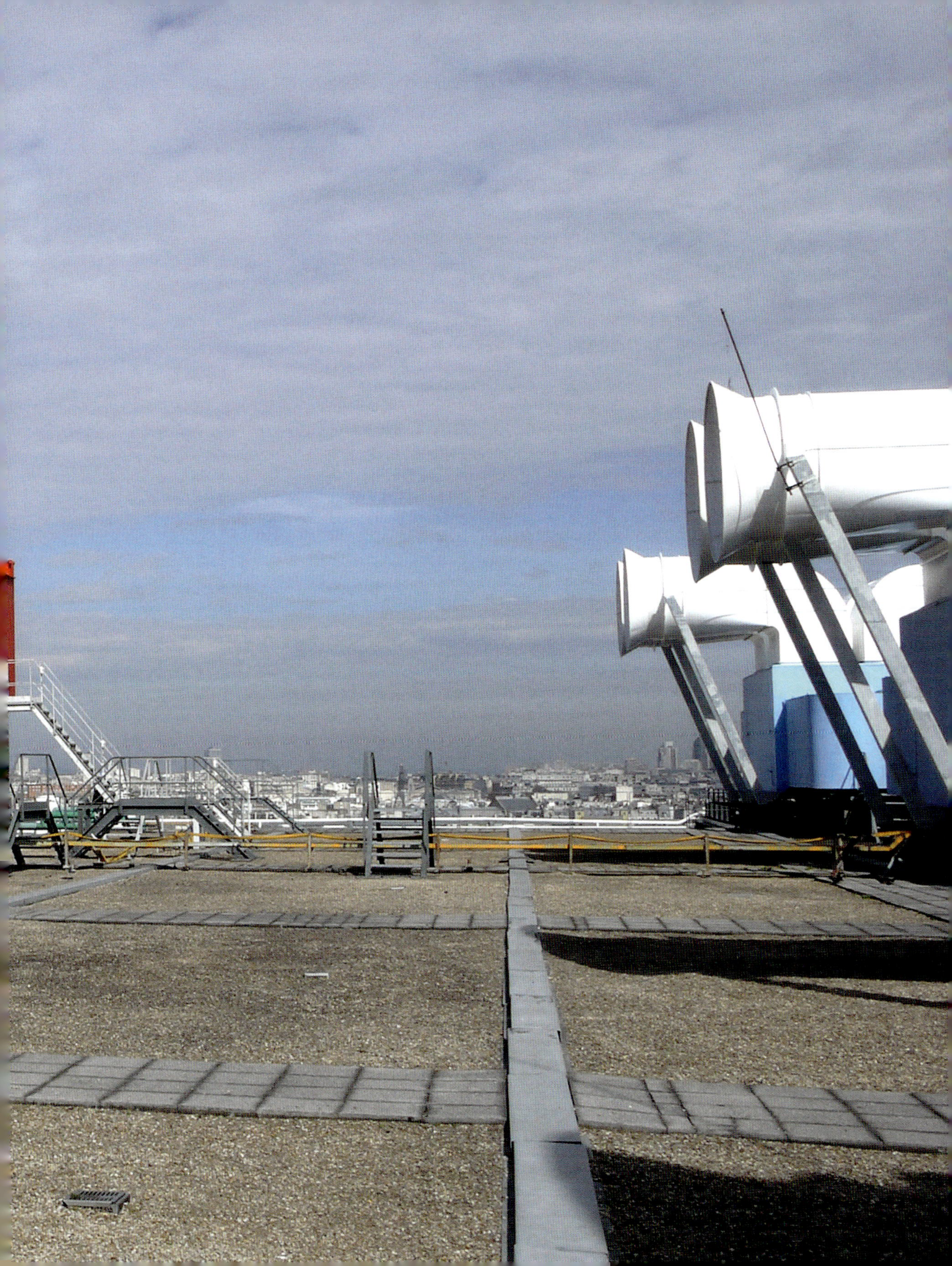

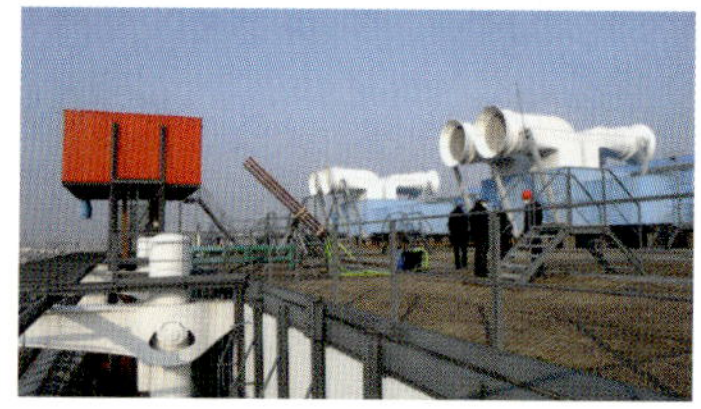

processes — how science understands itself, how it positions itself regarding the spiritual and the philosophical — have a strong influence on the role art plays in society. So the answer to your question is: yes, absolutely, I am very much involved in these changes.

BB En réponse à Roger Rotmann, tu laisses encore une fois entendre qu'il y a une influence de l'art dans le champ de la science…

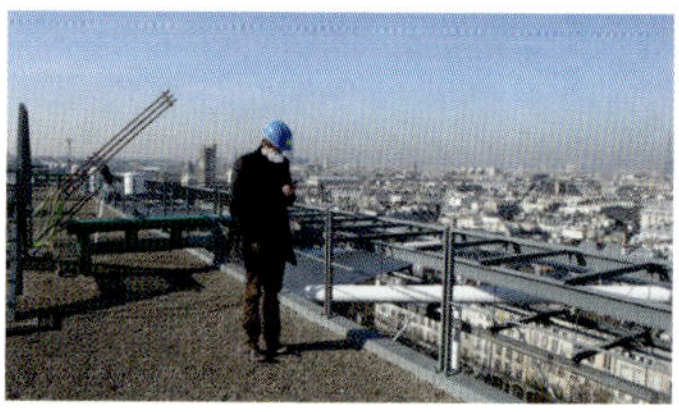

CK That is what I was alluding to with the anecdote about the Cabaret Voltaire, that there is always an interrelation, an influence — that of course you cannot fully track down — that literature and the arts exert on the factual sciences. They have an impact on how people, including scientists, can understand themselves being in the world. This is just an example of how scientists partake in cultural developments, often maybe without even being aware of it. So, yes, I think there is an interrelation. But what I was saying was different: it is not that I am not just searching for the effects of culture in science, but rather, I am interested in how the whole process of change is unfolding, and in how this might influence how art will look like in ten years from now, or twenty years from now. The preconditions of art are always changing.

BB Christoph est intéressé par le processus de changement de la science elle-même, et la manière dont cela affectera dans dix ou vingt ans, tout aussi bien son domaine propre que les domaines cognitifs auxquels elle renvoie.
Il y a une autre question qui me vient immédiatement à l'esprit. Tu as parlé de la photographie, tu as fait remarquer aussi que les premières images photographiques s'appuyaient non pas tant sur une dimension physique de l'image que sur une dimension chimique de celle-ci — alors, toi, comment est-ce que tu situes cette relation entre chimie-physique et art ?

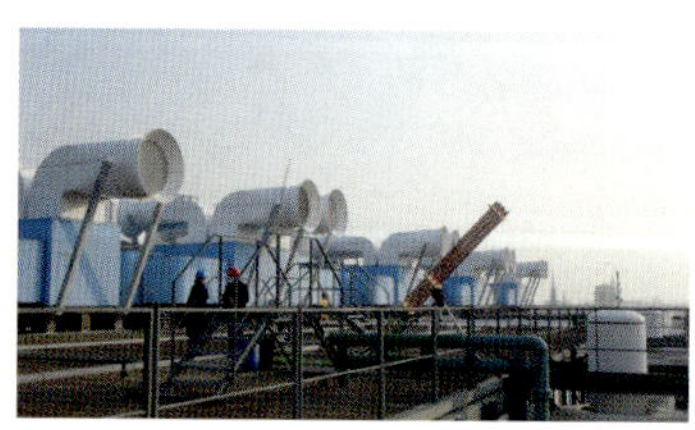

CK I chose the aether as a concept for the exhibition knowing that nobody can seriously expect all the questions raised here to be

answered in a simple way. Choosing the aether as a topic meant basically placing the question of the void in the center of the exhibition — which seemed to be a challenging point of departure for an art exhibition. Since the question around the aether cannot be answered simply, we've invited a lot of people to contribute to the exhibition with works and with talks. About the relationship, which you asked about, between physics, chemistry, and art: this is also a very broad topic, and I am not able to give you a short answer to that question either. But maybe I can tell you what I am interested in...

BB Vous l'avez compris, le sujet est trop large, trop ample pour qu'à travers l'expérience de l'éther, Christoph puisse répondre à la question. Il veut préciser ici ce qui d'abord l'intéresse.

CK The proposal of this exhibition is to encircle the aether, with different works of art and contributions by many people. Can you say "encerclement" in French?

BB S'approcher en "cerclant" autour de l'idée originelle, se rapprocher, en quelque sorte.

CK The relation of physics and chemistry to art is underscored by alchemy. The difference between alchemy and chemistry is that in chemistry, matter may change its state in a chemical reaction, whereas in alchemy, matter changes its state only by changing its concept as well. Basically, you have to undergo an inner process of change in order to be able to change a thing. And I think that is related to the way we see art. Art is not an objective quality; you can only make it work by changing yourself. That is also how I understand the experimental situation of an art exhibition, where you are offered the possibility to engage in an inner change, in a shift in the way you view something.

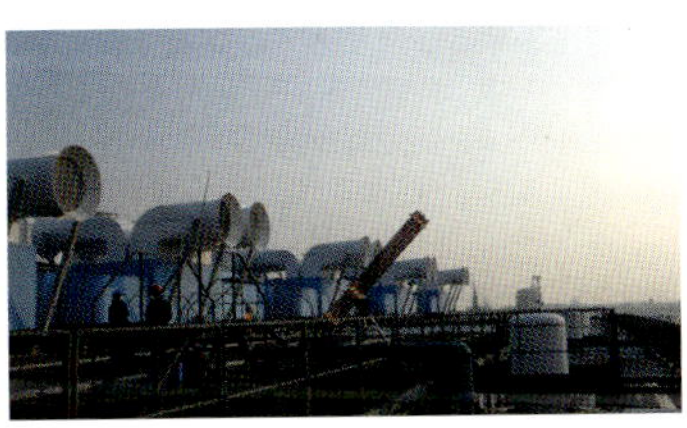

BB C'est extrêmement important d'envisager l'espace d'exposition comme un espace d'expérience et ce faisant, de se changer, se métamorphoser soi-même au travers de cette expérience. Il disait qu'entre chimie et physique, il y avait aussi cette dimension liée à ce qu'on appelle l'alchimie. A propos, tu n'utilises pas la notion d'alchimie avec prudence?

CK Why? I also use words like "vérité" or "transcendance" without being over cautious.

BB Il y a comme une dimension à la fois d'un passé, d'une vérité symboliste dans l'alchimie, que l'on utilise plus aujourd'hui.

CK Yes, but...

BB L'alchimie, c'est ce qui a le pouvoir de transformer!

CK I think that, as an artist, I wouldn't want to put myself into that position... I am not an alchemist! Joseph Beuys presented himself as a shaman sometimes, but I would never take that direction.

BB C'est très important d'un point de vue artistique... qu'un artiste de sa génération, lui en l'occurrence, ne revendique absolument pas la posture du chamane que Joseph Beuys, allemand également mais de deux générations son aîné, a revendiquée. D'ailleurs, je ne sais pas s'il l'a revendiquée vraiment ou si on lui a donné, collé cette posture du chamane?

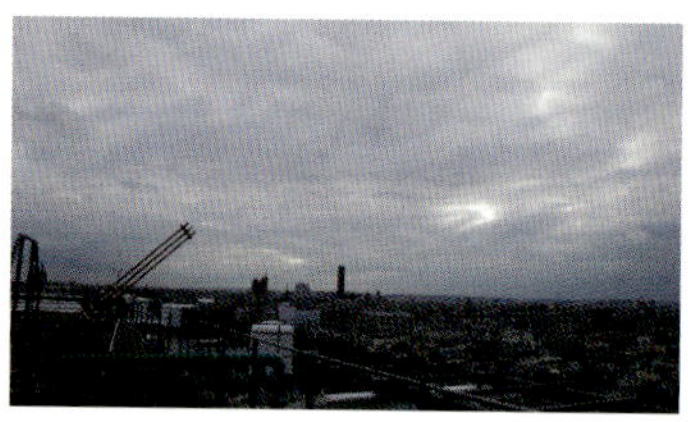

CK But if you enter a cage with a coyote, and a fur, and a stick, you do look like a shaman.

BB C'est peut-être parodique. Ç'est quelque chose d'autre, à mon avis. Beuys était plus critique au regard de l'alchimie que ce qu'on a essayé de lui faire dire. Au demeurant, dire de quelqu'un qu'il était tenté par l'alchimie dans les années 60 et 70, c'était peut-être lui faire une critique absolument radicale...

CK I don't want to dismiss Joseph Beuys. What I can say, on a more positive note, is that when I see an artwork, I am looking at the kind of relationship it establishes with me. The viewer always functions as a mediator, a me-

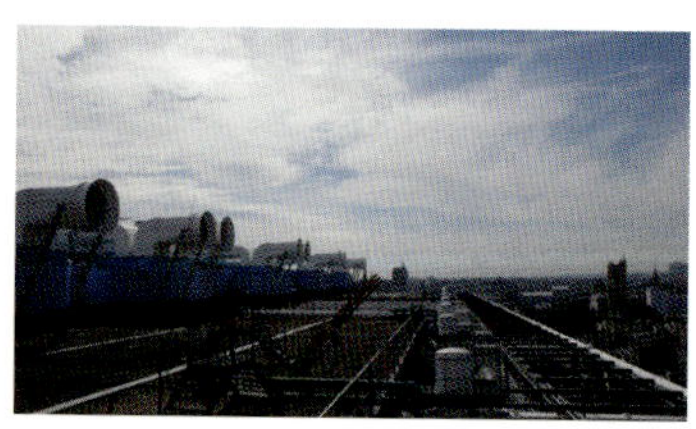

dium between the work and the artist. The question is: How does the artwork approach its counterpart? I like it when the viewer is perceived as a grown-up person by the work, like a scientist, with whom to share an experience.

BB La fameuse fonction du regardeur, de celui qui voit. Faut-il dire "regardeur," je ne sais pas, car quand vous dites regardeur, vous appuyez sur Marcel Duchamp et le rôle actif de ce regardeur comme interface entre la chose regardée et lui-même...

Audience Je voudrais interroger Christoph sur cette autre figure tutélaire, qui beaucoup plus que Beuys, paraît ici s'imposer par rapport au jeu sur le spiritisme, sur l'occultisme, sur la drogue, sur les états seconds, c'est évidemment Sigmar Polke... et sur l'alchimie aussi. C'est quelqu'un, j'imagine, qui aurait pu être présent ici. Quelle importance a-t-il à ses yeux?

BB Ce que l'on peut ajouter, c'est que Sigmar Polke commence une œuvre sur un arrière-plan que je dirais néo-dadaiste, dans une dimension extrêmement critique où les matériaux eux-mêmes sont pris au piège de leur propre devenir, jusqu'à introduire du curare dans certains tableaux qu'il a réalisés par la suite. Mais il apparaît comme une figure essentielle de la scène allemande depuis le début des années 60 critique par rapport au pop, jusqu'à sa mort l'année dernière. Alors, Sigmar Polke?

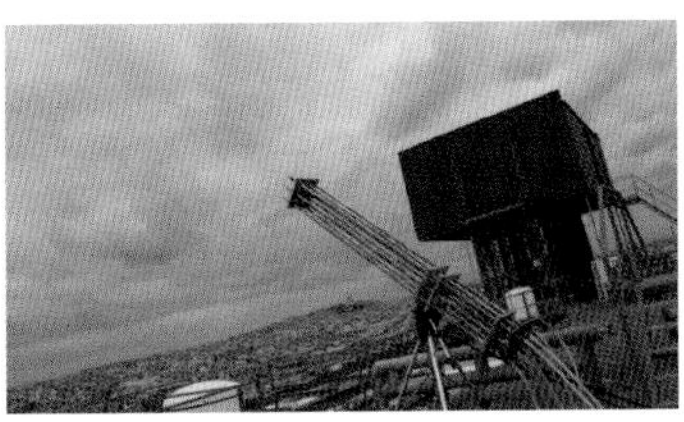

CK Your question was how much I was influenced by Beuys and Polke in my early years as an artist. I must say that my personal contestation with the dominant father figures of the Rheinland era is not so strong. I belong to the '90s Berlin generation and we were already detached from these father figures. We have a more historical view of Beuys — and same with Polke. Some of my works and especially this exhibition have more to do with the early avant-gardists, around and before Berlin Dada, which had a stronger influence on my early conception of art. Berlin Dadaism is, by the way, very different from the Parisian Dada. Even though they started together in Zurich and Tristan Tzara and Marcel Janco influenced Paris Dada, it was yet another new art movement here.

In Berlin the Dada movement was very political, anti-bourgeois, and anti-art even. It was also a very poor generation of artists often living in destitute situations.

BB Ce que Christoph met en évidence, c'est qu'il n'a rien à voir avec cette scène rhénane des années 60 et 70 qu'incarne Joseph Beuys. Lui est un berlinois des années 90 qui s'est affranchi de la relation qu'il aurait pu entretenir avec cette génération. De là sans doute, sa volonté de réinterroger, voire de s'approprier certains champs de la connaissance et domaines mal connus, voire négligés. De là sa volonté de s'appuyer aussi sur la spécificité de l'histoire de certains individus et de tenter de comprendre la perception qu'on a pu en avoir jusqu'à aujourd'hui. Je pense bien sûr à Wilhelm Reich, à sa posture, son histoire, ses investigations qui sont, certains d'entre vous le savent ici, des centres d'intérêt, d'analyse et d'investigations constants pour Christoph Keller que je remercie ici, tant pour la générosité de ses interventions que pour les pistes qu'il dessine à l'occasion de cette deuxième édition.

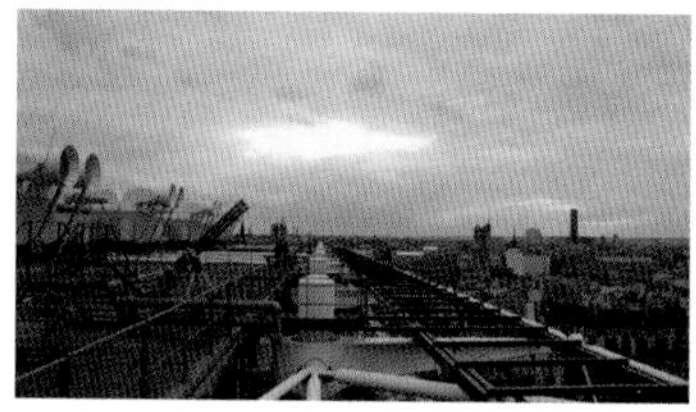

Œuvre parlée — transcript of the public talk between Christoph Keller and Bernard Blistène held at the "amphithéâtre" which was built into Espace 315 at Centre Pompidou for the exhibition "Æther — from Cosmology to Consciousness" (Nouveau festival du Centre Pompidou, second edition); February 16, 2011; English/French.

Æther

UNE PROPOSITION DE CHRISTOPH KELLER

DE LA COSMOLOGIE À LA CONSCIENCE

16.2.—7.3.2011, Espace 315
Nouveau festival du Centre Pompidou

La notion d'éther est un concept élusif, à la fois élément et substance. En philosophie, l'éther signifie l'absence du vide, le cinquième élément qui ne possède aucune qualité spécifique et dont l'existence, par définition, ne peut être exactement déterminée ou physiquement prouvée. Dans le domaine de la science, l'éther représente à la fois un élément et un médium qui ne pourrait être modifié et qui serait plus subtil que la lumière.

De plus, l'éther représente le médium de la modernité par excellence. Son rejet en tant que concept scientifique—conséquence de la théorie de la relativité d'Einstein—marque le moment où la physique se libère de l'occultisme encore omniprésent durant les recherches du XIXe siècle. Ce terrain abandonné par la science a très vite été réoccupé par les arts. Par conséquent, la chute de l'éther correspond au développement de la condition scientifique moderne et de sa vision rationnelle des choses, or la notion d'objectivité scientifique trouve sa complémentarité dans la subjectivité artistique et plus généralement dans la fonction sublimatoire assignée à l'expression culturelle. La mort de l'éther représente donc la naissance de l'art moderne ainsi que tous les pouvoirs irrationnels engendrés par celui-ci.

En choisissant l'éther comme concept central, ce projet propose de saisir—dans le cadre du Nouveau festival du Centre Pompidou—la relation ambivalente entre l'art et la science, dans laquelle l'art adhère au modèle scientifique tout en offrant une expérience qui transcende sa pure matérialité.

On peut dire de l'éther qu'il est l'inconnu.

Mais comment l'inconcevable peut-il être conçu ?

La réponse est multiple : du 5e élément de Platon jusqu'à Descartes, on trouve une multitude de théories scientifiques et philo-sophico-théologiques au sujet de l'éther. Plusieurs philosophes de la nature, comme Giordano Bruno, Christiaan Huygens et Isaac Newton, dont les travaux restent fondamentaux pour la science actuelle, ont fondé leurs théories sur l'hypothèse que l'éther était une donnée a priori.

Parallèlement au développement du siècle des Lumières, une quantité importante de théories sur l'éther fut publiée. Dans le Paris pré-révolutionnaire, le guérisseur Franz Anton Mesmer stipule que l'éther est un « fluide » , et il s'en sert comme un médium dans sa théorie psycho-physique sur le « magnétisme animal ». De plus, de nombreux cercles scientifiques et salons littéraires montrèrent de très fortes affinités pour ces conceptions et ces spéculations d'alchimistes. L'artiste et astronome français passionné du XIXe siècle, Étienne Léopold Trouvelot, réalisa des dessins impressionnants de ce que les puissants télescopes ne révélèrent que bien plus tard de l'espace, avant que la photographie n'ait été capable de capturer toutes ces données.

Par ailleurs, des écrivains romantiques comme Edgar Allan Poe et Friedrich Hölderlin ainsi que Emmanuel Kant étaient également des « aetheristes » écrivant de longs poèmes et traités à ce sujet.

Ensuite, bien entendu, est apparu le concept de l'« l'éther luminifère », une matière subtile, dont l'existence a été longuement discutée au cours du XIXe siècle. Des scientifiques aussi éminents que James Clerk Maxwell, Henri Poincaré et Nicolas Tesla ont défendu son existence, mais « l'experimentum crucis » de Michelson et Morley de 1887 a finalement démenti cette thèse.

Bien que souvent banni ou désapprouvé, l'éther continue, jusqu'à aujourd'hui, de réapparaître et de réemerger, tel un concept de continuité ou d'éventualité qui relierait le microcosme et l'universel. Qu'il s'agisse de « la physique orgone » de Wilhelm Reich, d'un « nouvel âge de l'ésotérisme » ou, comme on l'entend parfois, d'un « théorie du champ unifié » ou encore de la « matière noire », on constate que le terme lui-même reste soigneusement évité.

Enfin, cette approche ne saurait être complète sans évoquer la substance anesthésiante et bon marché que de nombreux acteurs de l'avant-garde consommèrent pour stimuler la perception et échapper à

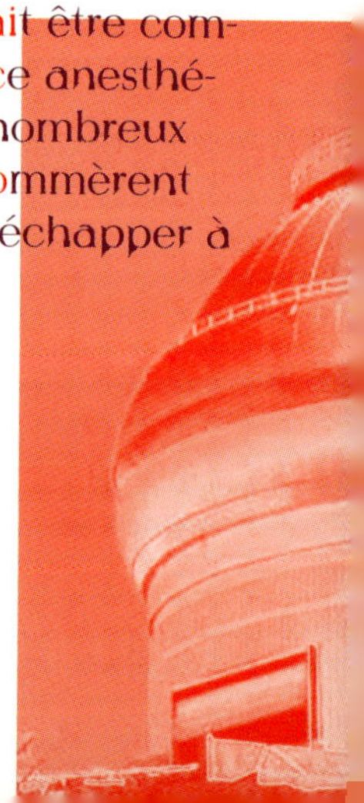

la réalité. L'usage de cette substance est devenu très populaire lorsque la bataille au sujet de l'éther était encore à son comble. Des artistes comme Henri Michaux, Gisèle Freund et Brassaï réalisèrent des œuvres de nature expérimentale faisant allusion aux « états altérés de la conscience » et Etienne-Jules Marey réalisa des expérimentations photographiques et obtint des images abstraites impressionnantes.

Ces explorations nous mènent, de façon quasi chronologique, vers le regard de nos contemporains tels Evariste Richer, Claude Lévêque, Thomas Ruff, Ugo Rondinone ou Wolfgang Tillmans (parmi d'autres) pour aboutir à un ensemble intitulé « le champ expérimental », réunissant une sélection de vidéos et de films contemporains qui renvoient de façons multiples à la notion d'éther. Parmi les œuvres présentées se trouvent des propositions de John Smith, Mariana Castillo Deball, Joachim Koester, Adolf Wölfli/Daniel Baumann, David Maljkovic et Cyprien Gaillard.

Dans le cadre du Nouveau festival du Centre Pompidou, vous êtes invités à un voyage à travers une exposition « mise en scène ». Le programme est articulé autour de la notion d'éther dans le discours contemporain : il questionne notre position en ce début du XXIe siècle, alors que la condition moderne est révolue mais que les questions essentielles de la science, de la réalité, de la transcendance et de l'art restent toujours sans réponses.

Christoph Keller

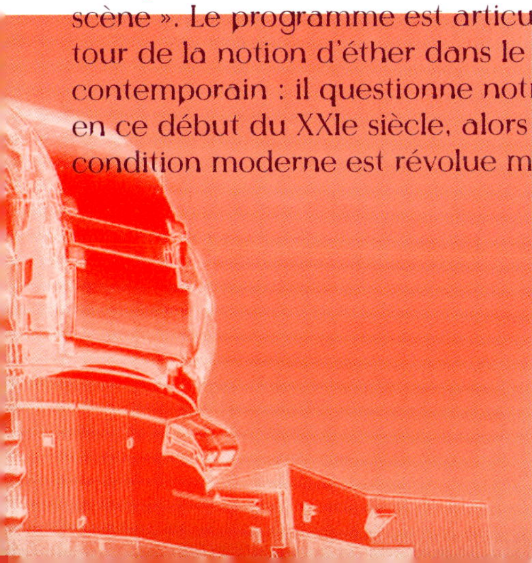

The perplexing thing about the theory of Anaxagoras is that his cosmogony seems repeatable in every particular thing in the world. That is, he speaks of all things being together in the beginning, present in one mass in infinitely small particles so that the whole would not seem to have any particular nature, except perhaps that of air or aether.

Ralph McInerny, A History Of Western Philosophy

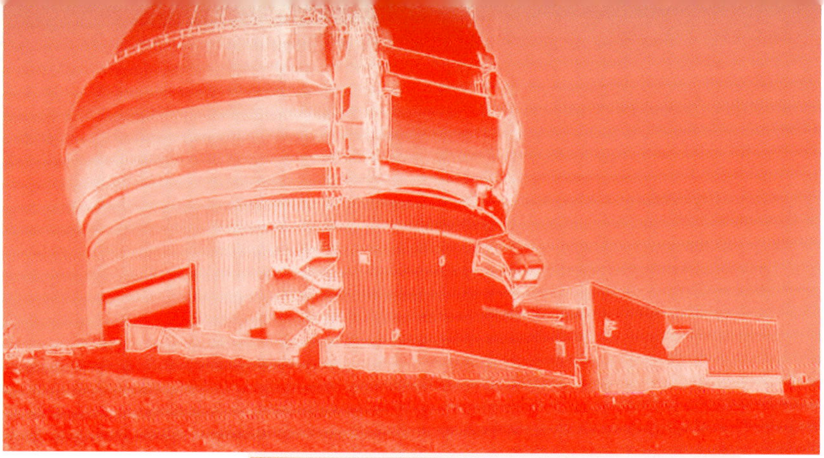

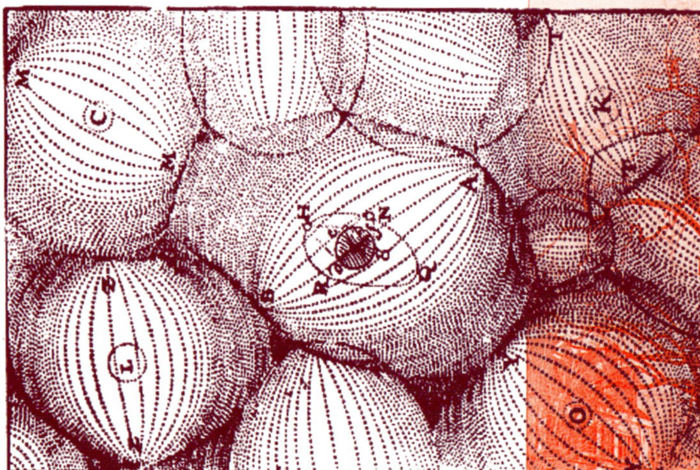

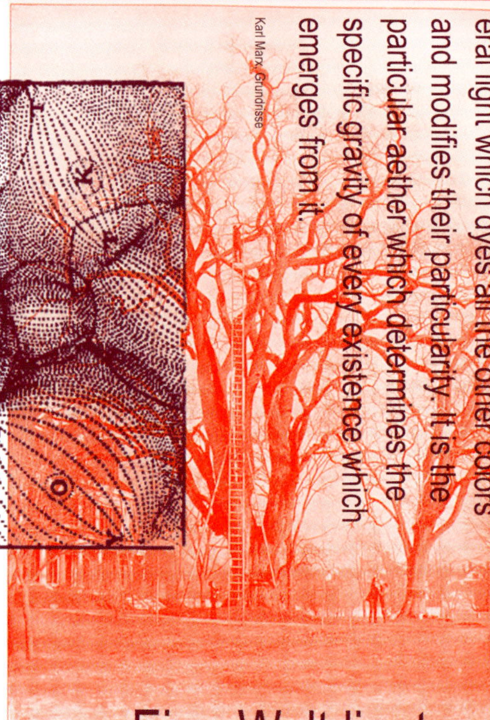

In all forms of society there is one determinate kind of production which assigns ranks and influence to all the others, and whose relations assign rank and influence to all other relations. It is the general light which dyes all the other colors and modifies their particularity. It is the particular aether which determines the specific gravity of every existence which emerges from it.

Karl Marx, Grundrisse

Äther

An die Scheiben schlägt
der Regen.
Eine Blume leuchtet rot.
Kühle Luft weht mir
entgegen.
Wach ich oder bin ich tot?

Eine Welt liegt weit ganz
weit,
Eine Uhr schlägt langsam
vier.
Und ich weiß von keiner Zeit,
In die Arme fall ich dir...

Emmy Hennings

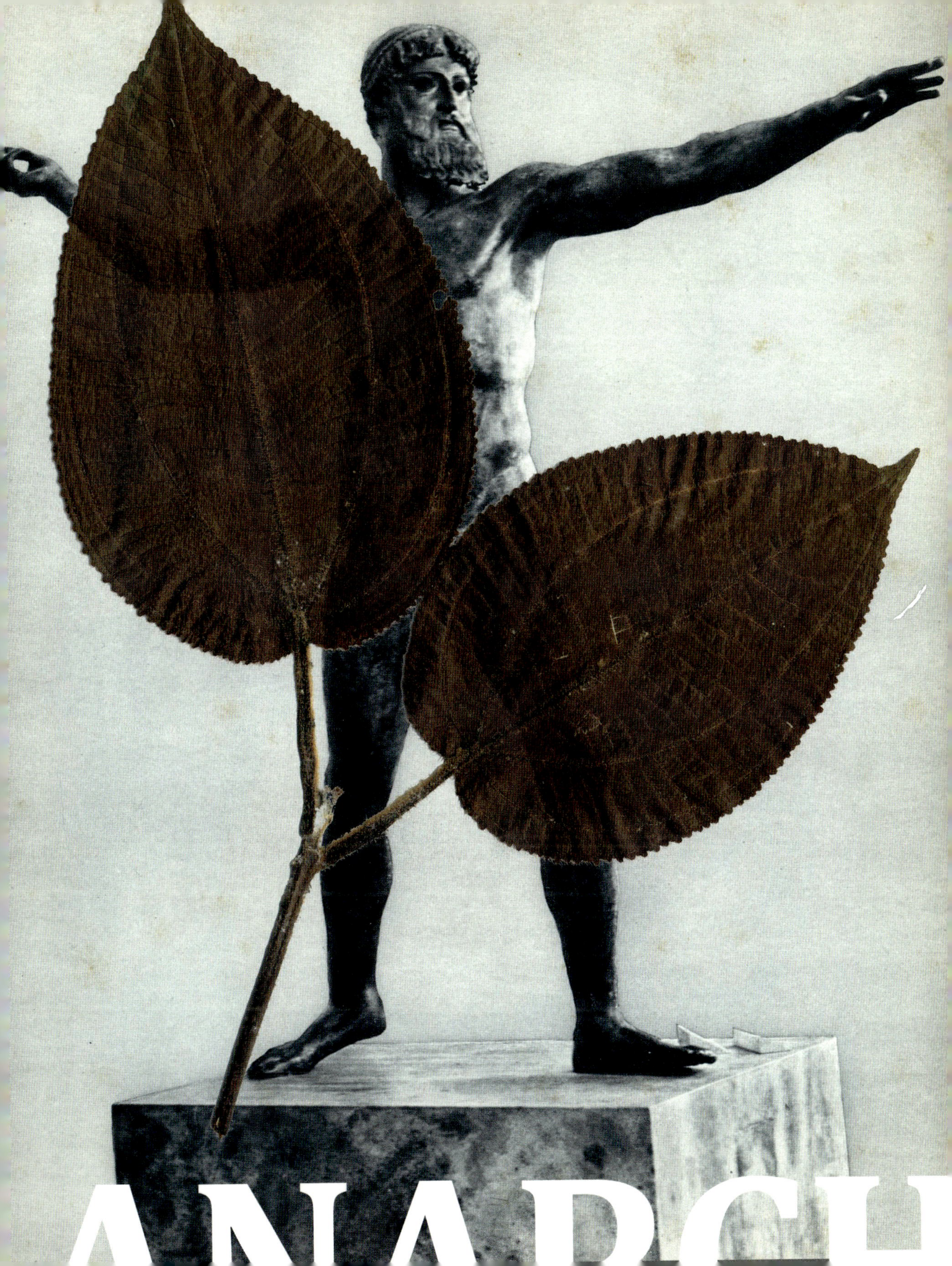

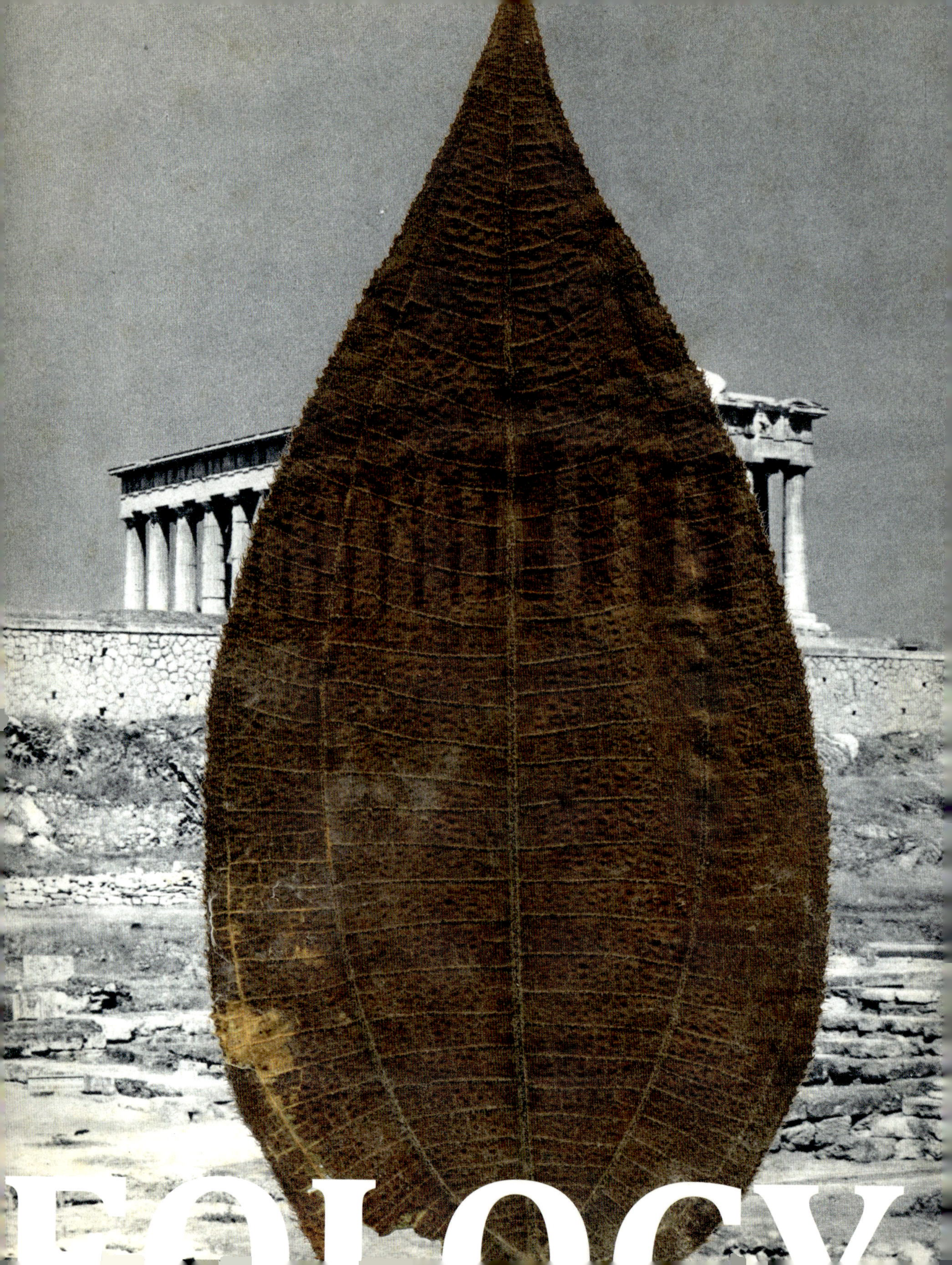

Anarcheology

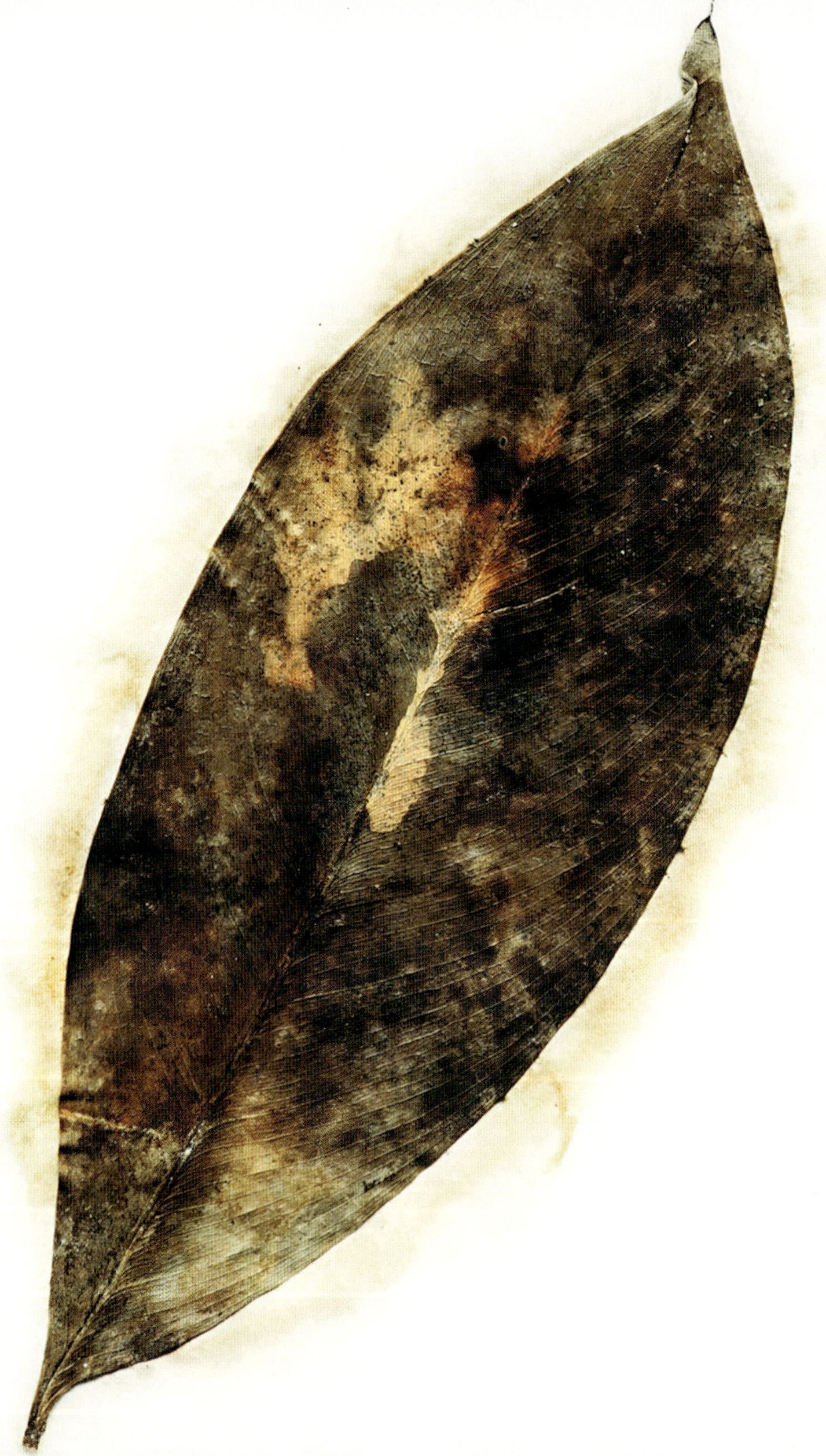

Anarcheology-Museum

We are entering a post-archeological situation, in which the narration that connects a fragment with its history needs to be questioned.

Archeology is linked to the national mythologies and narrations of the nineteenth century. They constituted an identity based on the assumption of the existence of a historical timeline.

The museums, and later the exhibitions, were the places where isolated fragments or objects were presented as carriers of extended meanings. Some objects in the museums could stand in for an entire epoch of history.

But without the framework and narration of the museum, the same object would just be an arbitrary object.

The question has been raised as to whether objects can be conceived of as existing from a past into a future, but without being dated and inscribed in the present, into a historicity.

Archeology has always started its narration with fragments. Its idea of history is linear. Some objects have made a jump in the archeological strata, for example when a vase from an earlier period has been excavated and then used again. Then the object is dated twice in an archeological sense.

The reality from the point of view of the object is not historical; rather it always exists in the here and now and all meanings and historical narrations are imposed from the outside.

This conception of the object as existing in its own time proposes a way to perceive a fragment as an object with different possible historical ties, in which the object itself allows the questioning of all these narrations.

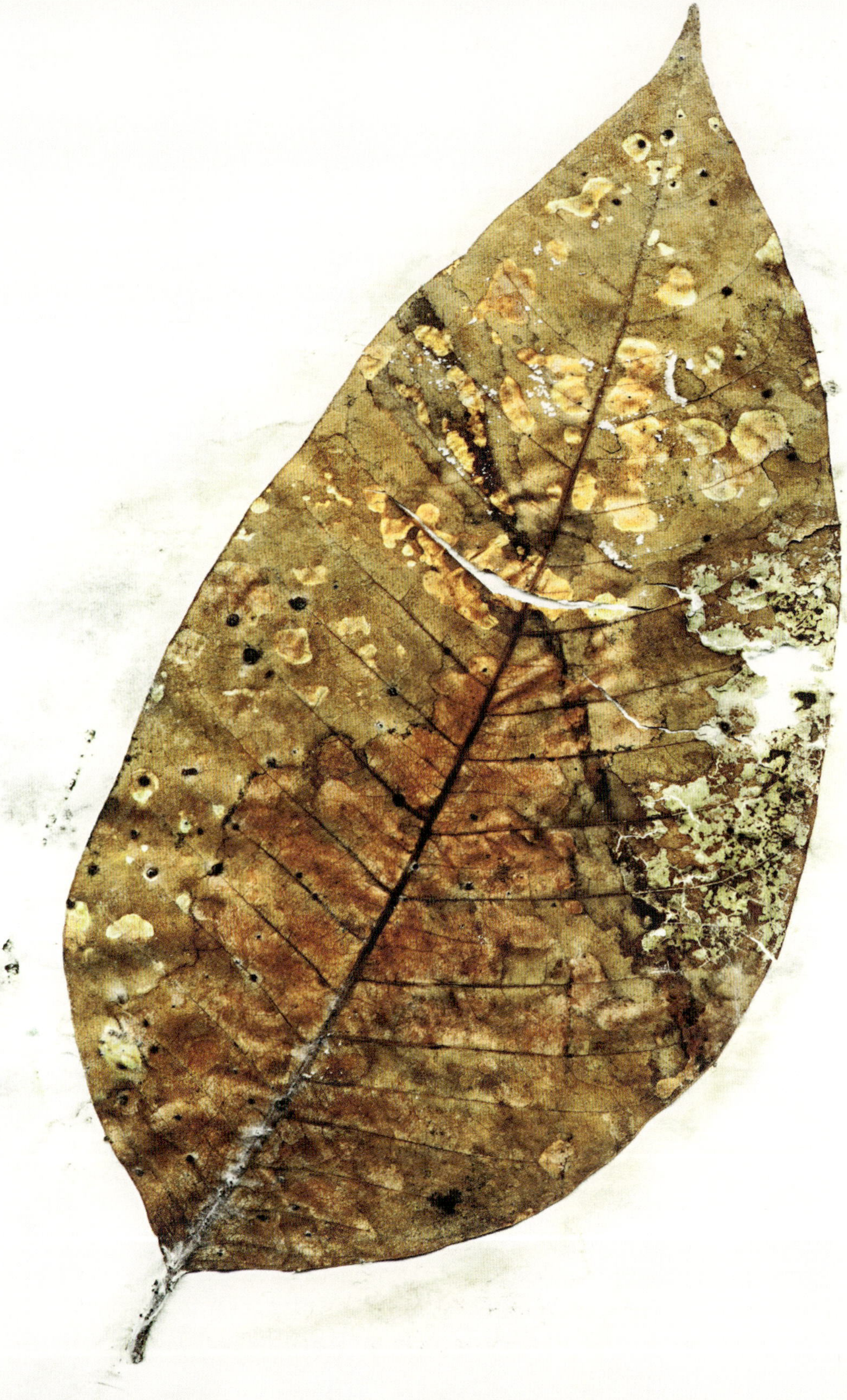

Ana Teixeira Pinto and Christoph Keller
On Anarcheology

Anarcheology, Christoph Keller's recent video work, is a travelogue on the fringes of what can be said or written—a text which deals with the spoken word and orality, in a film paradoxically silent. Juxtaposing three different rhetorical regimes, the video stages a performative contradiction between method and subject. The images suggest a voyage, departing from a bridge near Manaus and entering into the depths of Amazonia, a land apparently devoid of human traces. Black-and-white photographs alternate rhythmically with text inserts, leaving behind an afterimage that draws the viewer into an intermittent story.

Christoph Keller, *Anarcheology*, 2014 HD Video, 12:40 min, silent

Ana Teixeira Pinto: Can you elaborate a bit on the concept of Anarcheology?

Christoph Keller: Anarcheology is a semiotic divisor splitting the world into halves, the archeological and the non-archeological. It is a term that evokes something not yet known. But what could the non-archeological be? Michel Foucault introduced the term in his lectures, *Du gouvernement des vivants*, at the Collège de France in 1980, saying that it was a wordplay for anarchy or anarchism—an attitude "concerning the non-necessity of all power." The first part of the film touches on this.

In the film the only sign of a human presence is the concrete bridge of Manaus that appears in the very first images, almost like a symbol for an "archeological site of the future," which is then subsequently left behind. Is the bridge meant to signify the connection between archeology and the modern state?

The notion of archeology, generally speaking, is tied with nation-building. The discipline emerges in correlation with the nineteenth century occidental practice of legitimizing the power of nation-states by scientifically aligning their history with that of the ancient empires—most often from the south—which were hence publicly presented in museums or as displaced monuments. This practice recasts ancient objects as links in an evolutionary chain leading to the present powers, or more generally speaking, charges these objects as symbolic carriers of history. This archeological relation is still at work in many ways in which objects are displayed in exhibitions nowadays.

> The term "Anarcheology" also deals with another negative definition: the concept of "anti-psychiatry." Do you see anti-psychiatry as an anarcheological endeavor?

One could maybe say that both address a well-established dichotomy, in order to overcome it: the first between psychiatry and the "normal," the latter between archeology and its other. Also, there is clearly a parallel with the history of psychoanalysis, which is permeated by archeological metaphors.

> Your video has three, so to say, narrative blocks: the first describes a methodological conundrum, the second a personal story, and the third a Yanomami myth of origins. These three blocks refer to different temporalities. Does their juxtaposition signify the incommensurability between the present time of lived experience, the non-linear time of mythical tales, and the deferred time of written accounts?

These different temporalities are present everywhere all the time: a written text becomes a lived experience in the moment you read it and lend it an inner voice. And when you imagine its narrative, it may become a non-linear mythical tale. On the other hand, oral traditions also have the ability to pass on information over very long timespans, like books do.

> To write a text about orality is in a way a performative contradiction; is this why you felt the need to fictionalize the transition by interjecting a biographical narrative?

I wanted to turn this disparity between text and orality into a film or a filmic essay, where different textual and literary forms are brought into resonance on an equal level. I believe that storytelling can work as a collective device for sharing lived experience, for demythologizing and remythologizing knowledge, and perhaps even for reconciling trauma. In the middle part, when a personal story is told, the objectiveness of the preceding considerations collapses and the film turns into something closer to a personal letter. Many thoughts and ideas that went into this film are owed to the exchanges I had during a project in the Amazon, initiated by Capacete, with Helmut Batista and Amilcar Packer, and especially with Anne Ballester Soares. Anne is also the editor of a bilingual (Yanomami/Portuguese) transcription of the mythological history of the Yanomami group of the Parahiteri, an English-translated excerpt of which composes the last part of the film's text.

Excerpts included in *Anarcheology* are from:

Michael Hardt and Antonio Negri, *In Labor of Dionysus—A Critique of the State-Form* (Minneapolis: University of Minnesota Press, 1994): 292.

Michel Foucault, *Du gouvernement des vivants: Cours au College de France (1979–1980)* (Paris: Seuil – Hautes etudes, 2012): 76. Translated from French into English.

Anne Ballester Soares, "Os Espíritos—Horonami" in *Nohi Patama Parahiteri Pe Re Kuonowei Te A: História Mitológica do Grupo Parahiteri* (São Paulo: Hedra; ECidade, 2010): 133. Translated from Portuguese into English.

> Your work often explores the limits of scientific discourse. Could one say *Anarcheology* points to the Yanomami as the frontier of a possible archeology of knowledge?

In my view, the frontiers of a possible archeology of knowledge are the borders of our own archeological ways of thinking. That's why artists are often more attracted to the fringes of science than to its mainstream. The Yanomami speak for themselves and their frontier is not an abstract concept, but rather a struggle for political and cultural autonomy and for the integrity of their way of life in the Amazonian forest.

> Would you say that every human science constitutes a distinctive discursive practice, a particular modality of representation predicated on narrative?

At least you can attempt to understand human sciences as contemporary mythologies. Jean-François Lyotard has investigated the "metanarratives" to which the sciences and also the arts would contribute their partial stories. Paradoxically, the moment you address these metanarratives you have already begun to overcome them.

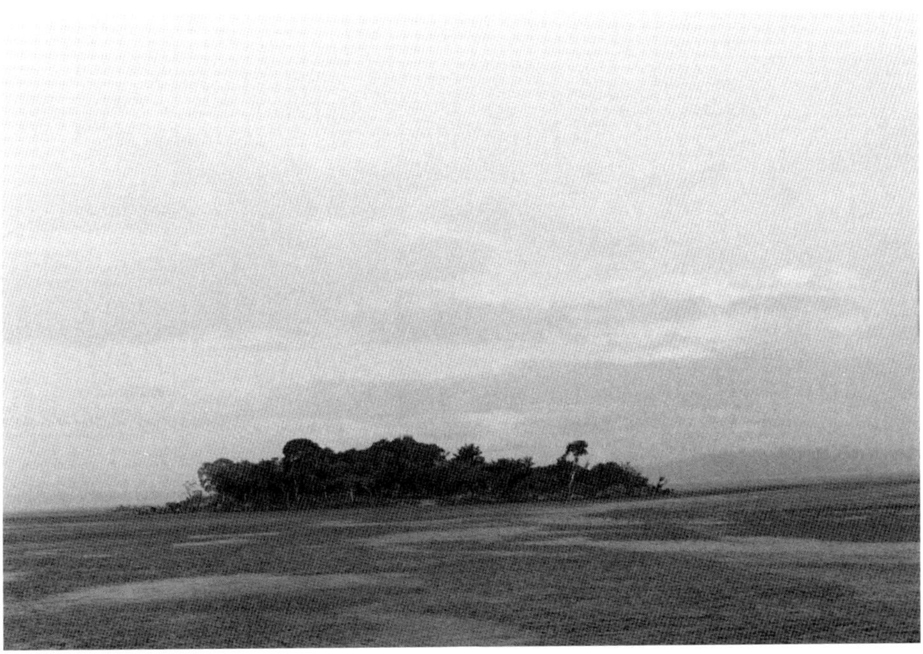

The text I want to write is about archeology as a paradigm in the Western tradition of art. A history of an art that is founded on what remains, on the traces that are left behind. According to anthropological findings, in some Yanomami cultures it is exactly the opposite: One strives to leave no trace. When a Yanomami dies, his or her name is no longer voiced by the family and the fellow villagers and all personal belongings are burned. In this belief, every link that remains on earth would be a burden on the voyage to the mythical spheres. I want to write a text about people living a life in the jungle based on oral tradition and mythology.

How can oral culture be translated into written language at all? There seems to be a border between the two worlds. One might argue that the world is made up of discourses, not of things. In oral cultures, for sure this is

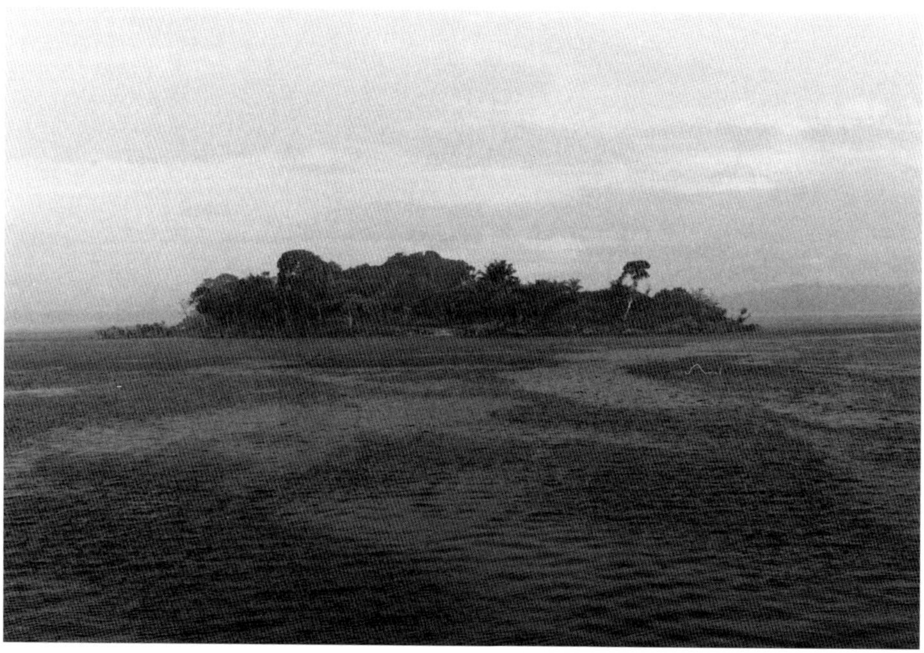

true. But writing changes it all. Writing is archeology, an archeology of language. In writing, writer and reader do not share a present time, as do speaker and listener in an oral culture. Instead you address somebody in an abstract future, an assumed posterity, who will someday find your words and reenact your speech.

History is written history, and the archeology of knowledge was derived from the history of ideas, which is confined to written knowledge almost exclusively. The inverse of which would be an an-archeology, pointing to all the rest: the mythological world, the living, the non-written. Michel Foucault used this term in the course he gave at the Collège de France named *Du gouvernement des vivants*. Some writers who have quoted the term have referred it to anarchism, as Anarcheology.

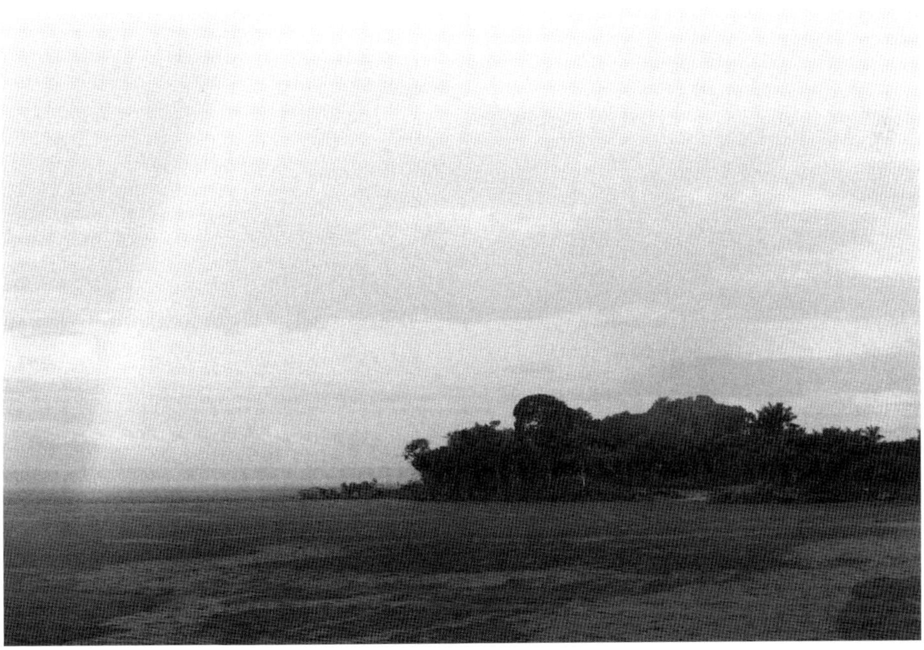

“I am not saying that all forms of power are unacceptable but that no power is necessarily acceptable or unacceptable. This is anarchism. But since anarchism is not acceptable these days, I will call it Anarcheology—the method that takes no power as necessarily acceptable.”

But connecting it with Foucault’s own methodological endeaveor, to introduce an archeology of knowledge, makes the wordplay of Anarcheology appear even more radical as an An-archeology: a non-history of thought!

Culture is obsessed with the remains of the past, so much so that cultural production itself is perceived as the production of future remnants of the present. But what could a non-history of thought be?

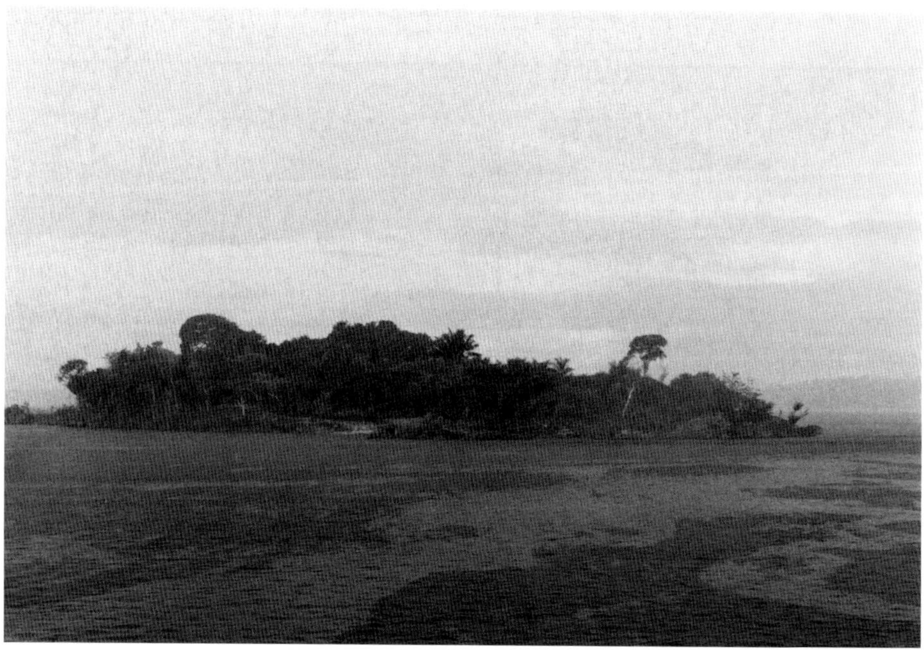

"There is no intrinsic legitimacy of power," says Foucault in *Du gouvernement des vivants*. "And assuming this position, the approach is to ask what happens with the subject and the coherence of knowledge when no power is founded in law or in need, since power never is based on the contingency and fragility of a history, that the social contract is a bluff and civil society a tale for children, there is no universal law, immediate and obvious, which could always and everywhere justify a notion of a power that should be there."

She told me her story when we had a quiet moment at the table in the shed where we usually cooked and ate. I began by saying I heard that she had been at La Borde, Guattari's anti-psychiatric hospital. She said she had been there

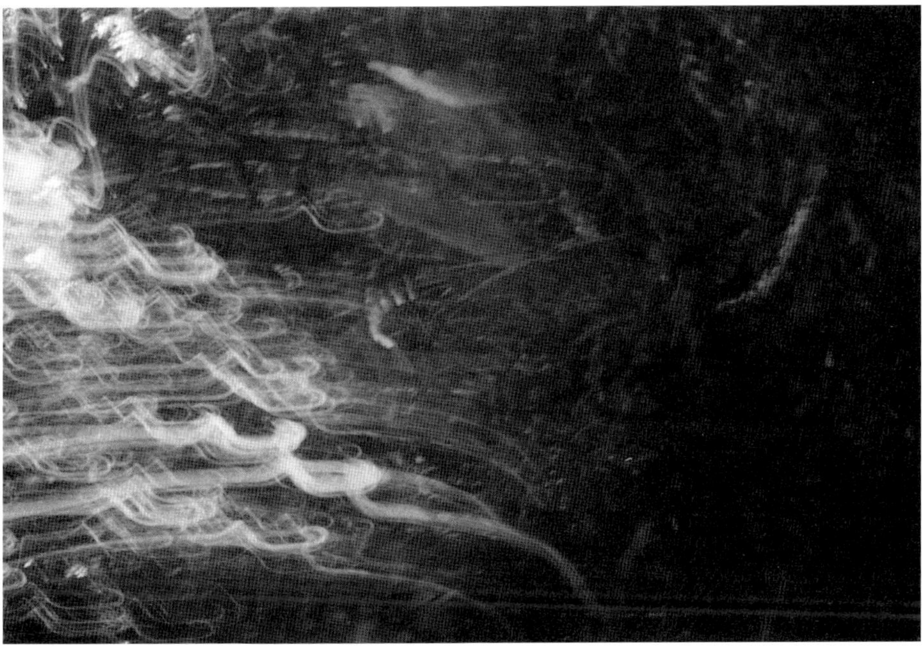

during her studies at the Beaux Arts. They went as a kind of a student excursion for about two to four weeks, she doesn't remember exactly how long. There were no fences and the patients walked to the neighboring village by themselves. Frequently, there were performances by artists and bands and then everybody gathered and listened to them. Her account of anti-psychiatry was critical. She was appalled that they still treated patients with electric shocks and cold water and that suicides occurred. She met somebody there, a patient, who had not come back from an LSD trip that he took six months previously. He was playing atonal sounds on his violin, which in his world was heavenly music. He was very sensitive and autistic, and something must have clicked between them. At one of the concert gatherings he took a ring off his finger and gave it to her. According to her, it had been an important gesture, a linking, in a way.

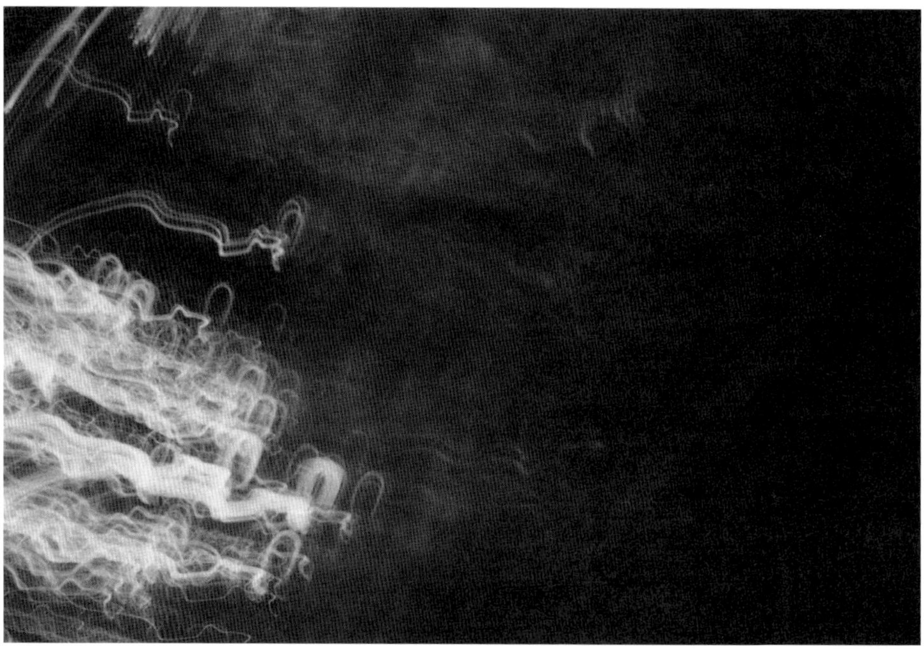

However, she dropped the ring the moment he gave it to her, or it fell (how could this have happened to her!) and then he was very upset and turned away from her. It was a lost cause, she never regained his trust.

Then I asked her why she had left France. She said that she was beaten by her father. She was a middle child and the black sheep of her family. When she was nine or ten years old, she already knew that she wanted to go away. She had an uncle, her godfather, who worked as a veterinarian in Africa at that time. As a young girl, this uncle in Africa strengthened her wish to go away. In a letter she asked him why had he left and he replied that he had always wanted to go away from France. Then he proposed that she visit him in Africa and it was the dream of her life. She was a young teenager by then, living in a boarding school away from home. But one day she found an

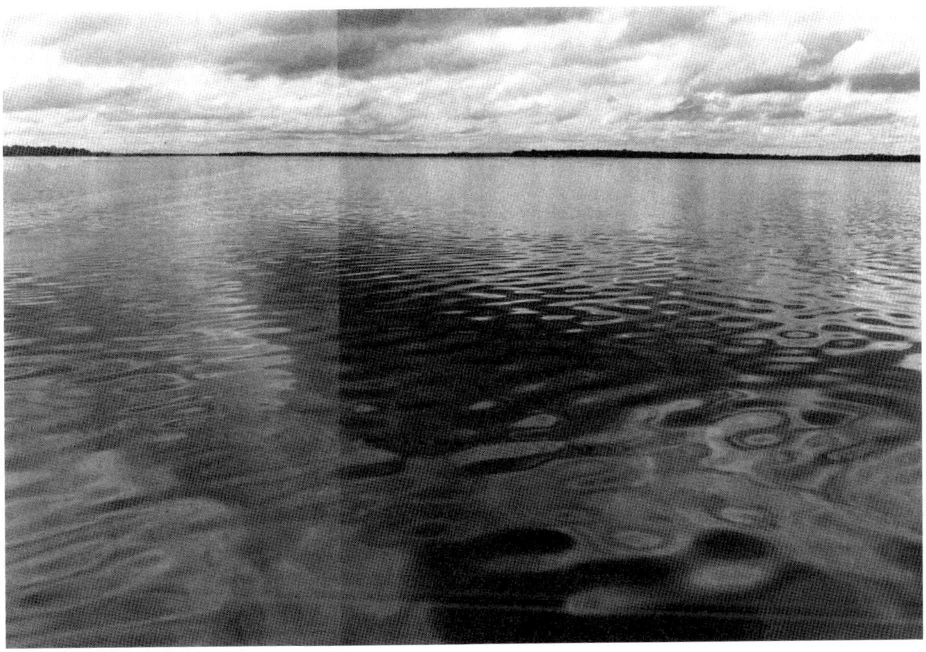

article in the local newspaper, which said that her uncle had died. She could not believe it. Her parents had to pick her up and take her home because she was in a state of shock. Later she travelled to the west coast of the USA to find out if the Californian dream was true. It wasn't, she said. But in the waiting line at the airport she met somebody who had the same way of thinking. Later she visited him in Canada. It was a friend of his who suggested that she travel to the Amazon and visit the people living in the remote jungle where she has now spent the past 20 years of her life. She hardly had any contact with her family ever since she left, especially not with her parents.

One day in a mission outpost, a letter arrived from her father. It was somehow surprising that a letter from France would even reach a place so far from what we call civilization. She suspected this would be the letter announc-

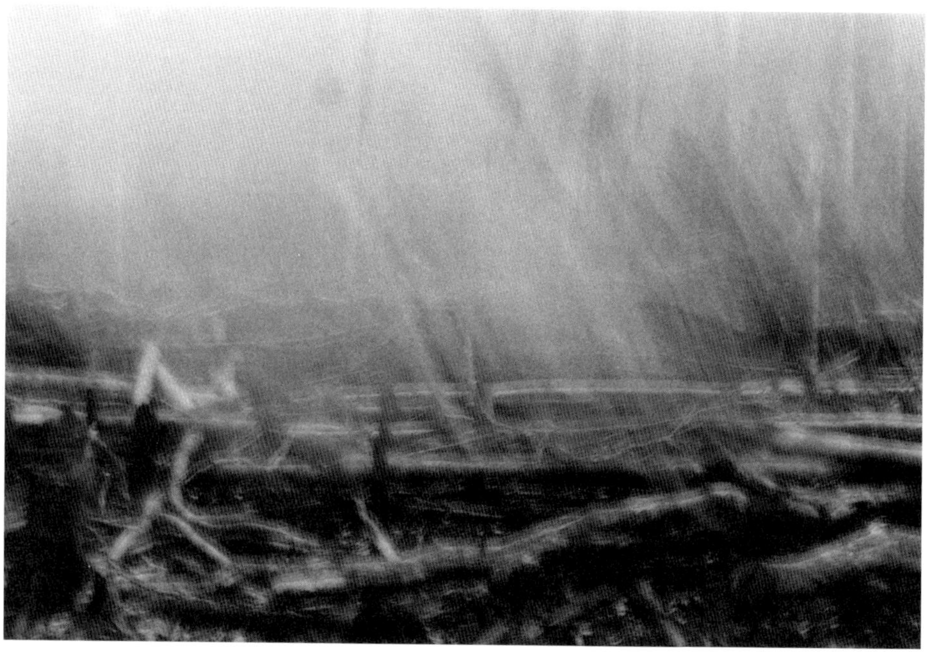

ing to her that her mother had passed away. When she opened the letter it read that her father begged her for forgiveness. It took some more time until she visited them for the first time at their home in France. Her friends here in the Amazon say that she has become calmer since then. She still can't understand why her mother did not protect her more when she was a child. Once when she visited her parents, an argument broke out at the coffee table and her old father left the house in rage. When he returned he hugged her and said for the first time in her life that he loved her.

Who made us?
This is the true story of our creation: When the forest was virgin Horonami appeared, the main character of our

history for his teachings. The great shaman Horonami Yanomami himself emerged, rising at the same time as the forest, and it was he who taught the Yanomami how to live in it. Thus was the beginning. There were no Yanomami like the ones of today, nor was there any other human being. He spread his wisdom so that our history would always be remembered and passed on as it is now.

All this happened a long time before the Yanomami leaders came to live as they do today. He was the first inhabitant of the forest and taught us how to live in it, and he also taught the Napë (whites). He had no father, yet he came into being. He sprung out of a wonderful forest.

Who lived with Horonami?

Horonami lived with his brother-in-law Wiyanawe who, despite not having married his sister, was truly his brother-in-law. Horonami always led them in wayumi (temporary nomadism practiced by the Yanomami villages) and taught the descendants to go in wayumi. Although she never gave birth to Horonami, because he appeared suddenly, the name of his mother was Yotoama.

The Horonami shaman inquired all about our food, about our knowledge of the forest and about the habitat of the animals, so that when the Yanomami went to the forest, they would be able to satiate their hunger for meat. He asked for the names of the animals back when they still lived like us. Although they are animals, at first they lived just as the Yanomami did.

How did he make the water appear, to soothe the thirst of the Yanomami?

He opened several creeks in the forest. He opened them in all directions so that they would never disappear and we would always have water to drink.

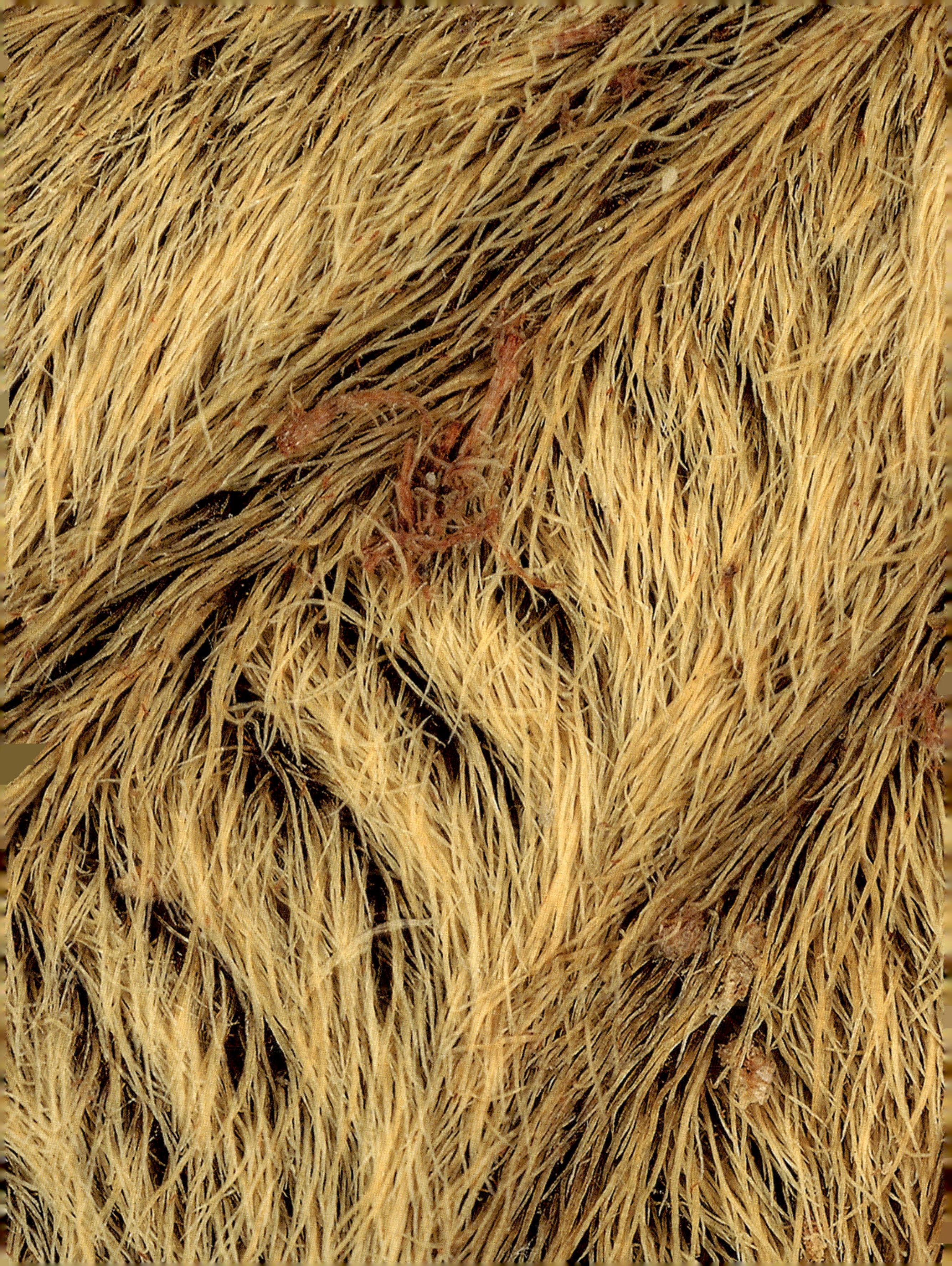

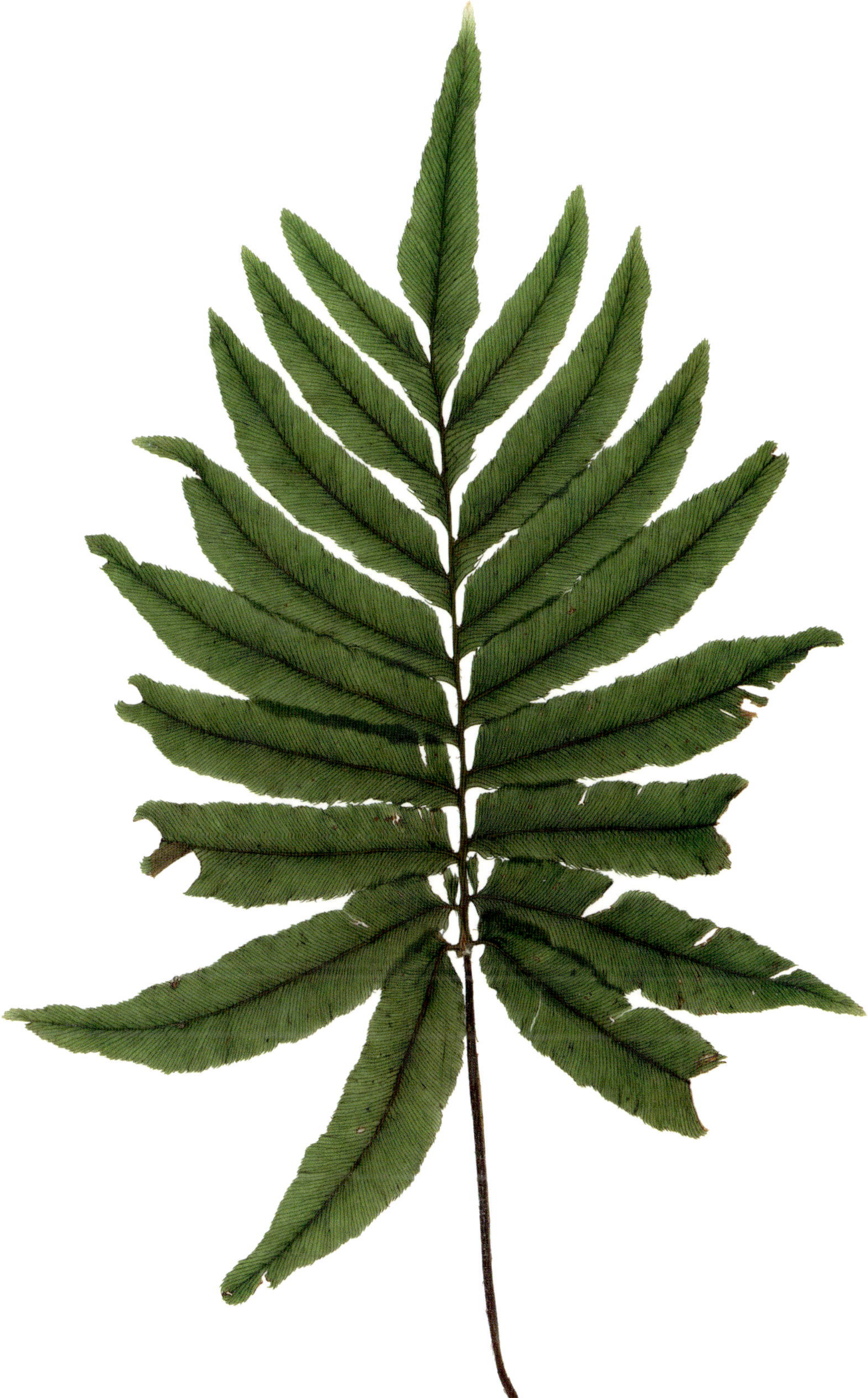

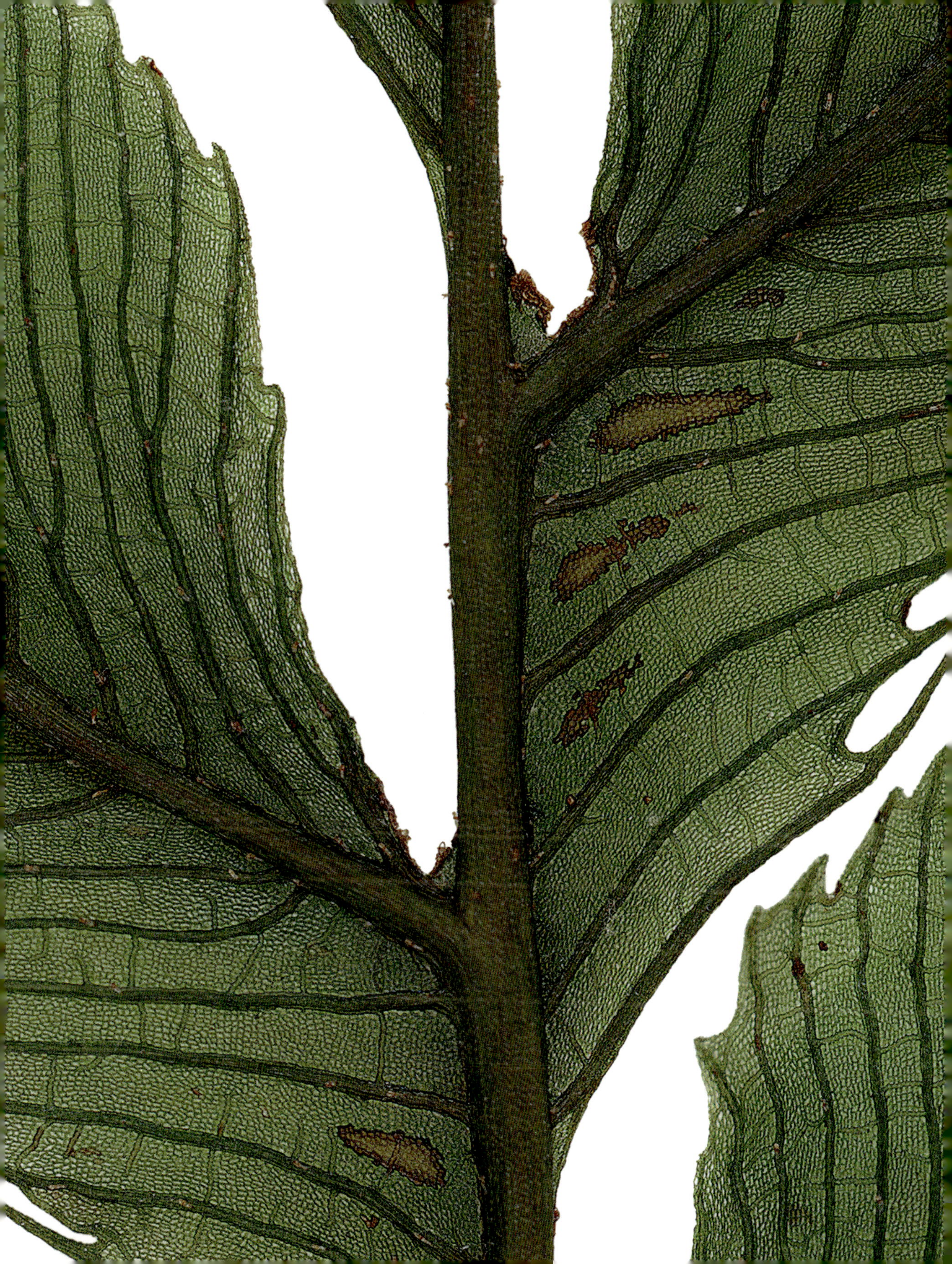

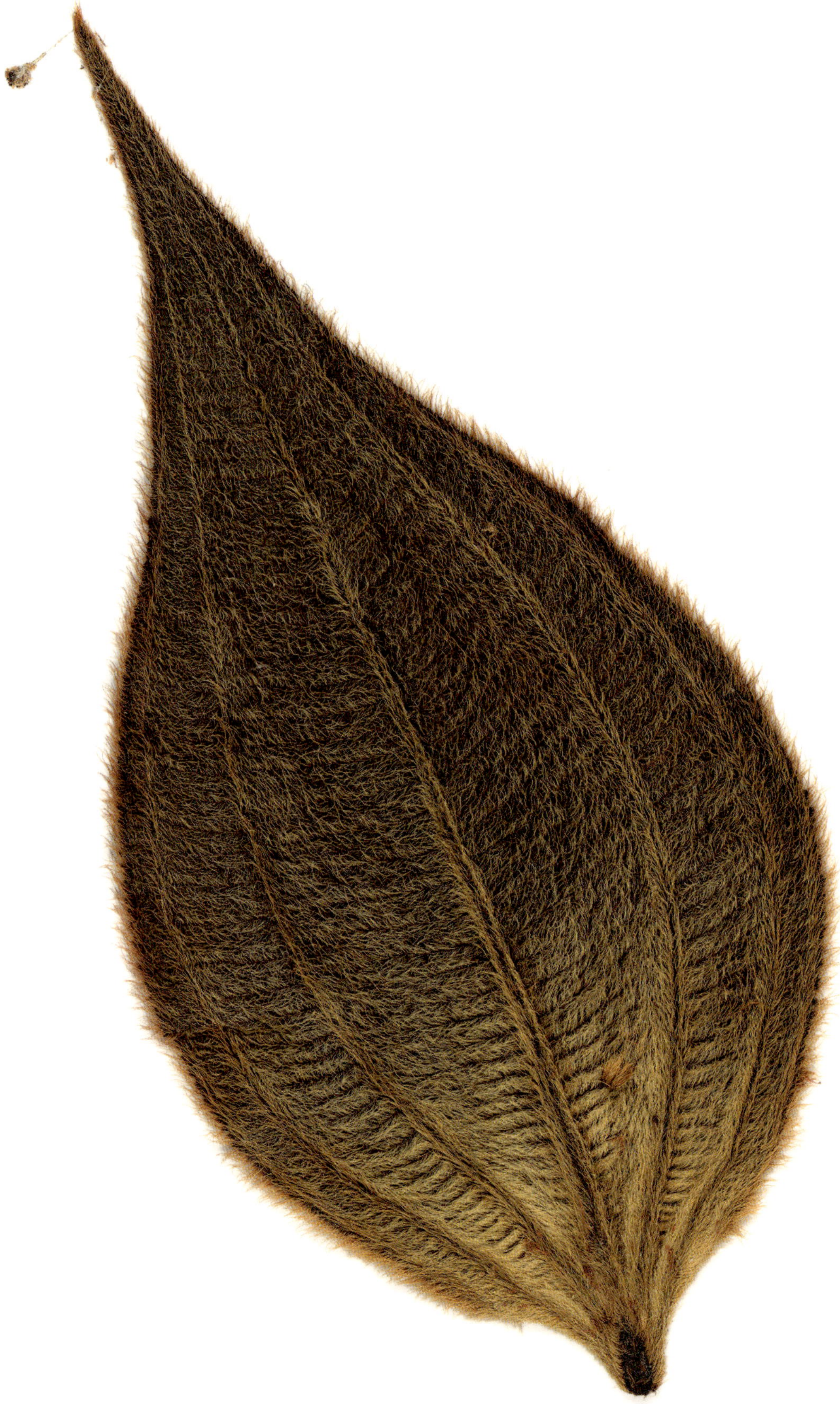

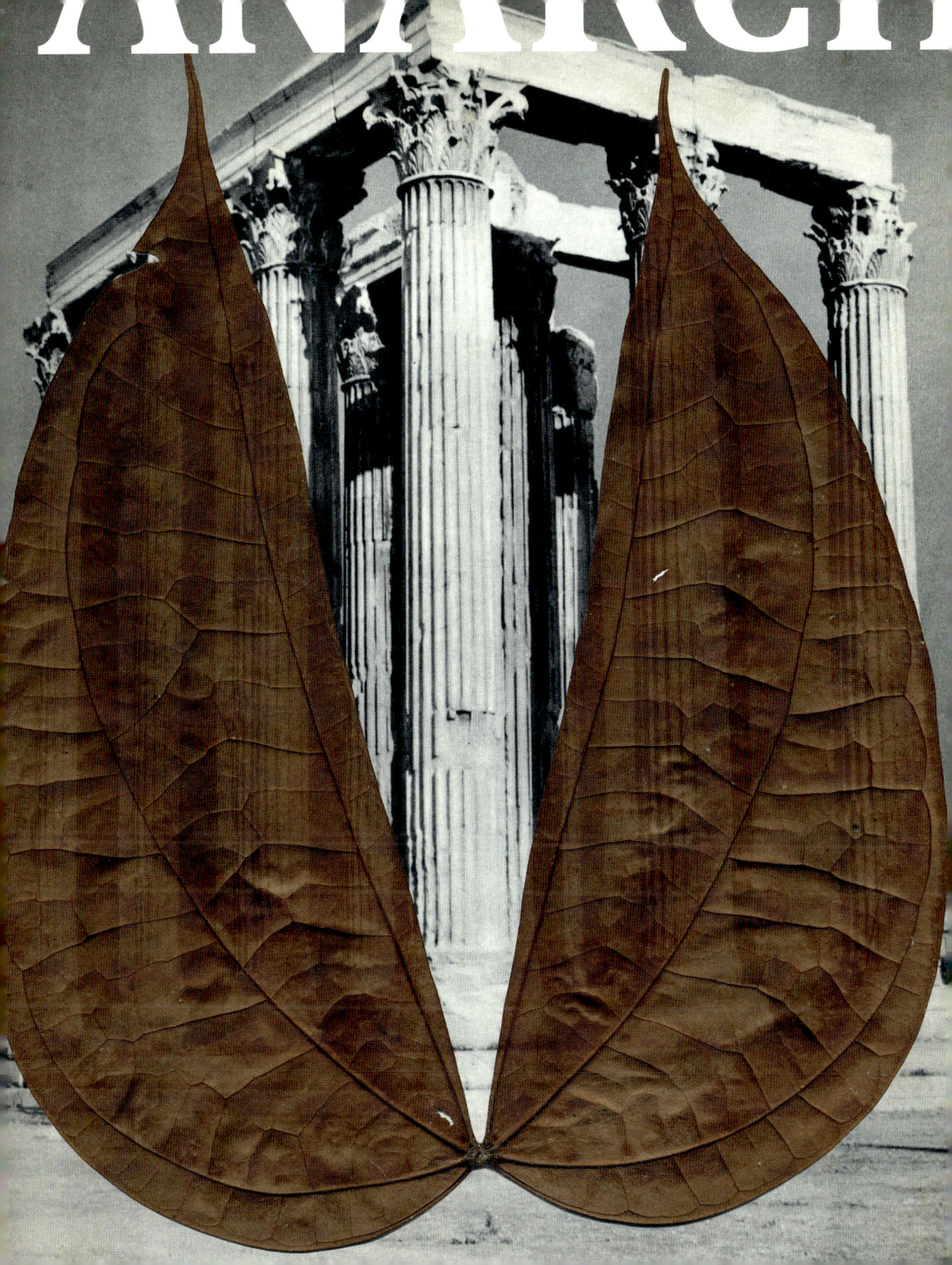

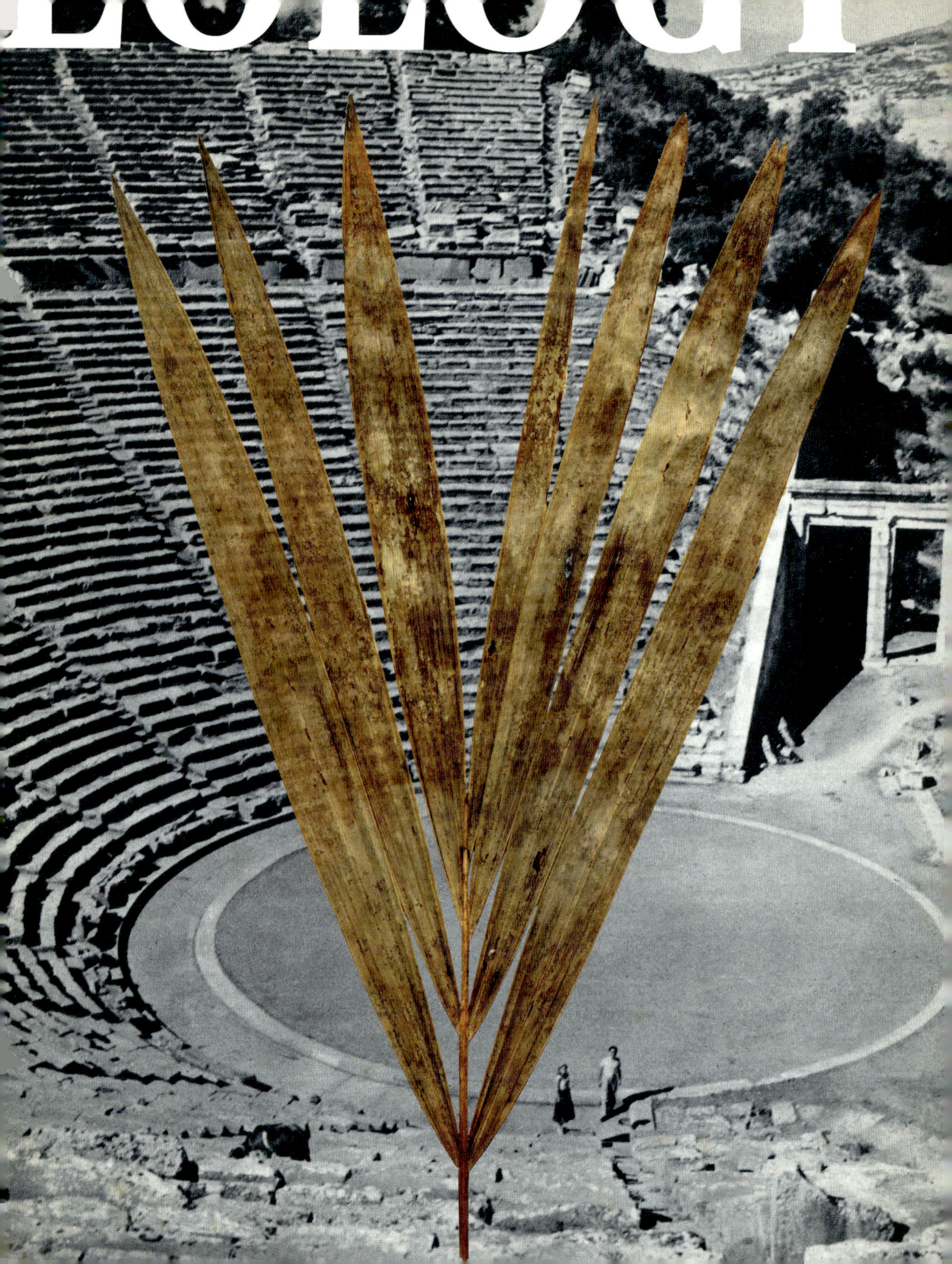

Small Survey on Nothingness

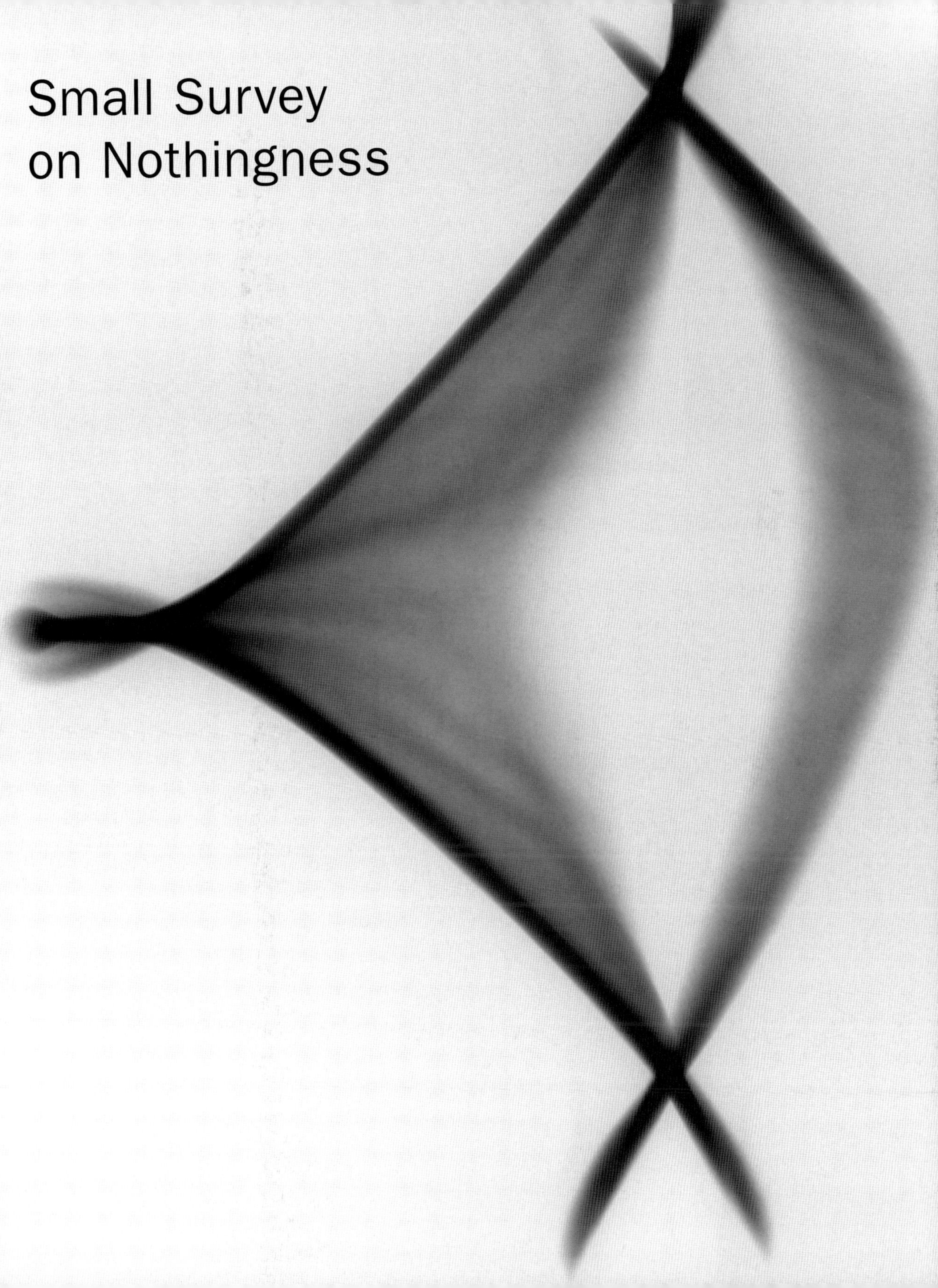

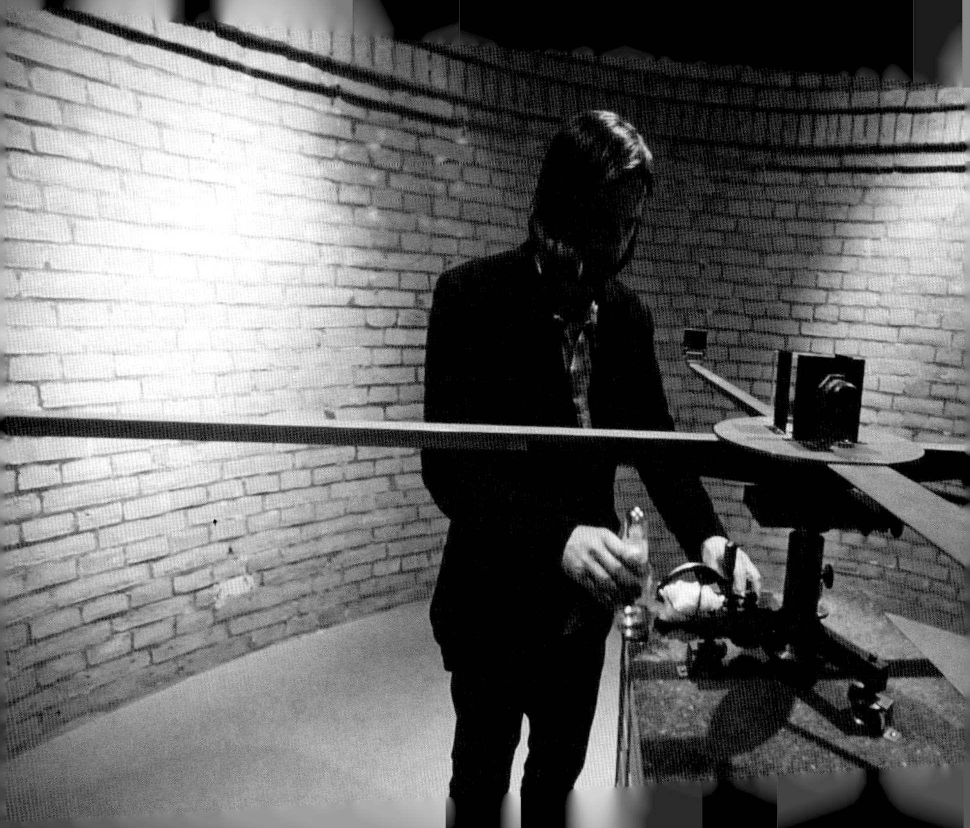

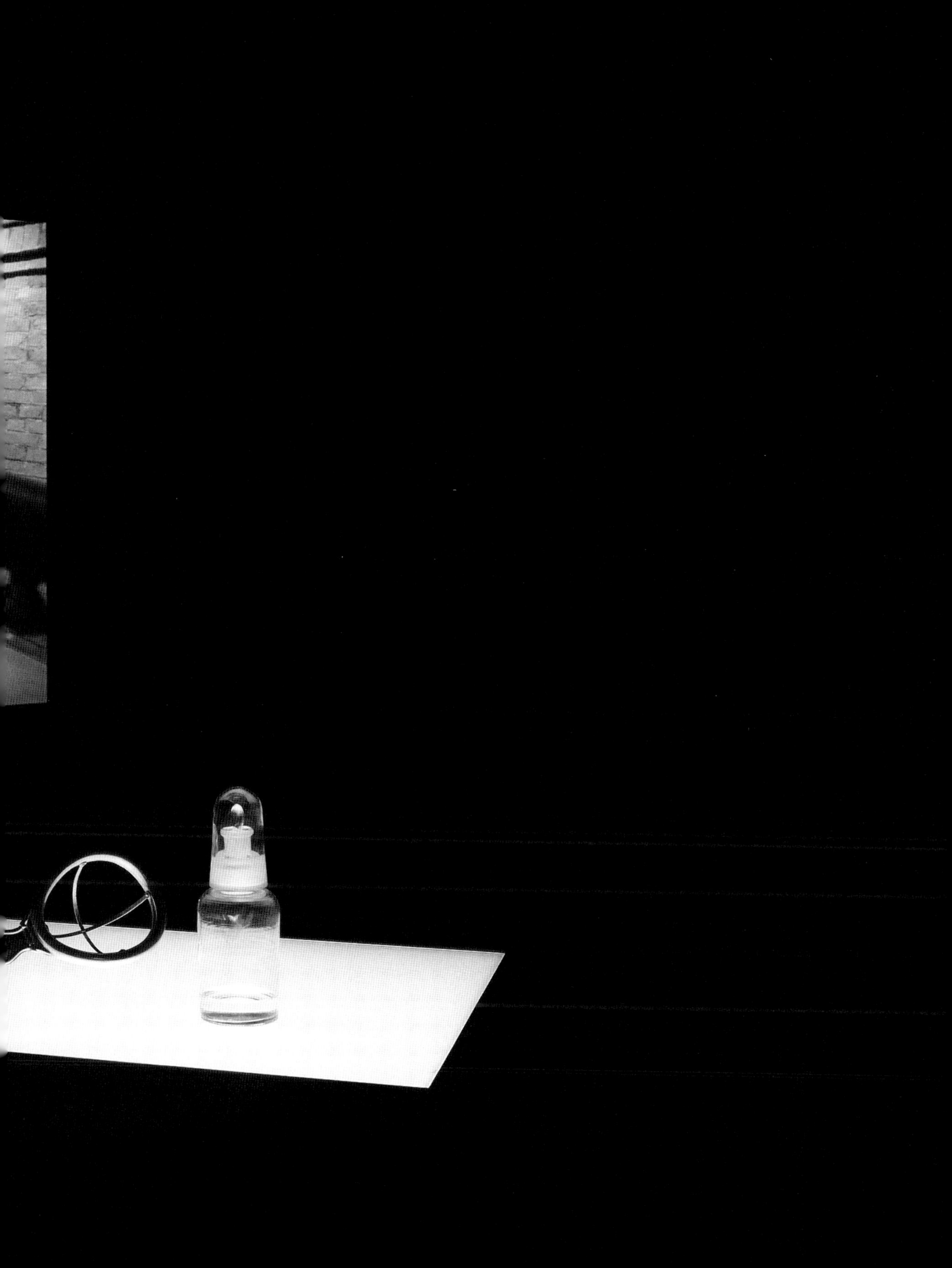

A Journey Through Nothing That Is

Heike Catherina Mertens

A black, almost completely dark room. The windows and doors admit no light, black carpeting covers the floor, and the ceiling is veiled with black, transparent gauze. The contours of the room disappear. Deep darkness envelops the visitor who has come to embark on a journey through Christoph Keller's exhibition "Small Survey on Nothingness." Three light sources provide orientation: a plinth on whose translucent, back-lit surface stands a glass bottle filled with ether; behind it, a wall-mounted flat-screen showing art-documentary interviews with a series of experts; and a big screen suspended diagonally in space where visitors can watch the artist perform an experiment on himself. These three light sources are the main exhibits and stages in Keller's 2014 show at the Schering Stiftung in Berlin.

Through two video productions and an open experiment for visitors, Christoph Keller investigates the relationship of nothingness to the ambivalent medium of the aether. In the entrance area of the exhibition diethyl ether, a chemical substance in a glass bottle, is offered to visitors to smell (*Aether Self Experiment*, 2014). Inhaling the fumes has an intoxicating effect, which—depending on the dosage—can range from strong emotional excitement to narcotization. Next to the ether bottle, the artist places a so-called ether mask, which was used in medical anesthetics until the 1970s. This historical display refers to one of the most important inventions in medical history ever. In Boston in 1846, American dentist William T. G. Morton administered ether to a patient for the first time. The effect—turning off both pain and consciousness for a period of time in a controlled manner—promised undreamed-of possibilities and became the medical standard worldwide.

For visitors of an exhibition, the possibility to test the effect of diethyl ether on themselves is a liminal experience. While some open themselves to the narcotizing effect of inhalation, others shrink from the very idea of surrendering to the narcotic. Again others start to feel sick after inhaling or remember long-repressed operations or surgeries they had as children or teenagers. The ether experiment is thus capable of activating our embodied memories, moving them from the level of the subconscious to the conscious.

After experiencing the intoxicating ether themselves, visitors next arrive at a video screen suspended in the middle of the room, where they can watch Keller in a self-administered experiment (*Aether Drift Experiment*, 2014) at a historically significant place: the main building of the Potsdam Astrophysical Observatory (today's Leibniz Institute for Astrophysics) on Telegrafenberg. It was there, in the basement, that Albert Abraham Michelson, in 1881, conducted his first interferometric experiment to prove the existence of the "aether wind." Michelson wanted to prove that aether was a carrier of light, assuming that light beams that move perpendicular to the aether arrive sooner than light beams moving parallel to the aether. This assumption turned out to be wrong. The speed of light remained constant. The existence of the aether wind was thus considered disproved. This *experimentum crucis* formed the basis for Albert Einstein's theory of special relativity of 1905, after which the aether, as a theory, completely vanished from physics research.

At the same time, this failed experiment also forms the basis for Keller's artistic experiment. For by disappearing from the natural sciences, the aether gained in importance among the artistic avant-garde, both in terms of its philosophical interpretation and, in a very mundane sense, as an intoxicant. We are here talking about two different forms of aether—the physical medium, whose existence Michelson wanted to prove through his experiment; and the chemical substance of ether, which is used as a narcotic and drug.

Christoph Keller brings together both forms of aether at this historic place. He soaks a piece of cloth with diethyl ether and brings it up to his face with the aid of the previously mentioned ether mask. The mask covers mouth and nose, so that the inhaled fumes have a particularly strong effect. He repeats this process again and again, until he risks losing consciousness. By proving the effect of the chemical ether at the site of the falsification of the physical aether, Keller subtly challenges the irrefutability of scientific research results.

The self-experiment is an important instrument in Keller's artistic practice. Many of his video works are based on self-administered experiments, such as, for example, hypnosis or trance states. In these works, his aim is always to expand the limits of consciousness and create new systems of reference.

Through his self-experiment at the interferometer, Keller invites the viewer to become a witness to both a historical and a contemporary experiment. The subtle camera work and the calmness of the protagonist who repeats the action of inhaling again and again make it possible for the viewer to closely experience Keller's changing state of consciousness. This change in consciousness is, at it were, an image for the aether's loss of significance in the history of science. The aether has an anesthetic effect and is being anesthetized.

Keller's second video work, which also provides the exhibition with its title, takes the viewer from the aether to nothingness. The film *Small Survey on Nothingness* (2014) starts with a 1913 poem by Dada artist Emmy Hennings, "Äther" (Aether), which is recited by film director Micah Magee. Hennings herself had been addicted to ether: "I want to give up the ether habit. It must be done. It's terrible. I have lost so many thoughts." As early as the nineteenth century, ether, as a cheap drug and alcohol substitute, had found many users. Hennings's poem harks back to the tradition of Romantic aether poetry, which, since the late eighteenth century, had paid tribute to the aether in its philosophical meaning as an omnipresent and eternal substance. But instead of Friedrich Hölderlin's "soul-giving air" or Friedrich Hebbel's poetic description of the aether as "that which is excluded from no ring of being," Hennings's hymn to the ether also hints at the drug's side-effects: "Cool air wafts towards me. Am I awake or am I dead?"

The motif of the wind, which is part of all aether poems, is taken up by the music that Christoph Keller has added to his film. First performed at the Berlin Philharmonic

Hall in 2013, his composition *Music for Clouds* frames the interviews conducted by the artist and at the same time opens up a space beyond the visible space of the film. Keller presents his conversations with physicists, philosophers, and a parapsychologist in uncut two-minute sequences. While the artist himself is neither visible nor audible, he is still present as the one asking the questions. The viewers take part in the intimacy of the conversation; while radio-controlled headphones allow them to move about freely in the dark space, they are physically very close to the speaker. “The Viewer as a Scientist” is the guiding motif.

By being mentally present in the spaces of conversation, the viewer is drawn into a vortex of perspectives on nothingness: Diego Blas, a theoretical physicist at CERN, throws out the idea of the vacuum that is empty of particles yet still has a structure; the philosopher Hanno Depner refers to the empty spaces between letters in a text without which there would be no writing or syntax; another CERN researcher, experimental physicist Tara Shears, talks about the Higgs Field as something that is beyond one’s ken.

Through this transdisciplinary gathering, Keller reflects on how the meaning of the ambivalent medium of the aether has shifted, against the background of the history of science and contemporary quantum physics, towards nothingness. Like the aether theory, the Higgs Field theory is based on the assumption that there is something invisible. In physics, it is called the invisible field and serves as a theoretical construct to explain the effect of atoms and electrons. Like the aether, the Higgs Field is nothing but a means to gain knowledge, to gain a better understanding of phenomena in the early stages of cosmic evolution. In the last analysis, it is about proving that nothing—that which is invisible—is a precondition for everything that exists in this universe.

The intellectual journey on which Christoph Keller takes the visitor in his *Small Survey on Nothingness* leads straight from ancient Greece to present-day Geneva, empowering the traveler to embark on further intellectual travels. Above all, however, the traveler learns that every scientific theory is a product of its time and that the impossible—thinking and showing nothingness—is the special task of art.

Keller's interpretation of nothingness by means of the exhibition's dark spatial arrangement fantastically corresponds to the black holes in astrophysics, whose gravitational force is so strong and whose mass concentration is so infinitely dense that neither light nor matter are able to escape from them. They are, therefore, not nothing, but rather condensed matter. In philosophy, Hegel equates pure being with pure nothingness. Contemporary poet Oswald Egger found an even more minimalist way of putting this equation: "Nothing that is." It is this very nothing, which is so much and much more, that Christoph Keller makes visible to us.

"Small Survey on Nothingness" is by no means what its title suggests—a small survey—but a wide, open space of knowledge and experience that inspires us to think, rethink, and think some more about nothingness.

Nothingness Is Not Nothing

Horst Bredekamp

A question that has, for ages, occupied humankind—which knows all too well how difficult it is to solve—is whether it's possible to conceive of nothingness, and whether nothingness could even be real beyond the realm of thought. Can nothingness exist? The question's formulation already leads to a paradox, because if something exists, then it can't be a something that is also nothing. Nothingness, therefore, cannot be nothing. This conclusion is by no means the mere product of a sophistic problem whose pure logic has nothing to do with the reality of the world and thus remains little more than a game with terms.

In 2013, the science pages of the major daily newspapers published exciting reports on a kind of cartography of the cosmos, based on data of the oldest traces of the Big Bang. These were prepared, analyzed, and visualized in an international collaboration between institutions for astrophysics led by the Max Planck Institute for Astrophysics in Garching, Germany. Traces of the explosion of the cosmos, known as the Big Bang, were brought together in an oval diagram that resembled the map projections in which the Earth's globe is converted to two dimensions.

With this kind of flattened cartography, however, two questions are glossed over. The first concerns the problem of why—if the data are not misleading—the cosmos is expanding in an accelerated manner. This would mean there exists an outside force causing an additional expansion beyond the original impulse of the Big Bang. This, in turn, presupposes the existence of a second cosmos that envelops the one we know and exerts its effect on it with its own physical laws.

The second question refers to the very first, in theoretical terms infinitely small, point of the Big Bang. In order to be able to explode, something has to be dynamic by nature—in other words, the product of a process that came before it, out of which it is driven to explode. This infinitely small point is commonly envisioned as the end product of a cosmos that has collapsed into itself in the manner of a black hole. This indication of a preexisting cosmos, however, rather than answer the question of origin, would merely pass it on, resulting in the notion that an infinite number of expanding, collapsing, and then once again exploding cosmoses might have existed. With this definition of an infinite sequence, however, the question of an original site returns and poses itself again and again, ad infinitum. As a result, we'd arrive at the very same knot that gives rise to the simple question of whether or not nothingness could exist.

In view of this initial position, which can be solved neither through logic nor fantasy, nearly all mythologies have agreed to quite simply avoid the question of nothingness. They operate from pre-established matter that is separate from the question of temporal development and hence predates the cosmos, and they've brought forth various different original scenes populated by an array of forms that serve as metaphors: the cosmic egg; the ocean; Tohu wa-bohu—chaos as a dark, completely unstructured, churning soup that is not produced in the act of creation, but is formed and shaped into the order of the cosmos. According to this view, the act of creation is by no means a creation out of nothingness, but rather a refinement of something chaotic. In the framework of this notion, the creator, the demiurge, was not a bearer, but a shaper, and in this sense the idea of the artist became situated close by. As a result of his dealings with stone, clay, color, and earth, the artist, while usually of a lower social order, could also, in contradiction to this degradation, be called a craftsman acting in parallel manner to the God creator: *as secundus deus*, a second God.

In contrast to this glossing over of the question of nothingness, the monotheistic religions, particularly Judaism, but also Christian religions, have placed this problem at their center. It became a matter of how to define omnipotence. If there was something that predated the act of creation, then the creator would not be omnipotent. This is why it says in the Old Testament, "In the beginning God created Heaven and Earth." The fact that this occurred out of nothing is not addressed, but implied. At least in this passage. Gnostic Christianity, in its radical form of Manicheism and its binary opposition between darkness and light, good and evil, particularly emphasized that a nothingness had to exist, in contrast to which creation appeared. The more moderate form of medieval theology as Thomas Aquinas magisterially formulated it issues from this. *Creare est aliquid ex nihilo facere*: "To create means to make something out of nothing." "Ex nihilo" is the established wording that sought to irrefutably define God's omnipotence.

Gershom Scholem developed this problem in a compact essay that is also essential for the artist Christoph Keller: "Schöpfung aus Nichts und Selbstbeschränkung Gottes" (Creation out of nothing and God's self-limitation). Scholem emphasizes that in the formulation in Genesis the original paradox is not overcome, but merely restated: in the second verse of the first chapter of Genesis that introduces the "darkness upon the face of the deep," the cosmic Tohu wa-bohu can be felt. Additional sections from the Old Testament add to this. Scholem mainly addresses the theological problem that God, in order to create out of nothingness, would have to be nothing Himself, because if He weren't, then nothingness would not exist.

Otto von Guericke's explanation for the vacuum contains entrancing formulations that address this problem. Guericke equates the vacuum with the almighty God in whom everything would be possible per se. Guericke, a seventeenth-century engineer and the mayor of Magdeburg, was also a great philosopher who ruminated on the validity of nothingness. God Himself, he thought, must be nothingness in order to be above all existence.

One might dismiss these thought processes as extreme movements in the history of theology, in themselves wonderful, but nonetheless obsolete following the loss of faith in a creator. Yet it's also possible that modern cosmology has not actually departed from the basic ideas expressed here, but merely touched them up. This particularly applies to the problem that Christoph Keller has been investigating since his 2011 Paris exhibition "Æther—from Cosmology to Consciousness" at Centre Pompidou, which researched the aether in all its forms and concepts. Until 1900 it was assumed that a very fine matter existed that induced light to motion. This aether might have been made obsolete by Albert Einstein's theory of relativity, but it never stopped exerting its effects on the thoughts, speculations, and even certainties of physicists. To this day one observes how problematic it is for people to accept that an absolute emptiness exists in outer space. It could well be that the so-called dark matter that is supposed to exist in outer space is merely a metaphor for the insolubility of the problem posed by thinking about nothingness.

Several years ago, I took part in a symposium at Stanford University dedicated to the concepts of emergence and convergence. I will never forget how the physicist Robert B. Laughlin asserted the existence of a primordial soup, by which he rehabilitated the aether in terms of quantum physics, while also blasting the Big Bang theory as a ridiculous fairy tale propagated by astrophysicists obsessed by money and influence. His anger was so vehement that his tirade ended in a kind of glossolalic negation. Laughlin received the Nobel Prize in 1998. Considerations on nothingness as they appear in mythologies and used to counter monotheistic creation theologies are by no means exhausted in the natural sciences. Again and again, new variations and attempts to prove these theories emerge.

Thus, Keller's reflection on the aether does not merely harbor the potential of a culture of remembrance; more than this, it articulates its argument parallel to the questions of our own time. Seemingly, our secular world is free from the theological foundation of these considerations, and they appear alien to it, at first glance. To date, however, it has not been possible to refute the paradoxes described here that raise the question of nothingness. One can only appease matters by glossing over them or hypothetically declaring them to be solved. Artists like Keller pull back this veil. In doing so, instead of opting for a diagram like that of the map mentioned at the beginning of this text, he rather chooses the depth of space.

Small Survey on Nothingness

(A film, first of all, tells the story of its conditions of production.)

MICAH MAGEE

— Shall we start?
— OK.
— Maybe we do one go to prepare.
— Yes.

Rain hits the window.
A flower shines red.
Cool air wafts in my direction.
Am I awake or am I dead?

A world is far, far away.
Slowly the clock strikes four.
And time has disappeared.
I fall into your arms...

That was nice.
I think...

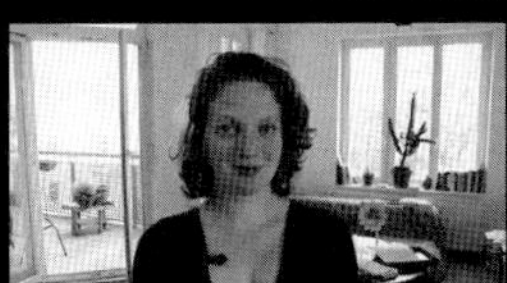

Maybe a bit slower, and...
For me it feels more like
the person is sitting down...
...and looking at things very far away.
That's why I thought

...that the balcony is actually good,
because
the world is so very, very, very far away.

DIEGO BLAS

This is something that is very present
in physics.
There are two things:
First, there is this idea of nothingness.
It could be maybe...
...translated, like you said,
as the idea of the vacuum.
Vacuum in physics, for us...
...means a state of the universe
when there are no particles.
It's empty.
But that doesn't mean that it's nothing.
The way we understand physics
nowadays...

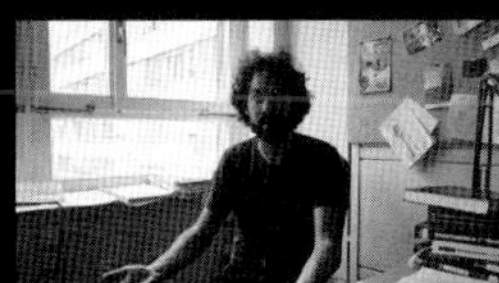

...is that there is no way...
...in which you can avoid very small...
...fluctuations, or very small—
yes, fluctuation would be the word
for this vacuum state.
So there is no perfect, pure state
which is not—
which is totally at rest—even the
vacuum.
Even if you don't have particles...
...even if there is nothing...
...this state has some structure

HANNO DEPNER

There is something in the project
Kant für die Hand...
...that does indeed deal with
nothingness.
For example, with the empty space
between letters.
Because it is the empty space between
letters...
...that makes science possible at all.
Since letters have space between
them...
There are scientific terms
to describe this semiotically.
Anyway, these empty spaces are what
allow us...
...to do things like form sentences...
...that express clear statements.
Statements that establish a particular
fact.
Thus, we can also form an opposite
statement...
...which negates the fact.
In this manner, we can also make logical
connections.
It has to do with these in-between
spaces.

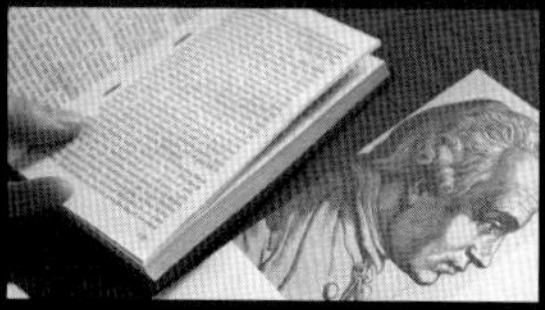

We can illustrate this...
...by comparing it...
...with an image, which has no
in-between spaces.
There is no spacing, like between
letters in a text.
Thus an image has no defined
statements...
...nor arguments, or logical
connections...
...which are possible in a text.
Simply because there are no
in-between spaces.
Of course, there are other images
that do have white spaces.
But actually, it is not the same.
The white between the letters is
different...
...from the white between the lines of
a drawing.
Because here the white has its own
meaning.
If you change the white,
or rather the thickness of the lines...
...the result would be a different image.
Or rather something else becomes
important.

It changes the essence.

Here, if you change the white spacing
or the letter's thickness...
...the content does not change.
You can change the lettering style:
this is Old German print.
You can use Roman lettering,
but the content remains the same.
Whereas in the drawing, if you
change the thickness of the lines...
...then you change the drawing itself.

These are just two ways
to speak about nothingness.

MATTHIAS MENGEL

Did you know this from physics class?
Yes, I think I did it in physics at school.
I only vaguely remember it.
But anyone who has studied physics
knows this experiment.
It's a classic experiment...
...which strongly influenced physics,
and how we see the world.
Well, the aim was to find out...
...if an aether exists.
And if...
...if our world is surrounded by...
...a universal...
...a kind of...
...what is called aether,
meaning a global reference frame.
The idea was to measure how
we move within this frame of reference.
And finally they determined...
...that it cannot be measured at all.
These were the first indicators that
perhaps...
...there is no global reference system
for our universe as a whole.
This led to the theory of special
relativity.
Essentially this states that...
...we cannot determine whether or not
we are moving in space...
...without making reference to another
object.

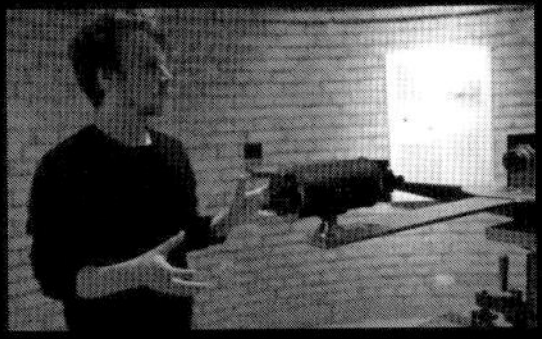

EBERHARD BAUER

I can't say anything about
the notion of aether in general.
It's such a broad subject, which,
for example, also has its roots in
physics.
I can only explain the references...
...which, for example, were used
in theosophy.
Such as by Blavatsky, Alice Bailey, etc.
The basic idea was that...
...there are different levels or layers
of the aetheric body, which...
...as according to Rudolf Steiner and
anthroposophy...
...have to do with the so-called
Body of Formative Forces.
Those are all contexts that play
a historical role here.

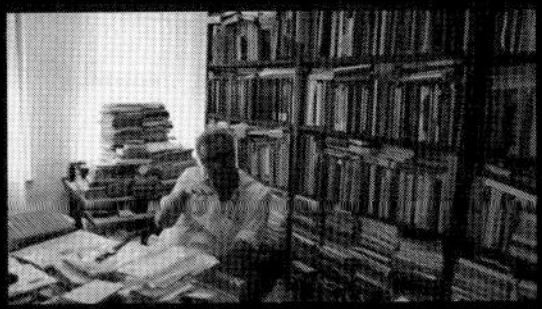

Personally, I am more interested in
concepts of occultism.
Perhaps you know about the "silver
cord"?
The idea is that there is a connection...
You've never heard of it?
Then I will have to show you an
illustration of it.
So you can see how these issues are
not uncommon.
Here is an excerpt from a famous book
by Muldoon and Carrington:
"The Projection of the Astral Body."

This is something you can basically find anywhere.
These are concepts that, in the context of the aetheric body and astral projection...
...play a very large role in occult literature.
They also play a role in the visual arts.
The self, as the bearer of experience, enters into a certain state...
...through dreaming, sleeping, or in a trance...
...and can move out into his fluid, subtle body.
There is a kind of silver cord, a connection...
...that links the aetheric body with the physical body.
And of course the big problem is what happens...
...when this silver cord somehow gets tangled or cut.

This possibility is often mentioned, for example, in early French occultism.
It is an entanglement...
...between the aetheric body and the physical body.
So that the aetheric body cannot return to the physical, physiological body.

OTTO E. RÖSSLER

Yesterday I happened to speak with a specialist...
...about American ways of thinking...
...or rather, Native American ways of thinking.
In Mexico.
He told me that there exists a certain belief...
...that time is always spiraling towards a point.
And the question is:
When it arrives, will time ever begin again?
And then a human sacrifice must be offered.
This person then knows that he will save the world...
...for he is sacrificed so that time can start over.
This concept was completely new to me.

TARA SHEARS

I think it's an interesting idea to call the Higgs Field "spirit."
But I don't know...
I have trouble making that jump...

...from a theory, an idea, of this...

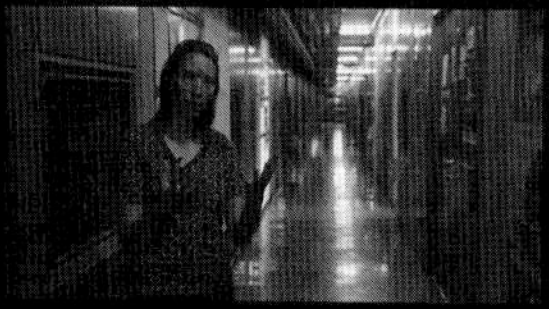

...all-pervasive somethingness
that I can't really picture in my head.
But I know mathematically what it does.
And I know that, mathematically,
it has shaped the outcome of the universe...

...and the way that everything is.
And so, to me...
...in my head, when I think of the Higgs Field...
...it's like a color...
...more than anything else, rather than a spirit.
A spirit to me implies...
...an ability...
...to affect an outcome that you can't predict.
To have...
To be able to have an influence on things...
...in a particular direction, of which you, as an observer, are perhaps unaware.
But it's something beyond your ken, completely.

LUIS ÁLVAREZ-GAUMÉ

In a quantum world...
...the black hole is not black, it emits things.
You can ask yourself: okay, we produce it.
But first of all, it will not be produced at rest.

So the probability that it
will be produced at zero velocity...
...is very small.
So mostly the black hole will just simply...
...go across the earth and into space.
Now, a black hole of that size,
even if produced at zero speed...
...will certainly begin to oscillate
and fall through the earth.
...until eventually it settles in the middle.
You can compute:
What is the probability that the black hole...
...which is really very, very small...
...will eat one atom of silicon...
...since most of the earth
is made of silicon or carbon.

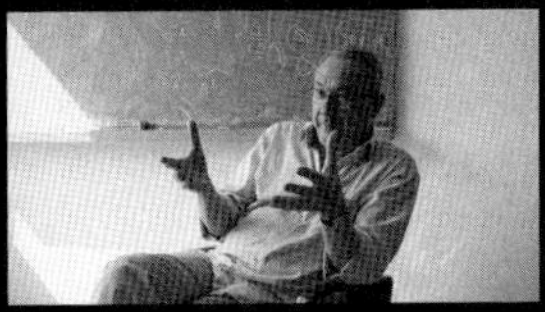

Well, it will take about four billion years...
...before it eats a single atom.
The reason is very simple.
An atom is infinitely big,
compared to a black hole.
So, quantum mechanics—it's a quantum phenomenon.
The thing is that...
...for this object to really
fall into this hole that is here...
...which is billions of times smaller...
Quantum mechanically, there is a barrier.
You know, Heisenberg, and so on.
It will happen. It will eat the atom.
But one atom will take four billion years.

DIEGO BLAS

In mathematics, zero is an element.
So when you derive this set...

...which is one of the most fundamental things in mathematics:
Set theory, sets,
collections of things.
The collection with a zero...
...is not empty; there is another element: zero.
You can't have a system where you don't have anything.
It is not a vacuum. There is something.
I don't know if this is nothing.
It is not nothingness, in a way.

The way we distinguish vacuum...
Now going back to physics:
When we don't have any element...
...there is still something, which is the system.
These small fluctuations.
And this system has some properties.
In the case of the universe,
this system has some small fluctuations.
In the case of mathematics, it is maybe zero,
but it may also have some properties.
Zero may have a color.
Zero-red, a red zero.
It may be helpful also to...
Or there may be different zeros,
and the zeros may be different from each other.
Because they correspond to different sets.

THOMAS MACHO

This beginning.
This idea was something that always fascinated Gershom Scholem.
Not only that creation had emerged from nothingness...
...but even more the question:
how did nothingness come into existence?
The idea that fascinated Scholem was first introduced
by the Kabbalist Isaac Luria in the sixteenth century.
He addressed the question of
what existed before creation.
Was there nothing or was there only God?
His answer was that there was only God.

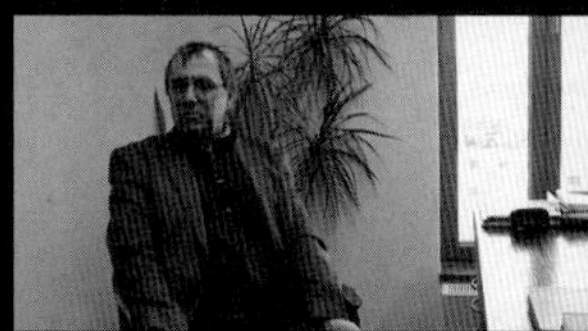

For some reason, God must have encountered an issue within himself.
So that God developed the wish
to create.
But in order to create something...
...God first had to create nothingness.
But how do you create nothingness?
And there Luria coined the notion of the Tzimtzum, which Scholem then also worked on.
Tzimtzum refers to a kind of divine contraction or self-inhalation by God.
God has to shrink in order
to make space for nothingness.
He needs nothingness, so that
from it, He can create a world.
Otherwise it would be impossible.

One can understand it as a process
like breathing:
To exhale, one must first inhale.
And one must exhale, in order to speak.
To say things like, "Let there be light,
Let there be day, Let there be the
sun," etc.

DETLEF THIEL

A priori is almost everything.
Aether is the prerequisite for
the possibility of experience.
If I experience something,
it must come from the outside.
From outside my body.
Even my body belongs to the
outside world.

In short: everything is aether.
Except for the plain will.
That which is purely immaterial.
If it exists: the spirit.
Everything else is aether.
Primary aether wafts diffusely all
around us.

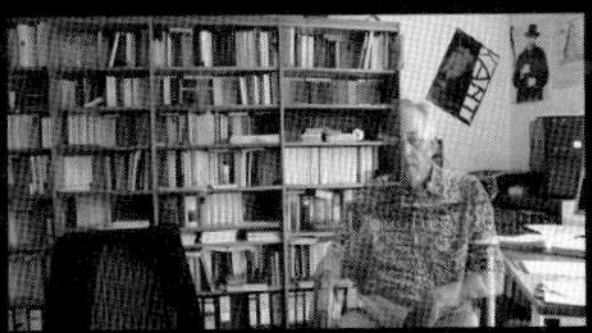

As soon as it congeals, coagulates...
This might be an alchemistic
expression,
I don't know the specifics of its origin.
But as soon as it densifies...

...temporarily, for a hundred years, for
all I know...
...everything emerges from this aether.
And that is how this is meant.

OTTO E. RÖSSLER

It is so obvious...
...to address that which is, rather than
its absence.
Of course, Schopenhauer said:
"Where I am, death is not.
And where death is, I am not."
This total separation from nothingness,
so to speak.
We live in the fiction that time goes on
and that we sometimes sleep and then
wake up.
But actually there are only the moments
of being awake.
And it is an ideology that we are
taught...

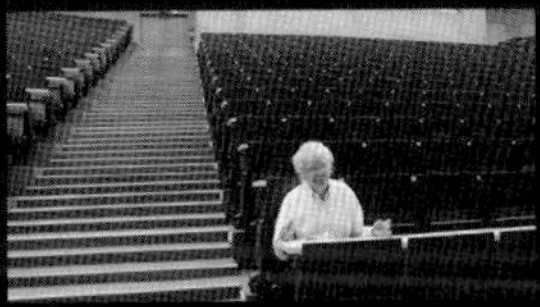

...that time continues in the meantime.
Every animal knows better!
But humans decided to accept this.
But...
Essentially the only thing we have
is the moment, the present.
No one talks about this.
Sometimes I call it the "gong of the
present."

It is very loud, but it is a taboo topic.
Death is like this:
When you know you must die.
Johnny Cash has a song about this:
"Three More Minutes to Go" comes to mind.
Well, now we have arrived at death...
...which doesn't exist.
Because in reality, we are dreamers.
And one cannot step out of a dream.
Just as one cannot stop dreaming.

Persons in the order of their appearance:

MICAH MAGEE, film director, reads the poem "Äther" by the early Berlin avant-garde artist and co-founder of the Cabaret Voltaire, Emmy Hennings.

DIEGO BLAS, mathematician and theoretical physicist at CERN, outlines the cosmological properties of a vacuum-aether in contemporary astrophysics and deduces the concept of zero.

HANNO DEPNER, philosopher and author of the handicraft book *Kant für die Hand* (Kant for the hand), speaks about the linguistic properties of nothingness.

MATTHIAS MENGEL, physicist, explains Michelson's Aether Drift Experiment at its historical site—in the cellar of an observatory at Potsdam Telegrafenberg.

EBERHARD BAUER, director of the Institut für Grenzgebiete der Psychologie, speaks about the concept of the aether-body in theosophy and occultism.

OTTO E. RÖSSLER, endophysicist and philosopher, speaks about human sacrifice, about being awake, and about the "gong of the present moment."

TARA SHEARS, experimental physicist at CERN, is asked if poet and aetherist E.A. Poe's idea that the aether might be termed spirit could also hold true for the Higgs Field.

LUIS ÁLVAREZ-GAUMÉ, theoretical physicist at CERN, explains why the experiments proving the existence of the Higgs Boson may only cause very small and harmless artificial black holes.

THOMAS MACHO, cultural scientist and philosopher, talks about the cabalistic concept of the "tzimtzum" and about nothingness as a prerequisite for God's creation.

DETLEF THIEL, philosopher and co-publisher of the estate of early Berlin avant-garde writer Salomo Friedlaender, speaks about the concept of aether in Immanuel Kant and Ernst Marcus.

Physics of Images – Images of Physics

Christoph Keller

The Images of Physics

"Thou scarcely move, yet swiftly seem to run; my son thou seest, here space and time are one." So begins the chapter about the Lorentz transformation in my physics textbook,[1] borrowing a line from Perceval. The textbook's author continues: "The Lorentz transformation shows that time can change into space and space into time." Developed by Dutch physicist Hendrik Antoon Lorentz at the end of the nineteenth century, the transformation is fundamental for the theory of special relativity. With it, one can calculate the relative time and the relative position of two observers moving relative to one another at a tempo approaching the speed of light.

If we were to isolate the perspectives of the two observers, each would see the other as through the viewfinder of a camera. Their perspectives are nevertheless joined to one another by an equal sign in the Lorentz transformation. There is thus a metaperspective of the formula itself, a way of thinking that unifies two irreconcilable, realistic images. But who is the observer occupying the viewpoint represented in this formula, which is supposed to show us that space and time are interwoven? What kind of self-conception and what kind of a worldview does this imply?

This is our picture: first of all, we have an observer who simultaneously occupies two different locations in different space and time systems. Secondly, we have material objects that, when seen from different perspectives, also have multiple space and time coordinates—each of which can nonetheless be perceived as one and the same. This picture is not at all impossible. All we need, bluntly put, is multiple personalities. What the Lorentz transformation changes is not the picture itself, but a realistic perspective of it. The metaobserver is motion. Since we still operate within a linear space-time, it is unavoidable that the observer experiences himself as spatially and temporally stretched.

Indeed, this is true to our everyday way of seeing: we are not really inertial observers that know only discreet points in time. The consequence of the relativist point of view is that the self only allows itself to be thought of in conjunction with a certain duration and through a certain movement in space. When I speak of the self, I no longer mean "I," here and now, in relation to an external situation—but rather the self as a temporal field experienced while traversing a certain field of situations. Thus the theory of relativity not only demonstrates that time and space are relative: what becomes relative is me.

The Physics of Images

The development of the photographic apparatus is an almost necessary result of the former hegemony of rationalism. It almost inescapably had to be invented in order to realize the images that had already been thought. In this respect, the development of photographic technology came surprisingly late. But through popular photography and film, photographic technologies came to be the central influence on modes of thought throughout modernity. And although many twentieth century scientific, artistic, or philosophic ideas rejected the dichotomy of realism and idealism, the vocabulary of the dominating discourse did not allow for a transgression of this dualistic worldview.

This is true, for example, in the early works of Duchamp, which had a tendency to convert realistic images or realistic objects into ideal ones (e.g., readymades). This process only functions, however, if the original dichotomy is maintained—it even reinforces it. Étienne-Jules Marey's chronophotography, a photographic technique that captured the movement of objects in serial prints, had a great impact on the physiology of medicine and on art at the turn of the century. In its reception, however, viewers were reluctant to see the works as simultaneously artistic *and* scientific—which had been Marey's original intent. Typical of the imperative of the two dominant schools of thought at the time, of realism and of idealism, the chronophotographs were inevitably described as belonging to either the one or the other.

In 1927, the 26-year-old quantum physicist Werner Heisenberg developed the uncertainty principle, which acknowledges that observer perception generally influences a scientific experiment. This epistemological statement is fundamental: the image of the "external" world is inextricably bound to its observation. Perception is an active procedure and in itself a material process. The philosophical implications of the uncertainty principle were however less pronounced at the time of its publication, as Heisenberg ultimately limited its formulation to a physical, external process, applying it solely to the behavior of particles.

These examples show how different modes of thought, or concepts of the self and of the world, may already exist without being prevalent in society, i.e., in the dominant discourse. Clearly the dichotomy of realism and idealism was too strong to allow for a third position. It is important to see that it is the mutual exclusivity of these oppositions that maintained this paradigm. Hence, paradoxically, it is idealism as the declared opponent of realism which guarantees its continued existence, and vice versa. Niels Bohr's motto for the complementarity principle in quantum physics thus applies to a completely different field: *Contraria non contradictoria sed complementa sunt*. Opposites don't contradict; they complement one another.

"Rundum" Photography

I arrived at Rundum photography through the Lorentz transformation. I placed a Rubik's Cube on a rotating plate and photographed it again and again, turning the plate by five degrees each time. Then I cut a strip from the middle of each of the photographs and glued these next to each other onto a piece of paper. This created an almost seamless picture of the Rubik's Cube, which nevertheless looked strange, as if the object were opened up on itself. The picture portrayed the cube from the perspective of a circle around the object. The circular perspective of the image was however purely arbitrary. Any other array of photographic viewpoints would potentially create a different image, a new perspective of the Cube. The composite image becomes more seamless as more photographs accrue and as the photo strips become more narrow. A strip camera brings this process to completion. Here, the camera steadily pulls film along a fixed exposure slit. It functions like a detached scanner, with which the surroundings are recorded through the movement of the apparatus. Though the resulting image on the filmstrip is static, it "contains" the entire movement of the camera during the recording. This process sets the self of the beholder virtually in motion. This is especially so when the beholder is informed as to the nature of the photographic reproduction, when he or she understands the image not only aesthetically as a strange deformation of a photograph, but on a technical level as well. The beholder's identification with the recording device is obviously a precondition for the transfer of reality onto the media of the image. The slit camera is a recording apparatus of motion — not only of the movement of the camera, but also of the moving objects in front of the camera's lens. If the camera is posed before an unmoving background, it reveals even, horizontal lines on the film. A picture ensues only through the movement of an object.

What results is a photographic diagram of movements. Fast objects are compressed, slow ones elongated. The spatial images may seem similar to the ones produced by a traditional photograph, yet the principle is essentially different. It is as if the observer perceives the world through a crack in a door, along which things pass by. In these images he or she can perceive the movements of an interval of time in an instant and thereby experience him- or herself in that moment as if being in motion. The self is thereby extended, spatially and temporally. The vertical axis of the Rundum picture corresponds to a realistic reproduction of the space. The horizontal axis of the picture, on the other hand, represents time and space — that is, motion. These pictures are by no means just visual strategies. They correlate in a certain way to our perceptual experience. Our eyes perceive only through movement: be it the movement of objects in our line of vision; the movement of our head, in order, for example, to perceive a room; or the movement of our pupils, to identify an object.

Captions

p. 24: Men searching for Gypsy Moth caterpillars in a large tree in Malden, close to Boston. From the book *The Gypsy Moth* by Edward H. Forbush and Charles H. Fernald, Wright & Potter Printing Co., 1896. Plate XXXVL. *Men at work on the Dexter elm, Malden. From a photograph.*

p. 26–27: Assemblage of images around the life story of Étienne Léopold Trouvelot, clockwise from the upper left corner:

Progressive spread of the Gypsy Moth (L. dispar) across the north-eastern US from 1900–2007, compiled from county data by US Forest Service. This image is in the public domain.

Total Eclipse of the Sun. Observed July 29, 1878, at Creston, Wyoming Territory (Plate III from *The Trouvelot Astronomical Drawings*, 1881–1882).

Étienne Léopold Trouvelot. Direct electric spark obtained with a Ruhmkorff coil or Wimshurst machine, also known as a "Trouvelot Figure." Photograph, ca. 1888.

The following four images are from the book *The Gypsy Moth* by Edward H. Forbush and Charles H. Fernald, Wright & Potter Printing Co., 1896.

Plate I. *Gypsy Moth, Fig. 2. Female Gypsy Moth with wings folded.*

Plate I. *Gypsy Moth, Fig. 6. Caterpillar, full grown.*

Plate II. *The Trouvelot house, 27 Myrtle Street, Glenwood, Medford, where the Gypsy Moth was first introduced into America. From a photograph taken in 1895.*

Plate XX. *Burning young caterpillars in infested brush land by means of the cyclone burner.*

Portrait photograph of Étienne Léopold Trouvelot, source and date unknown.

Etching taken from the article "The American Silk Worm" by Étienne Léopold Trouvelot, in *American Naturalist*, 1867.

Sketch of the 15-inch Great Refractor telescope at Harvard College Observatory near Boston. In 1847, the appearance of a comet became the stimulus to purchase what became the most important device for astronomical research in the United States for 20 years. It was active for nearly 75 years. Source and author unknown.

p. 28: Étienne Léopold Trouvelot, *Étincelle électrique directe* (Direct electric spark), 1885. Étienne Léopold Trouvelot, *Eclipse totale du Soleil* (Total eclipse of the sun), May 6, 1883, courtesy J-M. Kollar/ Observatoire de Paris.

p. 41: *Title Tool for an Imaginary Cinema*, 2015. Illuminated cinema display with exchangeable sets of letters. This work was part of the exhibition "Grey Magic" by Christoph Keller at Esther Schipper, Berlin, 2015. Photograph by Andrea Rossetti.

p. 42–51: *Magic Mirror Curtain*, 2015 125 polystyrene panels mirrored on one side and printed on the other, loosely hung on threads in a serpentine line through the gallery. Overall size approximately 2 × 25 m. Installation view at the exhibition "Grey Magic" at Esther Schipper, Berlin, 2015. Photograph by Andrea Rossetti.

p. 52–55: *Mental Radio*, 2015 Installation consisting of lamp, tripod, cot, pillow, pillowcase, blanket, custom-made goggles, wireless MP3 headphones, audio loop, questionnaire, clipboard, and egg timer. Photograph by Andrea Rossetti.

p. 56: Participant in *Mental Radio*, 2015. Photograph by Christoph Keller.

p. 60–79: Two-page questionnaire designed by Christoph Keller for *Mental Radio*, 2015. The depicted drawings were made by visitors during the exhibition "Grey Magic," Esther Schipper, Berlin, 2015. Participants agreed to take part in an anonymous, voluntary ganzfeld experiment. They underwent a ten-minute relaxation phase, lying down on a cot, looking into bright light while wearing translucent red goggles and listening to white noise over headphones. Subsequently they made drawings of what they had perceived during the experience and handed them out to the staff along with the questionnaire.

The *paranormal ideation questionnaire* reproduces text elements from Jiri Wackermann, Peter Pütz, and Carsten Allefeld, "Ganzfeld-Induced Hallucinatory Experience, Its Phenomenology and Cerebral Electrophysiology," *Cortex* no. 44 (2008), 1364–1378.

p. 81–85, 109–112: From the poster and reader distributed at the exhibition "Æther—from Cosmology to Consciousness," a proposition by Christoph Keller at the Nouveau Festival du Centre Pompidou, Paris, 2011, designed by Manuel Raeder.

p. 87-108: *Cloudbuster Project Pompidou*, 2011. Two large and thirty-one small photographs documenting the project by Christoph Keller on the rooftop of Centre Georges Pompidou in Paris. The work was part of the exhibition "Æther—from Cosmology to Consciousness" at the Nouveau festival du Centre Pompidou, 2011. Photograph by Christoph Keller.

p. 113-144: The following works were made with leaves collected by Christoph Keller at Rio Negro, Brazil, in 2013, and scanned by Mengershausen Editionen, Munich, in 2014.

p. 113-114, p. 143-144: *Archeology Plants Series (1-4)*, 2014. Four pigment prints: *Poseidon of Artemision, Hephaisteion, Olympieion, Epidaurus Theater*, 54 × 43 cm, framed.

p. 116, p. 118: *Herbarium Amazonas—Sheets (1-4)*, 2014. Two of four pigment prints, 110 × 85 cm, framed.

p. 123-130: The black-and-white analogue photographs are elements of the film *Anarcheology*, 2014. HD video, 12:40 minutes, black-and-white, silent.

p. 135-140: *Herbarium Amazonas (1-2)*, 2014. Two fine art prints, 225 × 150 cm, framed. Details of the images on pages 135 and 139.

p. 145: *Reflected Sunlight*, 2014. Inverted photograph, reflection of a sunbeam from a helioflex mirror, *helioflex—sun mirrors for dark urban habitations*, 1998–2010. Image used for the invitation of the exhibition "Small Survey on Nothingness," Schering Stiftung, Berlin, 2014.

p. 146-147: Installation view of the exhibition "Small Survey on Nothingness," 2014 at Schering Stiftung, Berlin, photographed by Andrea Rossetti, displaying the following works:

Aether Drift Experiment, 2014. HDV, 5:00 minutes, color, sound, projected on a screen and looped for installation.
The video shows the artist in an experiment: taking anesthetic diethyl ether at the historical site of Albert Abraham Michelson's 1881 Aether Drift Experiment at Potsdam Astrophysical Observatory on Telegrafenberg, near Berlin.

Aether Self Experiment, 2014. Illuminated pedestal with ether mask and flacon of diethyl ether for the use of the visitors, ca. 100 × 50 × 50 cm.

p. 159-166: Video stills from *Small Survey on Nothingness*, 2014, including images of Micah Magee, Diego Blas, Hanno Depner, Matthias Mengel, Eberhard Bauer, Otto E. Rössler, Tara Shears, Luis Álvarez-Gaumé, Thomas Macho, and Detlef Thiel.

All works courtesy of Christoph Keller and Esther Schipper, Berlin.

Notes

p. 8-11: Christoph Keller, *Paranomia*, 2016.

p. 13-23: *On Stammering*, interview between Christoph Keller and Joseph Vogl recorded in August 2010. This text was first edited, translated from the original German, and published in the booklet *Verbal/Nonverbal* on occasion of the exhibition "Verbal/Nonverbal," at Esther Schipper, Berlin, 2010, and it has been revised for this catalogue.

p. 25: Christoph Keller, *The Trouvelot Story*, 2016. Trouvelot's works and life story were one of the entry points to the exhibition "Æther—from Cosmology to Consciousness," proposed by Christoph Keller at the Nouveau festival du Centre Pompidou, Paris, 2011. For more information on Étienne Léopold Trouvelot, see also Jimena Canales, "Captured by Cinematography," in *A Tenth of a Second: A History* (Chicago University Press, 2010), 131–145.

p. 29-39: *The Viewer as a Scientist* is a conversation with Jimena Canales, Sarah Demeuse, and Christoph Keller. This text is an edited and revised transcript of a Skype conversation that took place in April 2016. Notes:
[1] Thomas Kuhn, *The Structure of Scientific Revolutions* (Chicago: University of Chicago Press, 1962).
[2] Jimena Canales, *The Physicist and the Philosopher: Einstein, Bergson, and the Debate That Changed Our Understanding of Time* (Princeton NJ: Princeton University Press, 2015).
[3] Bruno Latour, "Why Has Critique Run out of Steam? From Matters of Fact to Matters of Concern," *Critical Inquiry* 30, no. 2 (winter 2004): 225–248.
[4] Paul Feyerabend, *Wissenschaft als Kunst* (Berlin: Suhrkamp, 1984).
[5] Paul Feyerabend, *Against Method* (London: New Left Books, 1975).
[6] Étienne Léopold Trouvelot, *The Trouvelot Astronomical Drawings Manual* (New York: C. Scribner's Sons, 1882).

p. 47-48: *Eccentric Sensation: On the Aether Theory of Perception in Ernst Marcus and Salomo Friedlaender/Mynona*, Christoph Keller, 2015.

Originally published in German as an epilogue to the reproduction of Ernst Marcus's essay *Das Problem der exzentrischen Empfindung und seine Lösung* (The problem of eccentric sensation and its solution) first printed by Herwarth Walden's publishing house *Der Sturm*, Berlin, in 1918, published on occasion of Christoph Keller's exhibition "Grey Magic" at Esther Schipper, Berlin, 2015.

p. 53-59: This conversation on Ernst Marcus between Christoph Keller and Detlef Thiel is an edited and translated version of a 2014 interview on Ernst Marcus's *Exzentrische Empfindung*, Salomo Friedlaender/Mynona, and others, which was first published on occasion of the exhibition "Grey Magic" at Esther Schipper, Berlin, 2015.

p. 82-83, p. 109-111: *Æther—from Cosmology to Consciousness / Æther—de la cosmologie à la conscience*, Christoph Keller, 2011.

p. 84-85:
Ludwig Wittgenstein, *The Blue and Brown Books*, 1933–35, published in 1964.
Edgar Allan Poe, *Mesmeric Revelation*, 1844.
Jacques Lacan, *Anxiety: The Seminar of Jacques Lacan, Book X*, scripted 1962–63, published in 2014.
Immanuel Kant, loose pages, 1755.
Thomas Pynchon, *Gravity's Rainbow*, 1973.

p. 87-108: *On Æther—Œuvre parlée* is a transcript of the public conversation between Christoph Keller and Bernard Blistène held at the "amphithéâtre" built into Espace 315 at Centre Pompidou for the exhibition "Æther—from Cosmology to Consciousness," a proposition by Christoph Keller for the Nouveau festival du Centre Pompidou, Paris, February 16, 2011, in English and French. The bilingual talk was transcribed and edited preserving the informal character of the conversation.

p. 111-112:
Ralph McInerny, *A History of Western Philosophy*, 1963.
Karl Marx, *Grundrisse*, manuscript from 1858, published in 1939.
Emmy Hennings, *Äthergedichte*, 1913.

p. 117: Christoph Keller, *Anarcheology-Museum*, 2014.

p. 119-121: *On Anarcheology* is an interview between Ana Teixeira Pinto with Christoph Keller first published on vdrome.org, 2015. With thanks for permission to reprint to Vdrome and Filipa Ramos.

p. 123-133: Christoph Keller, *Anarcheology*, 2014. This text is from Christoph Keller's film *Anarcheology*, 2014. HD video, 12:40 minutes, black-and-white, silent. Text excerpts included in *Anarcheology* are from:
Michael Hardt and Antonio Negri, *In Labor of Dionysus—A Critique of the State-Form* (Minneapolis: University of Minnesota Press, 1994): 292.
Michel Foucault, *Du gouvernement des vivants: Cours au College de France (1979–1980)* (Paris: Seuil—Hautes etudes, 2012): 76. Translated from French into English.
Anne Ballester Soares, "Os Espíritos—Horonami" in *Nohi Patama Parahiteri Pe Re Kuonowei Te A: História Mitológica do Grupo Parahiteri* (São Paulo: Hedra; ECidade, 2010): 133. Translated from Portuguese into English.

Thanks to Siegfried Zielinski for his notion of *An-Archäologie der Medien* (an-archeology of media) in Siegfried Zielinski: *Archäologie der Medien. Zur Tiefenzeit des technischen Hörens und Sehens*, Reinbek, Hamburg, 2002.

p. 149-153: Heike Catherina Mertens, *A Journey Through Nothing That Is*, 2016.

p. 155-158: Horst Bredekamp, *Nothingness Is Not Nothing*, 2016. This text is based on the lecture "Das Nichts ist nicht nichts" (Nothingness is not nothing) by Horst Bredekamp in German, delivered on occasion of the opening of Christoph Keller's exhibition "Small Survey on Nothingness" on July 5, 2014, at Schering Stiftung, Berlin.

p. 159-166: This text represents the complete English titles and subtitles of Christoph Keller's film *Small Survey on Nothingness*, 2014. HD video, 23:00 minutes, color, sound, German and English with English subtitles. Credits: Johan Carlsen (editing), Jochen Jezussek (sound), Amy Patton (production).

p. 167-170: The essay *Physics of Images—Images of Physics* by Christoph Keller is based on the script of Keller's lecture performance *Bilder der Physik—Die Physik der Bilder* presented at Neuer Berliner Kunstverein in May 1996. It was first published as an exhibition booklet in 2002 by Christoph Keller, Kunsthaus Schloss Wendlinghausen e.V., and Schipper & Krome, and has been revised for this catalogue. Note:
[1] Jay Orear, *Physik* (Leipzig: Fachbuchverlag Leipzig, 1982).

Colophon

Christoph Keller: Paranomia

Published by Spector Books, Leipzig, 2016
www.spectorbooks.com

Edited by Christoph Keller

Copy editor: Tess Edmonson

Graphic design by Studio Manuel Raeder
(Miglė Kazlauskaitė, Manuel Raeder)

Editorial interlocutors: Sarah Demeuse,
Heike Catherina Mertens

Proofreaders: Ames Gerould, Sonya von
Amelunxen Merutka, Sydney Smith

Translations by Manuela Thurner, Joel Scott,
Ian Pepper, Andrea Scrima, Eva Wilson,
Alisa Kotmair

Additional text editing by Ana Teixeira Pinto,
Rebekka Ladewig, Charles McPhedran,
Ambroise Tièche

Printed by Vier-Türme GmbH, Benedict Press
Edition of 1500

Printed in Germany
ISBN 978-3-95905-100-2

This publication was made possible
with the generous support of:

SCHERING STIFTUNG

Additional support by:

Esther Schipper ERES STIFTUNG

Acknowledgments

Christoph Keller would like to thank the following people and institutions for their kind support:

Bernard Blistène, Jean-Marie Gallais, and
Laura Draghici-Foulon, Nouveau festival du
Centre Pompidou, Paris
Esther Schipper, Berlin
Arend and Brigitte Oetker, Berlin
Ulrich Sauerwein and Isabel Podeschwa, Berlin
Joachim Fischer, Ernst von Siemens Kunststiftung,
Munich
Helmut Batista, Capacete, Rio de Janeiro
Anne Ballester Soares, Rios Profundos
Sabine Adler, ERES-Stiftung, Munich

Heike Catherina Mertens and Martina Schrammek for their support for the exhibition "Small Survey on Nothingness," Schering Stiftung, Berlin, 2014, and for this book

Anja Dörken and Kirsten Niehuus, Medienboard Berlin-Brandenburg, for their support for the film *Small Survey on Nothingness*, 2014

All people appearing in *Small Survey on Nothingness*: Micah Magee, Diego Blas, Hanno Depner, Matthias Mengel, Eberhard Bauer, Otto E. Rössler, Tara Shears, Luis Álvarez-Gaumé, Thomas Macho, Detlef Thiel

Additional thanks to:
Linda Dalrymple Henderson, Tobi Maier, Solo Shows São Paulo, Filipa Ramos, Marie Muracciole, Manolis Daskalakis-Lemos, Hartmut Geerken and Sigrid Hauff, Jana Binder, Goethe-Institut São Paulo, Ulla Rossek, Mengershausen Editionen, Ariane Koek, Arts at CERN, Leah Turner, Amy Patton, Angela Anderson, Thomas Schnalke, Christina Weiss, the family of Emmy Hennings

Projects included in this book were supported by:

medienboard Berlin-Brandenburg

EvS ERNST VON SIEMENS KUNSTSTIFTUNG

Kulturkreis der deutschen Wirtschaft im BDI e.V.

SCHERING STIFTUNG

Short biographies of the authors

Bernard Blistène is a professor, curator, and museum director in Paris.

Horst Bredekamp is an art historian and professor in Berlin.

Jimena Canales is a historian of science, a writer, a physicist, and a professor in Illinois.

Sarah Demeuse is a Brooklyn-based curator, translator, and writer.

Christoph Keller is an artist working in Berlin.

Heike Catherina Mertens is a curator and managing director of a foundation in Berlin.

Ana Teixeira Pinto is a writer and cultural scientist in Berlin.

Studio Manuel Raeder is an interdisciplinary design studio based in Berlin and Mexico City.

Detlef Thiel is a philosopher and publisher of texts by Salomo Friedlaender/Mynona in Wiesbaden.

Joseph Vogl is a philosopher and professor in Berlin who writes on literature, culture, and media.

The publication features the following exhibition projects by Christoph Keller: "Æther—de la cosmologie à la conscience," Espace 315, Nouveau festival du Centre Pompidou, Paris, 2011; "Os Tropicos," Museu da Caixa Cultural, São Paulo, 2014; "Anarcheology," Esther Schipper, 2014; "Small Survey on Nothingness," Schering Stiftung, Berlin, 2014; "Grey Magic," Esther Schipper, Berlin, 2015.